806.66

rd

Books are to be returned on or before
the last date below.

19 MAR 2001

18 DEC 2007

Project Team

Managing Editor   Elizabeth Knowles

Senior Editor   Susan Ratcliffe

Reading Programme   Jean Harker
                          Helen Rappaport

Library Research   Ralph Bates
                          Marie G. Diaz

Proof-reading   Fabia Claris
                          Penny Trumble

We are grateful to Charlote Graves Taylor, Verity Mason, and
Penelope Newsome for additional contributions to the Reading
Programme, and to Sandra Vaughan for data capture.

Oxford
Love Quotations

Edited by
Susan Ratcliffe

OXFORD
UNIVERSITY PRESS

OXFORD
UNIVERSITY PRESS

Great Clarendon Street, Oxford OX2 6DP

Oxford University Press is a department of the University of Oxford.
It furthers the University's objective of excellence in research, scholarship,
and education by publishing worldwide in

Oxford New York

Athens Auckland Bangkok Bogotá Buenos Aires Calcutta
Cape Town Chennai Dar es Salaam Delhi Florence Hong Kong Istanbul
Karachi Kuala Lumpur Madrid Melbourne Mexico City Mumbai
Nairobi Paris São Paulo Singapore Taipei Tokyo Toronto Warsaw

with associated companies in Berlin Ibadan

Published in the United States
by Oxford University Press Inc., New York

Database right Oxford University Press (makers)

First published 1999

British Library Cataloguing in Publication Data

Data available

Library of Congress Cataloging in Publication Data

Data available

ISBN 0-19-860240-5

10 9 8 7 6 5 4 3 2

Typeset in Photina and Meta
by Interactive Sciences Ltd
Printed in Great Britain by
Mackays of Chatham plc
Chatham, Kent

Introduction

According to Jeanette Winterson, '"I love you" is always a quotation.' Certainly love has always been a major theme in dictionaries of quotations, but this selection shows just how universal and yet how different experience and comments on love can be, ranging from earliest times to the present, and across all continents.

The subjects encompassed here include not only the good times: **Falling in Love** ('whatever that may mean'—Charles, Prince of Wales), **Kissing** ('I still remember the chewing gum, tobacco, and beer taste of my first kiss, exactly 40 years ago, although I have completely forgotten the face of the American sailor who kissed me'—Isabel Allende), and **Memories** ('The memories of long love gather like drifting snow, poignant as the mandarin ducks who float side by side in sleep'—Murasaki Shikibu, a Japanese lady of the tenth century); but also the bad times: **Absence** ('I am reduced to a thing that wants Virginia'—Vita Sackville-West), **Jealousy** ('The French are jealous of their mistresses, but never of their wives'—Jacques Casanova), and **Unrequited Love** ('I wanted your soft verges But you gave me the hard shoulder'—Adrian Mitchell).

Love quotations fall into many themes, ranging from **Passion** 'One mad magenta moment and I have paid for it all my life' and **Sex** 'That was the most fun I ever had without laughing' through to **Cars** 'Though the various scents of garages, showrooms, and racetracks have pleasing associations for me, I've yet to hear a woman say, "Mmmmmmm, you smell like a car"' and **Individuality and Identity** 'PERSONALITY TITHE: A price paid for becoming a couple.' In **The Body** Leonard Cohen tells us 'A woman watches her body uneasily, as though it were an unreliable ally in the battle for love,' and in **Size and Shape** Arabella Weir confirms it: 'Does my bum look big in this?' At **Clothes and Fashion** Thoreau tells us to 'Beware of all enterprises that require new clothes' and indeed the **Wedding Dresses** range from 'gloomy...grey alpaca' to 'a big meringue'.

The words of famous literary lovers are often very familiar — Romeo's 'Good-night, good-night! parting is such sweet sorrow,' Jane Eyre's 'Reader, I married him'—but here too are the words of historical lovers: Héloise's 'When my self is not with you, it is nowhere', Joséphine writing to Napoleon 'How many times did I not wish to write to you! But I felt the reason of your silence, and I feared to be importunate by a letter,' and Henry VIII assuring Anne Boleyn of his affection in **Proposals** (sadly, her plea that he should not 'withdraw his princely favour' finds a home in **Breaking Up**). Modern lovers make their appearance too: 'I will not...sulk about having no boyfriend, but develop inner poise and authority and sense of self as woman of substance, complete without boyfriend, as best way to obtain boyfriend'—the unmistakable tones of Bridget Jones, while the poet Ted Hughes describes himself as 'a post-war, utility son-in-law! Not quite the Frog-Prince. Maybe the Swineherd.'

Byron's famous lines 'Man's love is of man's life a thing apart, 'Tis woman's whole existence' are often quoted. It is certainly true that women have had a great deal to say about love, and this is reflected in the high proportion of quotations by women in this book. Whether Byron was right, however, is open to question: today we are just as likely to hear 'A woman without a man is like a fish without a bicycle.' In **Remarriage**, for example, the women (with the exception of the Wife of Bath, perhaps) are much less enthusiastic than the men. Gertrude Stein thinks that 'Anyone who marries three girls from St Louis hasn't learned much', while Sacha Guitry tells his fifth wife 'The others were only my wives. But you, my dear, will be my widow.'

Tony Bennett said of Frank Sinatra 'We all fell in love, fell out of love, and fell in love again to the sound of his voice,' and songs have contributed many instantly recognizable quotations on love, summed up by Lennon and McCartney telling us all 'All you need is love.' Lines from films, too, have become part of our culture, from Mae West's 'Why don't you come up sometime, and see me' in 1933 to *Four Weddings and a Funeral* in 1994: 'All these years we've been single and proud of it—never noticed that two of us were to all intents and purposes married all this time.' Television quotations are rarely romantic: 'You may marry the man of your dreams, ladies, but 14 years later you're married to a couch that burps'—Roseanne Barr.

Many of these quotations are of happy moments: Mary Wordsworth writing to William 'It is not in my power to tell thee how I have been affected by this dearest of all letters—it was so unexpected—so new a thing to see the breathing of thy inmost heart upon paper'; others are more reminiscent of Jean Rhys' description: 'Love was a terrible thing. You poisoned it and stabbed at it and knocked it down into the mud—well down—and it got up and staggered on, bleeding and muddy and awful. Like—like Rasputin.' Every kind of love and lover can be found in these pages. But perhaps the last word should be given to Cher: 'If grass can grow through cement, love can find you at every time in your life.'

Susan Ratcliffe

Oxford, 1998

List of themes

A

Absence
Advice
Affairs
Age
Alcohol
Anniversaries
Armed Forces
Arranged Marriages
Assignations
Attraction

B

Bachelors
Beauty
Behaviour
The Beloved
The Best Man
Betrayal *see*
    Trust and Betrayal
The Body
Books and Literature
Breaking up
Bridegrooms
Brides
Bridesmaids

C

Cars
Charm
Chastity *see*
    Virtue and Chastity
Children *see*
    Pregnancy and Children
Choosing
Clothes and Fashion
Compatibility

Cooking *see*
    Food and Cooking
Cosmetics
Courtship

D

Dancing
Death
Deception
Declarations
Desire
Difficulties *see*
    Opposition and Difficulties
Divorce

E

Endearments
Engagements
Epitaphs

F

Falling in Love
The Family
Fashion *see*
    Clothes and Fashion
Fear
Fickleness
Fidelity
First Love
Flowers
Folly
Food and Cooking
Forgiveness *see*
    Quarrels and Forgiveness
Friendship

Absence

1 Absence makes the heart grow fonder.
Anonymous: proverb

2 O but I was mad to come here, even for money:
To have put myself at the mercy of the postman and the
    daydream,
That incorrigible nightmare in which you lie weeping or ill,
Or drowned in the arms of another.
W. H. Auden 1907–73: 'Love Letter'

3 Absence and letters are the forcing ground of love. What
renews it and confirms it is presence and bed.
Gerald Brenan 1894–1987: *Thoughts in a Dry Season* (1978)

4 Absence, that common cure of love.
Cervantes 1547–1616: *Don Quixote* (1605)

5 Our hours in love have wings; in absence, crutches.
Colley Cibber 1671–1757: *Xerxes* (1699)

6 Moonlight, a wood fire, my own good lamp. What can I
complain about? Only the absence of those I love.
Colette 1873–1954: letter, 3 January 1928

7 Our two souls therefore, which are one,
Though I must go, endure not yet
A breach, but an expansion,
Like gold to airy thinness beat.
John Donne 1572–1631: 'A Valediction: forbidding mourning'

8 I am shattered, numb, as though after a long orgy; I miss
you terribly. There is an immense void in my heart.
Gustave Flaubert 1821–80: letter to Louise Colet, 6–7 August 1846

9 *Partir c'est mourir un peu,*
C'est mourir à ce qu'on aime:
On laisse un peu de soi-même
En toute heure et dans tout lieu.

To go away is to die a little, it is to die to that which one loves: everywhere and always, one leaves behind a part of oneself.
Edmond Haraucourt 1856–1941: 'Rondel de l'Adieu' (1891)

10 When my self is not with you, it is nowhere.
Héloïse *c.*1098–1164: letter to Peter Abelard

11 He is gone, who knew the music of my soul.
Hsueh T'ao 768–831: 'Weaving Love Knots'

12 With leaden foot time creeps along
While Delia is away.
Richard Jago 1715–81: 'Absence'

13 The joy of life is variety; the tenderest love requires to be renewed by intervals of absence.
Samuel Johnson 1709–84: in *The Idler* no. 39

14 I wish you could invent some means to make me at all happy without you. Every hour I am more and more concentrated in you; every thing else tastes like chaff in my mouth.
John Keats 1795–1821: letter to Fanny Brawne, August 1820

15 Absence diminishes commonplace passions and increases great ones, as the wind extinguishes candles and kindles fire.
Duc de la Rochefoucauld 1613–80: *Maximes* (1678)

16 Where you used to be, there is a hole in the world, which I find myself constantly walking round in the daytime, and falling into at night. I miss you like hell.
Edna St Vincent Millay 1892–1950: Allen R. Macdougall (ed.) *Letters of Edna St Vincent Millay* (1952)

Absence

17 I do not love thee!—no! I do not love thee!
And yet when thou art absent I am sad.
Caroline Norton 1808–77: 'I do not love thee'

18 The longest absence is less perilous to love than the terrible
trials of incessant proximity.
Ouida 1839–1908: *Wisdom, Wit and Pathos* (1884)

19 I am reduced to a thing that wants Virginia.
Vita Sackville-West 1892–1962: letter to Virginia Woolf, 21 January 1926

20 I cannot love you and be perfectly satisfied at such a
distance from you.
Elizabeth Sheridan 1724–92: letter to her husband, 1776

21 Nothing reopens the springs of love so fully as absence, and
no absence so thoroughly as that which must be endless.
Anthony Trollope 1815–82: *The Last Chronicle of Barset* (1867)

Advice

1 A woman seldom asks advice before she has bought her
wedding clothes.
Joseph Addison 1672–1719: in *The Spectator* 4 September 1712

2 In matters of religion and matrimony I never give any
advice; because I will not have anybody's torments in this
world or the next laid to my charge.
Lord Chesterfield 1694–1773: letter to Arthur Charles Stanhope, 12
October 1765

3 He had polyester sheets and I wanted to get cotton sheets.
He discussed it with his shrink many times before he made
the switch.
*of the dependence of her former partner, Woody Allen, on
psychotherapists*
Mia Farrow 1945– : in *Independent* 8 February 1997 'Quote Unquote'

4 Never give away a tear,
   Never toss and pine;
   Should you heed my words, my dear,
   You're no blood of mine!
   Dorothy Parker 1893–1967: 'For a Favourite Granddaughter'

5 Advice to persons about to marry.—'Don't.'
   Punch: in 1845

Affairs see also Deception, Trust and Betrayal

1 I'm old-fashioned. I don't believe in extra-marital
   relationships. I think people should mate for life, like
   pigeons or Catholics.
   Woody Allen 1935– : *Manhattan* (1979 film)

2 A mistress kept at first is sweet,
   And joys to do the merry feat;
   But bastards come and hundreds gone,
   You'll wish you'd left her charms alone,
   Such breeding hussies are a pest,
   A neighbour's wife is far the best.
   Anonymous: *The Pearl* (1879–80)

3 Thou shalt not covet thy neighbour's wife.
   Bible: Exodus

4 Reading someone else's newspaper is like sleeping with
   someone else's wife. Nothing seems to be precisely in the
   right place, and when you find what you are looking for, it
   is not clear then how to respond to it.
   Malcolm Bradbury 1932– : *Stepping Westward* (1975)

5   Merely innocent flirtation,
   Not quite adultery, but adulteration.
   Lord Byron 1788–1824: *Don Juan* (1819–24)

6 If people will stop at the first tense of the verb 'aimer' they must not be surprised if one finishes the conjugation with somebody else.
Lord Byron 1788–1824: letter 13 January 1814

7 People who are so dreadfully devoted to their wives are so apt, from mere habit, to get devoted to other people's wives as well.
Jane Carlyle 1801–66: remark, c.1860; Michele Brown and Ann O'Connor *Hammer and Tongues* (1986)

8 I've looked on a lot of women with lust. I've committed adultery in my heart many times. This is something that God recognizes I will do—and I have done it—and God forgives me for it.
Jimmy Carter 1924– : in *Playboy* November 1976

9 Sara could commit adultery at one end and weep for her sins at the other, and enjoy both operations at once.
Joyce Cary 1888–1957: *The Horse's Mouth* (1944)

10 If you bed people of below-stairs class, they will go to the papers.
Jane Clark: in *Daily Telegraph* 31 May 1994

11 Do not adultery commit;
Advantage rarely comes of it.
Arthur Hugh Clough 1819–61: 'The Latest Decalogue' (1862)

12 There were three of us in this marriage, so it was a bit crowded.
Diana, Princess of Wales 1961–97: interview on *Panorama*, BBC1 TV, 20 November 1995

13 I had three concubines, who in three diverse properties diversely excelled. One, the merriest; another the wiliest; the third, the holiest harlot in my realm, as one whom no man could get out of the church lightly to any place but it were to his bed.
Edward IV 1442–83: Thomas More *The History of Richard III*, composed about 1513

Affairs

14 I say I don't sleep with married men, but what I mean is that I don't sleep with happily married men.
Britt Ekland 1942– : attributed, 1980s; Anne Stibbs (ed.) *Like a Fish Needs a Bicycle* (1992)

15 No, I shall have mistresses.
when Queen Caroline, on her deathbed in 1737, urged him to marry again; the Queen replied, 'Oh, my God! That won't make any difference'
George II 1683–1760: John Hervey *Memoirs of the Reign of George II* (1848)

16 No adultery is bloodless.
Natalia Ginzburg 1916–91: *The City and the House* (1985)

17 When you marry your mistress you automatically create a vacancy.
James Goldsmith: interview; in *Sunday Times* 12 March 1989

18 When a man steals your wife, there is no better revenge than to let him keep her.
Sacha Guitry 1885–1957: *Elles et toi* (1948)

19 There are few who would not rather be taken in adultery than in provincialism.
Aldous Huxley 1894–1963: *Antic Hay* (1923)

20 Adultery in your heart is committed not only when you look with excessive sexual desire at a woman who is not your wife, but also if you look in the same manner at your wife.
Pope John Paul II 1920– : speech at the Vatican Synod, October 1980

21 Adultery is a meanness and a stealing, a taking away from someone what should be theirs, a great selfishness, and surrounded and guarded by lies lest it should be found out. And out of the meanness and selfishness and lying flow love and joy and peace beyond anything that can be imagined.
Rose Macaulay 1881–1958: *The Towers of Trebizond* (1956)

Affairs

22 This curse pursues female adultery,
They'll swim through blood for sin's variety:
Their pleasure like a sea groundless and wide,
A woman's lust was never satisfied.
John Marston *c.*1575–1634: *The Insatiate Countess*

23 Our bourgeois, not having the wives and daughters of their
proletarians at their disposal, not to speak of common
prostitutes, take the greatest pleasure in seducing each
other's wives. Bourgeois marriage is in reality a system of
wives in common.
Karl Marx 1818–83 and **Friedrich Engels** 1820–95: *The Communist Manifesto* (1848)

24 You know, of course, that the Tasmanians, who never
committed adultery, are now extinct.
W. Somerset Maugham 1874–1965: *The Bread-Winner* (1930)

25 Adultery is the application of democracy to love.
H. L. Mencken 1880–1956: *Book of Burlesques* (1920)

26 Chaste to her husband, frank to all beside,
A teeming mistress, but a barren bride.
Alexander Pope 1688–1744: *Epistles to Several Persons* 'To a Lady' (1735)

27 Adultery introduces some energy into an otherwise dead
marriage.
Marcel Proust 1871–1922: *Remembrance of Things Past* (1922–31) 'The Prisoner'

28 Cuckoldry is an essential appendage of wedlock; your
shadow does not follow you more closely or naturally.
When you hear the three words: 'He is married,' add:
'Therefore he is, has been, will or may be cuckolded.' Do
this, and no one will ever accuse you of faulty logic.
François Rabelais *c.*1494–*c.*1553: *Gargantua and Pantagruel* (1534)

29 One man's folly is often another man's wife.
Helen Rowland 1875–1950: *Reflections of a Bachelor Girl* (1903)

30 Let's face it, I have been momentary.
A luxury. A bright red sloop in the harbour.
My hair rising like smoke from the car window.
Littleneck clams out of season.
Anne Sexton 1928–74: 'For my Lover, returning to his Wife'

31   Die: die for adultery! No:
The wren goes to't, and the small gilded fly
Does lecher in my sight.
Let copulation thrive.
William Shakespeare 1564–1616: *King Lear* (1605–6)

32 The first breath of adultery is the freest; after it, constraints
aping marriage develop.
John Updike 1932– : *Couples* (1968)

33 When he is late for dinner and I know he must be either
having an affair or lying dead in the street, I always hope
he's dead.
Judith Viorst 1935– : attributed

34 Just how difficult it is to write biography can be reckoned
by anybody who sits down and considers just how many
people know the truth about his or her love affairs.
Rebecca West 1892–1983: in *Vogue* 1 November 1952

35 I shall not say why and how I became, at the age of fifteen,
the mistress of the Earl of Craven.
Harriette Wilson 1789–1846: opening words of *Memoirs* (1825)

36 A mistress should be like a little country retreat near the
town, not to dwell in constantly, but only for a night and
away.
William Wycherley c.1640–1716: *The Country Wife* (1675)

Affairs

Age see also Old Age, Youth

1 Better be an old man's darling, than a young man's slave.
Anonymous: proverb

2 Accordingly we conclude that the appropriate age for
marriage is about the eighteenth year for girls and for men
the thirty-seventh year plus or minus.
Aristotle 384–322 BC: *Politics*

3 Being now in her twenty-first year, Maria Bertram was
beginning to think matrimony a duty.
Jane Austen 1775–1817: *Mansfield Park* (1814)

4 I gave my beauty and my youth to men. I am going to give
my wisdom and experience to animals.
Brigitte Bardot 1934– : attributed, June 1987

5 Women over thirty are at their best, but men over thirty
are too old to recognize it.
Jean-Paul Belmondo 1933– : attributed

6 The man of thirty who loves for the first time is usually the
embodiment of cautious discretion. He does not fall in love
with a violent descent, but rather lets himself gently down,
continually testing the rope.
Arnold Bennett 1867–1931: *Anna of the Five Towns* (1902)

7 What can a young lassie, what shall a young lassie,
What can a young lassie do wi' an auld man?
Robert Burns 1759–96: 'What can a Young Lassie do wi' an Auld Man'
(1792)

8 So, we'll go no more a-roving
So late into the night,
Though the heart be still as loving,
And the moon be still as bright.

For the sword outwears its sheath,
And the soul wears out the breast,
And the heart must pause to breathe,

And love itself have rest.
Lord Byron 1788–1824: 'So we'll go no more a-roving' (written 1817)

9   It is true from early habit, one must make love
mechanically as one swims, I was once very fond of both,
but now as I never swim unless I tumble into the water, I
don't make love till almost obliged.
Lord Byron 1788–1824: letter 10 September 1812

10   I was aware at the time that some people noted a certain
discrepancy in our ages—a bridegroom is not usually thirty
years *older* than his father-in-law.
on his marriage in 1957
Pablo Casals 1876–1973: attributed

11   If grass can grow through cement, love can find you at
every time in your life.
Cher 1946– : in *The Times* 30 May 1998

12   A man is as old as he's feeling,
a woman as old as she looks.
Mortimer Collins 1827–76: *The Unknown Quantity*

13   The age of a woman doesn't mean a thing. The best tunes
are played on the oldest fiddles.
Sigmund Z. Engel b. 1869: in *Newsweek* 4 July 1949

14   A diplomat is a man who always remembers a woman's
birthday but never remembers her age.
Robert Frost 1874–1963: attributed

15   There's a fascination frantic
In a ruin that's romantic;
Do you think you are sufficiently decayed?
W. S. Gilbert 1836–1911: *The Mikado* (1885)

16   O! sir, I must not tell my age. They say women and music
should never be dated.
Oliver Goldsmith 1728–74: *She Stoops to Conquer* (1773)

Age

17 It may be said that married men of forty are usually ready
and generous enough to fling passing glances at any
specimen of moderate beauty they may discern by the way.
Thomas Hardy 1840–1928: *Far from the Madding Crowd* (1874)

18 Personally, I think if a woman hasn't met the right man by
the time she's 24, she may be lucky.
Jean Kerr 1923– : attributed

19 My biological clock is ticking so loud I'm nearly deafened
by it. They search me going into planes.
Marian Keyes: 'Late Opening at the Last Chance Saloon' (1997)

20 The lovely thing about being forty is that you can
appreciate twenty-five-year-old men more.
Colleen McCullough 1937– : attributed

21 How absurd and delicious it is to be in love with somebody
younger than yourself. Everybody should try it.
Barbara Pym 1913–80: *A Very Private Eye (1984)*

22 He was rich and old and she
Was thirty-two or thirty-three.
She gave him fifteen years to live—
The only thing she meant to give.
Justin Richardson 1900–75: 'Wholly Matrimony' (1949)

23 How unnatural the imposed view, imposed by a puritanical
ethos, that passionate love belongs only to the young, that
people are dead from the neck down by the time they are
forty, and that any deep feeling, any passion after that age,
is either ludicrous or revolting.
May Sarton 1912– : *Journal of a Solitude* (1973)

24 Not so young, sir, to love a woman for singing, nor so old
to dote on her for any thing.
William Shakespeare 1564–1616: *King Lear* (1605–6)

25   Let still the woman take
An elder than herself, so wears she to him,
So sways she level in her husband's heart.
William Shakespeare 1564–1616: *Twelfth Night* (1601)

26 I have almost done with harridans, and shall soon become
old enough to fall in love with girls of fourteen.
Jonathan Swift 1667–1745: letter to Alexander Pope, September 1725

27 I think they deserve to have more than twelve years
between the ages of 28 and 40.
of women
James Thurber 1894–1961: in *Time* 15 August 1960

28 No woman should ever be quite accurate about her age. It
looks so calculating.
Oscar Wilde 1854–1900: *The Importance of Being Earnest* (1895)

29 It's never too late to have a fling,
For Autumn is just as nice as Spring,
And it's never too late to fall in love.
Sandy Wilson 1924– : 'It's Never Too Late to Fall in Love' (1954 song)

30 Oh, who could have foretold
That the heart grows old?
W. B. Yeats 1865–1939: 'A Song' (1919)

Alcohol

1 Alcohol is like love: the first kiss is magic, the second is
intimate, the third is routine. After that you just take the
girl's clothes off.
Raymond Chandler 1888–1959: *The Long Good-Bye* (1953)

2 And after wyn on Venus moste I thynke,
For al so siker as cold engendreth hayl,
A likerous mouth moste han a likerous tayl.
Geoffrey Chaucer c.1343–1400: *The Canterbury Tales* 'The Wife of Bath's
Prologue'

3 There is wan thing, an' on'y wan thing, to be said in favour iv dhrink, an' that is that it has caused manny a lady to be loved that otherwise might've died single.
Finley Peter Dunne 1867–1936: *Mr. Dooley Says* (1910)

4 I was in love with a beautiful blonde once, dear. She drove me to drink. That's the one thing I'm indebted to her for.
W. C. Fields 1880–1946: *Never Give a Sucker an Even Break* (1941 film)

5 The evil gin does would be hard to assess—
Besides, it's inclined to affect m'prowess.
Have some Madeira, m'dear.
Michael Flanders 1922–75 and **Donald Swann** 1923–94: 'Have Some Madeira, M'Dear' (c.1956 song)

6 If ever I marry a wife,
I'll marry a landlord's daughter,
For then I may sit in the bar,
And drink cold brandy and water.
Charles Lamb 1775–1834: 'Written in a copy of *Coelebs in Search of a Wife*'

7 No man is genuinely happy, married, who has to drink worse gin than he used to drink when he was single.
H. L. Mencken 1880–1956: *Prejudices* 'Reflections on Monogamy'

8 Candy
Is dandy
But liquor
Is quicker.
Ogden Nash 1902–71: 'Reflections on Ice-breaking' (1931)

9 I get no kick from champagne,
Mere alcohol doesn't thrill me at all,
So tell me why should it be true
That I get a kick out of you?
Cole Porter 1891–1964: 'I Get a Kick Out of You' (1934)

10 A little in drink, but at all times yr faithful husband.
Richard Steele 1672–1729: letter to his wife, 27 September 1708

11 'But you married?' 'Yes, mum. But it was in the war, and
he was very drunk.'
Evelyn Waugh 1903–66: *Decline and Fall* (1928)

12 Liquor and love
rescue the cloudy sense
banish its despair
give it a home.
William Carlos Williams 1883–1963: 'World Narrowed to a Point'

13 The lips that touch liquor must never touch mine.
George W. Young 1846–1919: title of verse (*c.*1870)

Anniversaries

1 John Gilpin's spouse said to her dear
—Though wedded we have been
These twice ten tedious years, yet we
No holiday have seen.

Tomorrow is our wedding day
And we will then repair
Unto the Bell at Edmonton
All in a chaise and pair.
William Cowper 1731–1800: 'John Gilpin' (1785)

2 No, I haven't any formula. I can just say it's been a very
happy experience . . . a successful marriage I think gets
happier as the years go by, that's about all.
on his 43rd wedding anniversary
Dwight D. Eisenhower 1890–1969: news conference, 1 July 1959

3 I know a lot of people didn't expect our relationship to
last—but we've just celebrated our two months
anniversary.
Britt Ekland 1942– : attributed

4 I think everybody really will concede that on this, of all
days, I should begin my speech with the words 'My
husband and I'.
Elizabeth II 1926– : speech at Guildhall on her 25th wedding anniversary,
20 November 1972

5 Please don't be too effusive.
*adjuration to the Prime Minister, at their weekly meeting on
the speech he was to make to celebrate her golden wedding*
Elizabeth II 1926– : in *Daily Telegraph* 21 November 1997

6 Ten years after your death
I meet on a page of your journal, as never before,
The shock of your joy.
Ted Hughes 1930–98: *Birthday Letters* (1998) 'Visit'

7 She had celebrated her silver wedding and renewed her
intimacy with her husband by waltzing with him to Mr
Power's accompaniment.
James Joyce 1882–1941: *Dubliners* (1914)

8 The secret of our relationship is that we hardly ever see
each other.
*on the eve of the silver anniversary of his marriage to Joanne
Woodward*
Paul Newman 1925– : attributed

Armed Forces

1 Mademoiselle from Armenteers,
Hasn't been kissed for forty years,
Hinky, dinky, parley-voo.
Anonymous: 'Mademoiselle from Armenteers', song of the First World War,
variously attributed to Edward Rowland and to Harry Carlton

2 *Nous en rêvons la nuit, nous y pensons le jour,
Ce n'est que Madelon, mais pour nous, c'est l'amour.*
We dream of her by night, we think of her by day,

It's only Madelon, but for us, it's love.
Anonymous: 'Quand Madelon' (1914), French soldiers' song of the First World War

3 She very soon married this short young man
Who talked about soldiers all day
But who wasn't above
Making passionate love
In a coarse, rather Corsican way.
Noël Coward 1899–1973: 'Josephine' (1946)

4 A good uniform must work its way with the women, sooner or later.
Charles Dickens 1812–70: *Pickwick Papers* (1837)

5 For here the lover and killer are mingled
who had one body and one heart.
And death, who had the soldier singled
has done the lover mortal hurt.
Keith Douglas 1920–44: 'Vergissmeinnicht, 1943'

6 I could not love thee, Dear, so much,
Loved I not honour more.
Richard Lovelace 1618–58: 'To Lucasta, Going to the Wars' (1649)

7 The Duke returned from the wars today and did pleasure me in his top-boots.
Sarah, Duchess of Marlborough 1660–1744: attributed

8 When I was in the military, they gave me a medal for killing two men and a discharge for loving one.
Leonard Matlovich d. 1988: attributed

9 I . . . know why most societies don't allow women in combat. Combat is just a battle to the death. You don't want to turn it into something really ugly like a marriage.
P. J. O'Rourke 1947– : *Age and Guile* (1995)

Armed Forces

10   We are soldiers;
And may that soldier a mere recreant prove,
That means not, hath not, or is not in love!
William Shakespeare 1564–1616: *Troilus and Cressida* (1602)

11 When the military man approaches, the world locks up its
spoons and packs off its womankind.
George Bernard Shaw 1856–1950: *Man and Superman* (1903)

12 Overpaid, overfed, oversexed, and over here.
of American troops in Britain during the Second World War
Tommy Trinder 1909–89: associated with Trinder, but probably not his
invention

Arranged Marriages

1 They only who have felt it know the misery of being forced
to marry where they do not love; of being yoked for life to a
disagreeable person and imperious temper, where
ignorance and folly (the ingredients of a cockscomb, who is
the most insufferable fool) tyrannizes over wit and sense.
Mary Astell 1668–1731: *Reflections upon Marriage* (1700)

2 Love matches are formed by people who pay for a month of
honey with a life of vinegar.
Countess of Blessington 1789–1849: *Desultory Thoughts and Reflections*
(1839)

3 To take a wife merely as an agreeable and rational
companion, will commonly be found to be a grand mistake.
Lord Chesterfield 1694–1773: *Letters* (1765)

4 As to marriage on the part of a man, my dear, Society
requires that he should retrieve his fortunes by marriage.
Society requires that he should gain by marriage. Society
requires that he should found a handsome establishment by
marriage. Society does not see, otherwise, what he has to
do with marriage.
Charles Dickens 1812–70: *Little Dorrit* (1857)

5 To be sure a love match was the only thing for happiness, where the parties could any way afford it.
Maria Edgeworth 1767–1849: *Castle Rackrent* (1800)

6 Personally, I can't see why it would be any less romantic to find a husband in a nice four-colour catalogue than in the average downtown bar at happy hour.
Barbara Ehrenreich 1941– : *The Worst Years of Our Lives* (1991)

7 Marriages would in general be as happy, and often more so, if they were all made by the Lord Chancellor, upon a due consideration of characters and circumstances, without the parties having any choice in the matter.
Samuel Johnson 1709–84: James Boswell *Life of Samuel Johnson* (1791)
22 March 1776

8 What I say is what business have the likes of us with love? It is enough to have to find the bite to eat.
speech of the matchmaker, Thomasheen Seán Rua
John B. Keane 1928– : *Sive* (1959)

9 Any one must see at a glance that if men and women marry those whom they do not love, they must love those whom they do not marry.
Harriet Martineau 1802–76: *Society in America* (1837)

10 I have chosen such a good boy for Savita, and all everyone does is complain.
Vikram Seth 1952– : *A Suitable Boy* (1993)

11 I do need your help. Getting you married is not easy.
Vikram Seth 1952– : *A Suitable Boy* (1993)

12 Here [in Tangier], marriage is contracted by the parents of the parties to it. There are no valentines, no stolen interviews, no riding out, no courting in dim parlours, no lovers' quarrels and reconciliations—no nothing that is proper to approaching matrimony.
Mark Twain 1835–1910: *The Innocents Abroad* (1869)

Arranged

13 People who wish to get married should actually have met
before deciding to do so.
William Whitelaw 1918– : speech, House of Commons, 14 November 1979

Assignations see also **Meeting**

1 In the licorice fields at Pontefract
My love and I did meet
And many a burdened licorice bush
Was blooming round our feet.
John Betjeman 1906–84: 'The Licorice Fields at Pontefract' (1954)

2 We loved, sir—used to meet:
How sad and bad and mad it was—
But then, how it was sweet!
Robert Browning 1812–89: 'Confessions' (1864)

3 Never the time and the place
And the loved one all together!
Robert Browning 1812–89: 'Never the Time and the Place' (1883)

4 Here of a Sunday morning
My love and I would lie,
And see the coloured counties,
And hear the larks so high
About us in the sky.
A. E. Housman 1859–1936: *A Shropshire Lad* (1896)

5 Look for me by moonlight;
Watch for me by moonlight;
I'll come to thee by moonlight, though hell should bar the
way!
Alfred Noyes 1880–1958: 'The Highwayman' (1907)

6 Meet me in St Louis, Louis,
Meet me at the fair.
Andrew B. Sterling: 'Meet Me in St Louis' (1904 song)

7 Why don't you come up sometime, and see me?
usually quoted as, 'Why don't you come up and see me
sometime?'
Mae West 1892–1980: *She Done Him Wrong* (1933 film)

8 Down by the salley gardens my love and I did meet;
She passed the salley gardens with little snow-white feet.
She bid me take love easy, as the leaves grow on the tree;
But I, being young and foolish, with her would not agree.
W. B. Yeats 1865–1939: 'Down by the Salley Gardens' (1889)

Attraction

1 That's it baby, when you got it, flaunt it.
Mel Brooks 1926– : *The Producers* (1968 film)

2 You see a pair of laughing eyes,
And suddenly you're sighing sighs,
You think there's something wrong,
You string along,
And then—snap!
Those eyes, those sighs, they're part of the tender trap.
Sammy Cahn 1913–93: 'The Tender Trap' (1955 song)

3 Nothing is more attractive to a man than a bored,
beautiful, but safely married woman—all fun and no fear.
Jilly Cooper 1937– : *How to Stay Married* (1977)

4 Sex-appeal isn't just straight teeth, a square jaw and a solid
torso. Look at me. I'm sixty-three and first thing in the
morning I have a face like a woollen mat. And yet I am the
most desirable man in the world. Indeed, if I put my mind
to it I am sure I could pass the supreme test and lure Miss
Taylor away from Mr Burton.
Noël Coward 1899–1973: Dick Richards *The Wit of Noel Coward* (1968)

5 (i do not know what it is about you that closes
and opens; only something in me understands
the voice of your eyes is deeper than all roses)

nobody, not even the rain, has such small hands.
e. e. cummings 1894–1962: 'somewhere I have never travelled' (1931)

6 Rule 1. Be a 'creature unlike any other'.
Ellen Fein and Sherrie Schneider: *The Rules: Time-Tested Secrets for Capturing the Heart of Mr Right* (1995)

7 Fish got to swim and birds got to fly
I got to love one man till I die,
Can't help lovin' dat man of mine.
Oscar Hammerstein II 1895–1960: 'Can't Help Lovin' Dat Man of Mine' (1927 song)

8 When I'm not near the girl I love,
I love the girl I'm near.
  . . . When I can't fondle the hand I'm fond of
I fondle the hand at hand.
E. Y. Harburg 1898–1981: 'When I'm Not Near the Girl I Love' (1947 song)

9 'Tisn't beauty, so to speak, nor good talk necessarily. It's
just It. Some women'll stay in a man's memory if they once
walked down a street.
Rudyard Kipling 1865–1936: *Traffics and Discoveries* (1904)

10 Sex appeal is fifty per cent what you've got and fifty per
cent what people think you've got.
Sophia Loren 1934– : Leslie Halliwell (ed.) *Halliwell's Filmgoer's Companion* (1984)

11 Coquettes know how to please, not how to love, which is
why men love them so much.
Pierre Marivaux 1688–1763: *Lettres sur les habitants de Paris* (1717–8)

12 No matter how happily a woman may be married, it
always pleases her to discover that there is a nice man who
wishes she were not.
H. L. Mencken 1880–1956: *Chrestomathy* (1949)

13 A man doesn't dream about a woman because he thinks
    her 'mysterious'; he decides that she is 'mysterious' to
    justify his dreaming about her.
    Henry de Montherlant 1896–1972: 'The Goddess Cypris' (1944)

14 Lolita, light of my life, fire of my loins. My sin, my soul.
    Lo-lee-ta: the tip of the tongue taking a trip of three steps
    down the palate to tap, at three, on the teeth. Lo. Lee. Ta.
    Vladimir Nabokov 1899–1977: *Lolita* (1955)

15 A woman without the vanity which delights in her power
    of attracting would be by that very fact without power to
    attract.
    Coventry Patmore 1823–96: *Religio Poetae* (1893)

16 When I find a woman attractive, I have nothing at all to
    say. I simply watch her smile. Intellectuals take apart her
    face in order to explain it bit by bit, but they no longer see
    the smile.
    Antoine de Saint-Exupéry 1900–44: *Pilote de Guerre* (1942)

17 If most men and women were forced to rely upon physical
    charm to attract lovers, their sexual lives would be not only
    meagre but in a youth-worshipping country like America
    painfully brief.
    Gore Vidal 1925– : in *New York Review of Books* 31 March 1966

Bachelors see also Men, The Single Life

1 It is a truth universally acknowledged, that a single man in
   possession of a good fortune, must be in want of a wife.
   Jane Austen 1775–1817: *Pride and Prejudice* (1813)

2 A man in love is incomplete until he has married. Then he's finished.
Zsa Zsa Gabor 1919– : in *Newsweek* 28 March 1960

3 'It is very pleasant dining with a bachelor,' said Miss Matty, softly, as we settled ourselves in the counting-house. 'I only hope it may not be improper; so many pleasant things are!'
Elizabeth Gaskell 1810–65: *Cranford* (1853)

4 Oh, is it true, I ask again,
The world's still full of single men,
Ubiquitous as Cellophane,
As commonplace as slumber,
Who hail you taxis in the rain
And ask you for your number?
Phyllis McGinley 1905– : 'Letter from a Winter Resort'

5 Bachelors know more about women than married men. If they did not they would be married too.
H. L. Mencken 1880–1956: *Chrestomathy* (1949)

6 We are a select group, without personal obligation, social encumbrance, or any socks that match.
P. J. O'Rourke 1947– : *The Bachelor Home Companion* (1987)

7 Bachelors know all about parties. In fact, a good bachelor is a living, breathing party all by himself.
P. J. O'Rourke 1947– : *The Bachelor Home Companion* (1987)

8 Somehow a bachelor never quite gets over the idea that he is a thing of beauty and a boy forever.
Helen Rowland 1875–1950: *A Guide to Men* (1922)

9 Never trust a husband too far or a bachelor too near.
Helen Rowland 1875–1950: *The Rubaiyat of a Bachelor* (1915)

10 A young man married is a man that's marred.
William Shakespeare 1564–1616: *All's Well that Ends Well* (1603–4); cf. **Epitaphs** 7

11 Nothing perhaps is so efficacious in preventing men from
   marrying as the tone in which married women speak of the
   struggles made in that direction by their unmarried friends.
   Anthony Trollope 1815–82: *The Way We Live Now* (1875)

Beauty see also The Body, Cosmetics, Hair

1 Love is a great beautifier.
   Louisa May Alcott 1832–88: *Little Women* (1868–9)

2 Girl, when rejecting me you never guessed
   I gave you all the beauty you possessed.
   Now that I've ceased to love you, you remain
   At once, a creature singularly plain.
   Martin Armstrong 1882–1974: 'To a Jilt'

3 Love . . . the delightful interval between meeting a beautiful
   girl and discovering that she looks like a haddock.
   John Barrymore 1882–1942: attributed

4 A pretty girl is like a melody
   That haunts you night and day.
   Irving Berlin 1888–1989: 'A Pretty Girl is like a Melody' (1919 song)

5 Who is she that looketh forth as the morning, fair as the
   moon, clear as the sun, and terrible as an army with
   banners?
   Bible: Song of Solomon

6 Beauty. The power by which a woman charms her lover
   and terrifies her husband.
   Ambrose Bierce 1842–c.1914: *The Devil's Dictionary* (1911)

7 It is better to be first with an ugly woman than the
   hundredth with a beauty.
   Pearl S. Buck 1892–1973: *The Good Earth* (1931)

8 She walks in beauty, like the night
   Of cloudless climes and starry skies.
   Lord Byron 1788–1824: 'She Walks in Beauty' (1815)

9 Ask me no more where Jove bestows,
When June is past, the fading rose;
For in your beauty's orient deep
These flowers, as in their causes, sleep.
Thomas Carew c.1595–1640: 'A Song' (1640)

10 'Oh, Julia,' he said, opening his eyes very wide with
reproach, 'how can you be so shameless?'
    'Ah, Ned,' I answered, 'Because you are so beautiful.'
Sarah Caudwell 1939– : *Thus Was Adonis Murdered* (1981)

11 And she was fayr as is the rose in May.
Geoffrey Chaucer c.1343–1400: *The Legend of Good Women* 'Cleopatra'

12 When a woman isn't beautiful, people always say, 'You
have lovely eyes, you have lovely hair.'
Anton Chekhov 1860–1904: *Uncle Vanya* (1897)

13 She is not fair to outward view
As many maidens be;
Her loveliness I never knew
Until she smiled on me.
Hartley Coleridge 1796–1849: 'She is not fair' (1833)

14 Beauty is the lover's gift.
William Congreve 1670–1729: *The Way of the World* (1700)

15 Love built on beauty, soon as beauty, dies.
John Donne 1572–1631: 'The Anagram' (c.1595)

16 Plain women he regarded as he did the other severe facts of
life, to be faced with philosophy and investigated by
science.
George Eliot 1819–80: *Middlemarch* (1871–2)

17 One girl can be pretty—but a dozen are only a chorus.
F. Scott Fitzgerald 1896–1940: *The Last Tycoon* (1941)

18 He was afflicted by the thought that where Beauty was,
nothing ever ran quite straight, which, no doubt, was why
so many people looked on it as immoral.
John Galsworthy 1867–1933: *In Chancery* (1920)

19 I have a left shoulder-blade that is a miracle of loveliness.
People come miles to see it. My right elbow has a
fascination that few can resist.
W. S. Gilbert 1836–1911: *The Mikado* (1885)

20 A poor beauty finds more lovers than husbands.
George Herbert 1593–1633: *Outlandish Proverbs* (1640)

21 This Adonis in loveliness was a corpulent man of fifty.
of the Prince Regent
Leigh Hunt 1784–1859: in *The Examiner* 22 March 1812

22 Beauty in London is so cheap, and consequently so
common to the men of fashion, (who are prodigiously fond
of novelty) that they absolutely begin to fall in love with
the ugly women, by way of change.
Elizabeth Inchbald 1753–1821: *Appearance is Against Them* (1785)

23 She is magnificently ugly—deliciously hideous . . . Now in
this vast ugliness resides a most powerful beauty which, in
a very few minutes, steals forth and charms the mind, so
that you end as I ended, in falling in love with her.
of George Eliot
Henry James 1843–1916: letter to his father Henry James, 10 May 1869

24 Was this the face that launched a thousand ships,
And burnt the topless towers of Ilium?
Sweet Helen, make me immortal with a kiss!
Christopher Marlowe 1564–93: *Doctor Faustus* (1604)

25 She fair, divinely fair, fit love for gods.
John Milton 1608–74: *Paradise Lost* (1667)

26 No power on earth, however, can abolish the merciless class distinction between those who are physically desirable and the lonely, pallid, spotted, silent, unfancied majority.
John Mortimer 1923– : *Clinging to the Wreckage* (1982)

27 If you are really Master of your Fate,
It shouldn't make any difference to you whether
Cleopatra or the Bearded Lady is your mate.
Ogden Nash 1902–71: 'The Anatomy of Happiness' (1938)

28 The flowers anew, returning seasons bring;
But beauty faded has no second spring.
Ambrose Philips c.1675–1749: *The First Pastoral* (1708)

29 Art is not the application of a canon of beauty but what the instinct and the brain can conceive beyond any canon. When we love a woman we don't start measuring her limbs.
Pablo Picasso 1881–1973: interview with Christian Zervos, 1935; A. H. Barr *Picasso: Fifty Years of his Art* (1946)

30 I always say beauty is only sin deep.
Saki 1870–1916: *Reginald* (1904)

31 O! she doth teach the torches to burn bright.
It seems she hangs upon the cheek of night
Like a rich jewel in an Ethiop's ear;
Beauty too rich for use, for earth too dear.
William Shakespeare 1564–1616: *Romeo and Juliet* (1595)

32 My mistress' eyes are nothing like the sun;
Coral is far more red than her lips' red:
If snow be white, why then her breasts are dun;
If hairs be wires, black wires grow on her head.
William Shakespeare 1564–1616: sonnet 130

33 Beauty is all very well at first sight; but who ever looks at it when it has been in the house three days?
George Bernard Shaw 1856–1950: *Man and Superman* (1903)

34 For she was beautiful—her beauty made
   The bright world dim, and everything beside
   Seemed like the fleeting image of a shade.
   Percy Bysshe Shelley 1792–1822: 'The Witch of Atlas' (written 1820)

35 What woman whose beauty time has at last ravaged can
   hear without tears the song that her lover once sung for
   her?
   Mme de Staël 1766–1817: *Lettres sur les ouvrages et le caractère de J. J.*
   Rousseau (1788)

36 If beauty is truth, why don't women go to the library to
   have their hair done?
   Lily Tomlin 1939– : Sally Feldman (ed.) *Woman's Hour Book of Humour*
   (1993)

37 The beauty myth moves for men as a mirage; its power lies
   in its ever-receding nature. When the gap is closed, the
   lover embraces only his own disillusion.
   Naomi Wolf 1962– : *The Beauty Myth* (1990)

38 A woman of so shining loveliness
   That men threshed corn at midnight by a tress,
   A little stolen tress.
   W. B. Yeats 1865–1939: 'The Secret Rose' (1899)

Behaviour

1 Most vices may be committed very genteelly: a man may
   debauch his friend's wife genteelly: he may cheat at cards
   genteelly.
   James Boswell 1740–95: *Life of Samuel Johnson* (1791)

2 In short, he was a perfect cavaliero,
   And to his very valet seemed a hero.
   Lord Byron 1788–1824: *Beppo* (1818)

(B)

3 It doesn't matter what you do in the bedroom as long as
you don't do it in the street and frighten the horses.
Mrs Patrick Campbell 1865–1940: D. Fielding *Duchess of Jermyn Street*
(1964)

4 Careless she is with artful care,
Affecting to seem unaffected.
William Congreve 1670–1729: 'Amoret'

5 A little disdain is not amiss; a little scorn is alluring.
William Congreve 1670–1729: *The Way of the World* (1700)

6 I believe we should all behave quite differently if we lived in
a warm, sunny climate all the time.
Noël Coward 1899–1973: *Brief Encounter* (1945)

7 I get too hungry for dinner at eight.
I like the theatre, but never come late.
I never bother with people I hate.
That's why the lady is a tramp.
Lorenz Hart 1895–1943: 'The Lady is a Tramp' (1937)

8 Oh, when I was in love with you,
Then I was clean and brave,
And miles around the wonder grew
How well I did behave.

And now the fancy passes by,
And nothing will remain,
And miles around they'll say that I
Am quite myself again.
A. E. Housman 1859–1936: *A Shropshire Lad* (1896)

9 Ceremony is an invention to take off the uneasy feeling
which we derive from knowing ourselves to be less the
object of love and esteem with a fellow-creature than some
other person is.
Charles Lamb 1775–1834: *Essays of Elia* (1823) 'A Bachelor's Complaint of
the Behaviour of Married People'

10 Delicacy is to love what grace is to beauty.
Madame de Maintenon 1635–1719: *Maximes de Mme de Maintenon* (1686)

11 CHARMIAN: In each thing give him way, cross him in
nothing.
CLEOPATRA: Thou teachest like a fool; the way to lose him.
William Shakespeare 1564–1616: *Antony and Cleopatra* (1606–7)

12 Manners are especially the need of the plain. The pretty can
get away with anything.
Evelyn Waugh 1903–66: in *Observer* 15 April 1962

13 The best way to hold a man is in your arms.
Mae West 1892–1980: Joseph Weintraub *Peel Me a Grape* (1975)

14 The amount of women in London who flirt with their own
husbands is perfectly scandalous. It looks so bad. It is
simply washing one's clean linen in public.
Oscar Wilde 1854–1900: *The Importance of Being Earnest* (1895)

15 Talk to every woman as if you loved her, and to every man
as if he bored you, and at the end of your first season you
will have the reputation of possessing the most perfect
social tact.
Oscar Wilde 1854–1900: *A Woman of No Importance* (1893)

16 Hysteria is a natural phenomenon, the common
denominator of the female nature. It's the big female
weapon, and the test of a man is his ability to cope with it.
Tennessee Williams 1911–83: *The Night of the Iguana* (1961)

The Beloved

1 When, after all, what reason have you to love me,
Who have neither the prettiness and moisture of youth, the
appeal of the baby,
The fencing wit of the old successful life,
Nor brutality's fascination?
W. H. Auden 1907–73: 'Love Letter'

2 To love someone is to isolate him from the world, wipe out every trace of him, dispossess him of his shadow, drag him into a murderous future. It is to circle around the other like a dead star and absorb him into a black light.
Jean Baudrillard 1929– : *Fatal Strategies* (1983)

3 Love-thirty, love-forty, oh! weakness of joy,
The speed of a swallow, the grace of a boy,
With carefullest carelessness, gaily you won,
I am weak from your loveliness, Joan Hunter Dunn.
John Betjeman 1906–84: 'A Subaltern's Love-Song' (1945)

4 As the apple tree among the trees of the wood, so is my beloved among the sons.
Bible: Song of Solomon

5 He's more myself than I am. Whatever our souls are made of his and mine are the same.
Emily Brontë 1818–48: *Wuthering Heights* (1847)

6 I would that you were all to me,
You that are just so much, no more.
Robert Browning 1812–89: 'Two in the Campagna' (1855)

7 To see her is to love her,
And love but her for ever;
For Nature made her what she is
And never made anither!
Robert Burns 1759–96: 'Bonnie Lesley' (1798)

8 I am not at all the sort of person you and I took me for.
Jane Carlyle 1801–66: letter to Thomas Carlyle, 7 May 1822

9 I shall ever remember the gentleness of your manners and the wild originality of your countenance.
Claire Clairmont 1798–1879: letter to Lord Byron, 1816

10 And yet I love this false, this worthless man,
With all the passion that a woman can;
Dote on his imperfections, though I spy

Nothing to love; I love, and know not why.
Ephelia: 'To one that asked me why I loved J. G.' (1679)

11 Who calls her two-faced? Faces, she has three:
The first inscrutable, for the outer world;
The second shrouded in self-contemplation;
The third, her face of love,
Once for an endless moment turned on me.
Robert Graves 1895–1985: 'The Three-Faced'

12 One alone to be my own,
I alone to know her caresses,
One to be eternally
The one my worshipping soul possesses.
Oscar Hammerstein II 1895–1960 and **Otto Harbach** 1873–1963: 'One Alone' (1926 song) from *The Desert Song*

13 The ones we choose to love become our anchor
when the hawser of the blood-tie's hacked, or frays.
Tony Harrison 1953– : *v* (1985)

14 I was more pleased with possessing your heart than with
any other happiness . . . the man was the thing I least
valued in you.
Héloise *c.*1098–1164: first letter to Abelard, c.1122

15 That was the proverb. Let my mistress be
Lazy to others, but be long to me.
Robert Herrick 1591–1674: 'Long and Lazy'; cf. **Women 1**

16 A fool there was and he made his prayer
(Even as you and I!)
To a rag and a bone and a hank of hair
(We called her the woman who did not care)
But the fool he called her his lady fair—
(Even as you and I!)
Rudyard Kipling 1865–1936: 'The Vampire' (1897)

(B)

17 I loved you, so I drew these tides of men into my hands and
    wrote my will across the sky in stars
To earn you freedom, the seven pillared worthy house, that
    your eyes might be shining for me
When we came.
T. E. Lawrence 1888–1935: *The Seven Pillars of Wisdom* (1926) dedication

18 There are the lover and the beloved, but these two come
from different countries.
Carson McCullers 1917–67: *Ballad of the Sad Cafe* (1951)

19 Difficult or easy, pleasant or bitter, you are the same you: I
cannot live with you—or without you.
Martial AD *c.*40–*c.*104: *Epigrammata*

20 You're the Nile,
You're the Tow'r of Pisa,
You're the smile
On the Mona Lisa.
I'm a worthless check, a total wreck, a flop,
But if, baby, I'm the bottom
You're the top!
Cole Porter 1891–1964: 'You're the Top' (1934 song)

21   It were all one
That I should love a bright particular star
And think to wed it, he is so above me.
William Shakespeare 1564–1616: *All's Well that Ends Well* (1603–4)

22 Run, run, Orlando: carve on every tree
The fair, the chaste, and unexpressive she.
William Shakespeare 1564–1616: *As You Like It* (1599)

23 To her! To that magnificent and appalling creature! I
should as soon have thought of making love to the
Archbishop of Canterbury!
*responding to Samuel Rogers's suggestion that Sheridan might
'make open love' to Mrs Siddons*
Richard Brinsley Sheridan 1751–1816: Henry Colborn (ed.) *Sheridaniana*
(1826)

24 How many loved your moments of glad grace,
    And loved your beauty with love false or true,
    But one man loved the pilgrim soul in you,
    And loved the sorrows of your changing face.
W. B. Yeats 1865–1939: 'When You Are Old' (1892)

The Best Man

1 Ride softly on, said the best young man,
    For I think our bonny bride looks pale and wan.
Ballad: 'The Cruel Brother'

2 My lucky appearance saved the bridegroom from having to
    sally out into the streets in search of a best man.
Arthur Conan Doyle 1859–1930: *The Adventures of Sherlock Holmes* (1892)

3   For Best Man—my squire
    To hold the meanwhile rings—
    We requisitioned the sexton.
Ted Hughes 1930–98: *Birthday Letters* (1998) 'A Pink Wool Knitted Dress'

4   The trouble
    with being best man is, you don't get a chance to prove it.
Les A. Murray 1938– : *The Boys Who Stole the Funeral* (1989)

5 The best man's principal responsibility, however, is to talk
    the groom into running away to Ibiza, at the last minute
    after all.
P. J. O'Rourke 1947– : *Modern Manners* (1984)

6 He pretended five times that he had lost the ring, and just
    as we were setting out he mislaid it in earnest; but his
    lordship, with his customary detective ability, discovered it
    and took charge of it personally.
Dorothy L. Sayers 1893–1957: *Busman's Honeymoon* (1937)

Betrayal see Trust and Betrayal

The Body see also Beauty, Cosmetics, Hair, Size and Shape

1 My brain? It's my second favourite organ.
Woody Allen 1935– : *Sleeper* (1973 film, with Marshall Brickman)

2 A man cannot marry before he has studied anatomy and has dissected at the least one woman.
Honoré de Balzac 1799–1850: *Physiology of Marriage* (1829)

3 Red hair she had and golden skin,
Her sulky lips were shaped for sin,
Her sturdy legs were flannel-slack'd,
The strongest legs in Pontefract.
John Betjeman 1906–84: 'The Licorice Fields at Pontefract' (1954)

4 He has adopted a most graceful and decorative attitude, leaning back against the top of the seat with just sufficient to emphasize the charming hollow of the left hip. But I haven't been able to see his face.
Sarah Caudwell 1939– : *Thus Was Adonis Murdered* (1981)

5 I let go of her wrists, closed the door with my elbow and slid past her. It was like the first time. 'You ought to carry insurance on those,' I said.
Raymond Chandler 1888–1959: *The Little Sister* (1949)

6 The more serious the face, the more beautiful the smile.
François-René Chateaubriand 1768–1848: *Mémoires d'Outre-Tombe* (1849–50)

7 A woman watches her body uneasily, as though it were an unreliable ally in the battle for love.
Leonard Cohen 1934– : *The Favourite Game* (1963)

8 When she raises her eyelids, it is as if she is undressing.
Colette 1873–1954: *Claudine Goes Away* (1931)

9 i like my body when it is with your
body. It is so quite new a thing.
Muscles better and nerves more.
i like your body. i like what it does,
i like its hows.
e. e. cummings 1894–1962: 'Sonnets–Actualities' no. 8 (1925)

10 The average man is more interested in a woman who is
interested in him than he is in a woman—any woman—
with beautiful legs.
Marlene Dietrich 1901–92: attributed, 1954

11 But O alas, so long, so far
Our bodies why do we forbear?
They're ours, though they're not we, we are
The intelligencies, they the sphere.
John Donne 1572–1631: *Songs and Sonnets* 'The Ecstasy'

12 Grishkin is nice: her Russian eye
Is underlined for emphasis;
Uncorseted, her friendly bust
Gives promise of pneumatic bliss.
T. S. Eliot 1888–1965: 'Whispers of Immortality' (1919)

13 In my sex fantasy, nobody ever loves me for my mind.
Nora Ephron 1941– : attributed

14 Of course, she's only a digestive tube, like all of us.
Yes, but look what it's attached to!
Gavin Ewart 1916–95: 'A Dialogue between the Head and the Heart'

15 Being a woman is worse than being a farmer—There is so
much harvesting and crop spraying to be done: legs to be
waxed, underarms shaved, eyebrows plucked, feet
pumiced, skin exfoliated and moisturized, spots cleansed,
roots dyed, eyelashes tinted, nails filed, cellulite massaged,
stomach muscles exercised . . . Is it any wonder girls have
no confidence?
Helen Fielding 1958– : *Bridget Jones's Diary* (1996)

Body

16 Love's tongue is in the eyes.
Phineas Fletcher 1582–1650: *Piscatory Eclogues* (1633)

17 Anatomy is destiny.
Sigmund Freud 1856–1939: *Collected Writings* (1924)

18 I like the hair upon your shoulders,
Falling like water over boulders.
I like the shoulders, too: they are essential.
Your collar-bones have great potential
(I'd like all your particulars in folders
Marked *Confidential*).
John Fuller 1937– : 'Valentine'

19 When our organs have been transplanted
And the new ones made happy to lodge in us,
Let us pray one wish be granted—
We retain our zones erogenous.
E. Y. Harburg 1898–1981: 'Seated One Day at the Organ' (1965)

20 Fain would I kiss my Julia's dainty leg,
Which is as white and hairless as an egg.
Robert Herrick 1591–1674: 'On Julia's Legs' (1648)

21 I'm tired of all this nonsense about beauty being only skin-
deep. That's deep enough. What do you want—an
adorable pancreas?
Jean Kerr 1923– : *The Snake has all the Lines* (1958)

22 Between her breasts is my home, between her breasts.
Three sides set on me space and fear, but the fourth side
rests
Sure and a tower of strength, 'twixt the walls of her
breasts.
D. H. Lawrence 1885–1930: 'Song of a Man Who is Loved'

23 The light that lies
In woman's eyes,
Has been my heart's undoing.
Thomas Moore 1779–1852: 'The time I've lost in wooing' (1807)

24 I'd like to borrow his body for just 48 hours. There are
three guys I'd like to beat up and four women I'd like to
make love to.
of Muhammad Ali
Jim Murray: attributed

25 I have gone marking the blank atlas of your body
with crosses of fire.
My mouth went across: a spider, trying to hide.
In you, behind you, timid, driven by thirst.
Pablo Neruda 1904–73: 'I Have Gone Marking' (1924)

26 Men seldom make passes
At girls who wear glasses.
Dorothy Parker 1893–1967: 'News Item' (1937)

27 Had Cleopatra's nose been shorter, the whole face of the
world would have changed.
Blaise Pascal 1623–62: *Pensées* (1662)

28 You can't expect too much of it, it's seen a lot of service.
But I'm still a bargain.
Edith Piaf 1915–63: comment, *c.*1959; Simone Berteaut *Piaf* (1970)

29 The body of a young woman is God's greatest
achievement . . . Of course, He could have built it to last
longer but you can't have everything.
Neil Simon 1927– : *The Gingerbread Lady* (1970)

30 I let down my silken hair
Over my shoulders
And open my thighs
Over my lover.
'Tell me, is there any part of me
That is not lovable?'
Tzu Yeh *c.*300 AD: 'Song'; K. Rexroth and Ling Chung eds. *The Orchid Boat,
Women Poets of China* (1972)

31 My love is like Mies van der Rohe's
'Machine for living'; she,
Divested of her underclothes,

Body

Suggests efficiency.
John Updike 1932– : 'Dea Ex Machina' (1985)

32 *Dixit et avertens rosea cervice refulsit,*
Ambrosiaeque comae divinum vertice odorem
Spiravere; pedes vestis defluxit ad imos,
Et vera incessu patuit dea.

Thus she spoke and turned away with a flash of her rosy
neck, and her ambrosial hair exhaled a divine fragrance;
her dress flowed right down to her feet and her true
godhead was evident from her walk.
Virgil 70–19 BC: *Aeneid*

33 Big breasts à la Pamela Anderson are one thing but ones
that look more like old socks with tangerines dropped in the
bottom are an entirely different kettle du poisson.
Arabella Weir: *Does My Bum Look Big in This?* (1997)

Books and Literature see also Poets

1 Began the second part of *Little Women* . . . Girls write to ask
who the little women marry, as if that was the only end
and aim of a woman's life. I *won't* marry Jo to Laurie to
please anyone.
Louisa May Alcott 1832–88: *Journals* (1868)

2 We men have got love well weighed up; our stuff
Can get by without it.
Women don't seem to think that's good enough;
They write about it.
Kingsley Amis 1922–95: 'A Bookshop Idyll' (1956)

3 I'm interested in the Gothic novel because it's very much a
woman's form. Why is there such a wide readership for
books that essentially say, 'Your husband is trying to kill
you'?
Margaret Atwood 1939– : in an interview, July 1978; Earl G. Ingersoll
(ed.) *Margaret Atwood: Conversations* (1990)

4 I'd rather have cloth-of-gold wedding dresses, quotations from *Urne Buriall* and tigerish passion in crime writers acquitted of murder, than brown frocks, knitted socks in clerical grey, and cauliflower cheese.
comparing Dorothy L. Sayers and Barbara Pym as providers of escape literature
A. S. Byatt 1936– : in 1986; *Passions of the Mind* (1991); cf. **Wedding Dresses 3**

5 I never wrote anything worth mentioning till I was in love.
Lord Byron 1788–1824: *Conversations* (1824)

6 The reading or non-reading a book—will never keep down a single petticoat.
Lord Byron 1788–1824: letter to Richard Hoppner, 29 October 1819

7 In our culture, love needs a mixer before it qualifies as a subject for literature. Pour it out neat, and you get Mills & Boon.
John Carey 1934– : in *Sunday Times* 11 February 1996

8 If, as Dr Johnson said, a man who is not married is only half a man, so a man who is very much married is only half a writer.
Cyril Connolly 1903–74: *Enemies of Promise* (1938)

9 I have met with women whom I really think would like to be married to a poem and to be given away by a novel.
John Keats 1795–1821: letter to Fanny Brawne, 8 July 1819

10 Surely the sex business isn't worth all this damned fuss? I've met only a handful of people who cared a biscuit for it.
on reading Lady Chatterley's Lover
T. E. Lawrence 1888–1935: Christopher Hassall *Edward Marsh* (1959)

11 Literature is mostly about having sex and not much about having children. Life is the other way round.
David Lodge 1935– : *The British Museum is Falling Down* (1965)

12 My only books
Were woman's looks,
And folly's all they've taught me.
Thomas Moore 1779–1852: 'The time I've lost in wooing' (1807)

13 Writing is like getting married. One should never commit
oneself until one is amazed at one's luck.
Iris Murdoch 1919– : *The Black Prince* (1973)

14 Writing a poem is like a short love affair, writing a short
story like a long love affair, writing a novel like a marriage.
Amos Oz 1939– : in *Observer* 21 July 1985

15 What time the gifted lady took
Away from paper, pen, and book,
She spent in amorous dalliance
(They do these things so well in France).
Dorothy Parker 1893–1967: 'George Sand'

16 The principle of procrastinated rape is said to be the ruling
one in all the great best-sellers.
V. S. Pritchett 1900–97: *The Living Novel* (1946)

17 There *is* sex in the Discworld books, but it usually takes
place two pages after the ending.
Terry Pratchett 1948– : Terry Pratchett and Stephen Briggs *The Discworld
Companion* (1994)

18 Reading about sex in yesterday's novels is like watching
people smoke in old films.
Fay Weldon 1931– : in *Guardian* 1 December 1989

19 Beware you be not swallowed up in books! An ounce of
love is worth a pound of knowledge.
John Wesley 1703–91: Robert Southey *Life of Wesley* (1820)

20 LORD ILLINGWORTH: The Book of Life begins with a man
and a woman in a garden.
MRS ALLONBY: It ends with Revelations.
Oscar Wilde 1854–1900: *A Woman of No Importance* (1893)

Breaking Up see also **Heartbreak, Loss, Parting**

1 O waly, waly, gin love be bonnie
   A little time while it is new!
   But when 'tis auld it waxeth cauld,
   And fades awa' like morning dew.
   Ballad: 'Waly, Waly'

2 I leave before being left. I decide.
   Brigitte Bardot 1934– : in *Newsweek* 5 March 1973

3 You have chosen me, from a low estate, to be your queen
   and your companion, far beyond my desert or desire. If
   then, you find me worthy of such honour, good your
   Grace, let not any light fancy, or bad counsel of mine
   enemies, withdraw your princely favour from me.
   Anne Boleyn 1507–36: letter to Henry VIII, 1536

4 And I shall find some girl perhaps,
   And a better one than you,
   With eyes as wise, but kindlier,
   And lips as soft, but true,
   And I daresay she will do.
   Rupert Brooke 1887–1915: 'The Chilterns'

5 It is difficult suddenly to lay aside a long-cherished love.
   Catullus c.84–c.54 BC: *Carmina*

6 1 Don't see him. Don't phone or write a letter.
   2 The easy way: get to know him better.
   Wendy Cope 1945– : 'Two Cures for Love'

7 Two spheres on meeting may so softly collide
   They stay, as if kissing, side by side.
   Lovers may part for ever—the cause so small
   Not even a lynx could see a gap at all.
   Walter de la Mare 1873–1956: 'Divided'

8 Farewell! Be the proud bride of a ducal coronet, and forget
me! . . . Unalterably, never yours, Augustus.
Charles Dickens 1812–70: *Martin Chuzzlewit* (1844)

9 How do you know love is gone? If you said that you would
be there at seven and you get there by nine, and he or she
has not called the police yet—it's gone.
Marlene Dietrich 1901–92: *Marlene Dietrich's ABC* (1962)

10 Love, for both of them, had ceased to be a journey, an
adventure, an essay of hope. It had become an infection, a
ritual, a drama with a bloody last act, and they could both
foresee the final carnage.
Margaret Drabble 1939– : *The Middle Ground* (1980)

11 When love grows diseased, the best thing we can do is put
it to a violent death; I cannot endure the torture of a
lingering and consumptive passion.
George Etherege c.1635–91: *The Man of Mode* (1676)

12 The love we thought would never stop
now cools like a congealing chop.
The kisses that were hot as curry
are bird-pecks taken in a hurry.
Gavin Ewart 1916–95: 'Ending'

13 Two separate, distinct personalities, not separate at all, but
inextricably bound, soul and body and mind, to each other,
how did we get so far apart so fast?
Judith Guest 1936– : *Ordinary People* (1976)

14 I'm gonna wash that man right outa my hair.
Oscar Hammerstein II 1895–1960: title of song (1949) from *South Pacific*

15 The end of love should be a big event.
It should involve the hiring of a hall.
Why the hell not? It happens to us all.
Why should it pass without acknowledgement?
Sophie Hannah 1971– : 'The End of Love'

16 Love frequently dies of time alone—much more frequently of displacement.
Thomas Hardy 1840–1928: *A Pair of Blue Eyes* (1873)

17 When love congeals
It soon reveals
The faint aroma of performing seals,
The double crossing of a pair of heels.
I wish I were in love again!
Lorenz Hart 1895–1943: 'I Wish I Were in Love Again' (1937 song)

18 There are few people who are not ashamed of their love affairs when the infatuation is over.
Duc de la Rochefoucauld 1613–80: *Maximes* (1678)

19 He loved me absolutely, that's why he hates me absolutely.
Frieda Lawrence 1879–1956: letter to Edward Garnett, c.1914

20 Love never dies of starvation, but often of indigestion.
Ninon de Lenclos 1616–1705: *Letters* (1870)

21 After all, my erstwhile dear,
My no longer cherished,
Need we say it was not love,
Now that love is perished?
Edna St Vincent Millay 1892–1950: 'Passer Mortuus Est' (1921)

22 You who seek an end of love, love will yield to business: be busy, and you will be safe.
Ovid 43 BC–AD c.17: *Remedia Amoris*

23 Ah, the relationships we get into just to get out of the ones we are not brave enough to say are over.
Julia Phillips 1944– : *You'll Never Eat Lunch in This Town Again* (1991)

24 In a separation it is the one who is not really in love who says the more tender things.
Marcel Proust 1871–1922: *Remembrance of Things Past* (1922–31) 'The Captive'

Breaking

25 It is seldom indeed that one parts on good terms, because if
one were on good terms one would not part.
Marcel Proust 1871–1922: *Remembrance of Things Past* (1922–31) 'The
Fugitive'

26 I loved you; and perhaps I love you still,
The flame, perhaps, is not extinguished; yet
It burns so quietly within my soul,
No longer should you feel distressed by it.
Alexander Pushkin 1799–1837: 'I Loved You' (1829)

27 I made a home for you in my heart.
it didn't have four walls
but it had a door
so you left.
Jade Reidy 1962– : 'Home is Where the Heart Is'

28 If you never want to see a man again, say, 'I love you, I
want to marry you. I want to have children . . . '—They
leave skid marks.
Rita Rudner: attributed; Regina Barreca (ed.) *The Penguin Book of Women's
Humour* (1996)

29 I beg of you, don't say goodbye
Can't we give our love another try
Come on, baby, let's start anew
'Cause breaking up is hard to do.
Neil Sedaka 1939– : 'Breaking Up Is Hard To Do' (1959 song)

30 I hated her now with a hatred more fatal than indifference
because it was the other side of love.
August Strindberg 1849–1912: *A Madman's Defence* (1968)

31 And I would have, now love is over,
An end to all, an end:
I cannot, having been your lover,

Stoop to become your friend!
Arthur Symons 1865–1945: 'After Love' (1892)

32 Marriages stop. Marriages change. People are always
saying a marriage 'failed'. It's such a negative way of
putting it . . . Failure is terribly important. Perhaps that's
why I'm saying: the notion that failure is a negative thing
is wrong.
Emma Thompson 1959– : in *Vanity Fair* February 1996

33 *Non! rien de rien,*
Non! je ne regrette rien,
Ni le bien, qu'on m'a fait,
Ni le mal—tout ça m'est bien égal!

No, no regrets,
No, we will have no regrets,
As you leave, I can say—
Love was king, tho' for only a day.
Michel Vaucaire: 'Non, je ne regrette rien' (1960 song); sung by Edith Piaf

34 I don't want anyone to notice that I've been chucked, well,
not even chucked, to be chucked you have to have been
going out with someone, I've been . . . sort of sampled.
Arabella Weir: *Does My Bum Look Big in This?* (1997)

35 We remain bestest of friends.
on her relations with her former husband in the week of her
divorce
Sarah, Duchess of York 1959– : in *Observer* 21 April 1996 'Sayings of the
Week'

Bridegrooms

1 A delectable sward, shaved as close as a bridegroom and
looking just as green.
Basil Boothroyd 1910–88: *Let's Move House* (1977)

2 I am about to be married—and am of course in all the
misery of a man in pursuit of happiness.
Lord Byron 1788–1824: letter 15 October 1814

3 But for his funeral train which the bridegroom sees in the
    distance,
Would he so joyfully, think you, fall in with the marriage-
    procession?
Arthur Hugh Clough 1819–61: *Amours de Voyage* (1858)

4 O God, and the wedding! All her family and her friends
and only a handful of mine all scroungy and bearded
just wait to get at the drinks and food.
Gregory Corso 1930– : 'Marriage' (1960)

5 What she remembers
Is his glistening back
In the bath, his small boots
In the ring of boots at her feet.
Seamus Heaney 1939– : 'Mother of the Groom' (1966)

6 I'm getting married in the morning,
Ding! dong! the bells are gonna chime.
Pull out the stopper;
Let's have a whopper;
But get me to the church on time!
Alan Jay Lerner 1918–86: 'Get Me to the Church on Time' (1956 song)

7 For the poor craven bridegroom said never a word.
Sir Walter Scott 1771–1832: *Marmion* (1808)

8   I will be
A bridegroom in my death, and run into 't
As to a lover's bed.
William Shakespeare 1564–1616: *Antony and Cleopatra* (1606–7)

Brides see also **Wedding Dresses**

1 Happy is the bride that the sun shines on.
Anonymous: proverb

2 That is ever the way. 'Tis all jealousy to the bride and good
wishes to the corpse.
J. M. Barrie 1860–1937: *Quality Street* (1913)

3 Bride. A woman with a fine prospect of happiness behind
her.
Ambrose Bierce 1842–c.1914: *The Devil's Dictionary* (1911)

4 The bride hath paced into the hall,
Red as a rose is she.
Samuel Taylor Coleridge 1772–1834: 'The Rime of the Ancient Mariner'
(1798)

5 Girls usually have a papier mâché face on their wedding
day.
Colette 1873–1954: *Earthly Paradise* (1966)

6 I saw that the bride within the bridal dress had withered
like the dress, and like the flowers, and had no brightness
left but the brightness of her sunken eyes.
of Miss Havisham
Charles Dickens 1812–70: *Great Expectations* (1861)

7 The flowers in the bride's hand are sadly like the garland
which decked the heifers of sacrifice in old times.
Thomas Hardy 1840–1928: *Jude the Obscure* (1896)

8 It has been said that a bride's attitude towards her
betrothed can be summed up in three words: Aisle. Altar.
Hymn.
Frank Muir 1920–98: Frank Muir and Denis Norden *The Complete and Utter
'My Word' Collection* (1983)

9 Her feet beneath her petticoat,
Like little mice, stole in and out,
As if they feared the light.
John Suckling 1609–42: 'A Ballad upon a Wedding' (1646)

10 Calypso shone triumphant in a white coat and skirt, satin
shirt, a wreath of gardenias on her sleek head.
   'I've never seen anyone look so smug,' one twin in Air
Force uniform whispered to the other.
Mary Wesley 1912– : *The Camomile Lawn* (1984)

Bridesmaids

1 Why am I always the bridesmaid,
Never the blushing bride?
Fred W. Leigh d. 1924: 'Why Am I Always the Bridesmaid?' (1917 song,
with Charles Collins and Lily Morris)

2   Behold, down the rich aisle,
With sweet and fixèd smile,
The bridesmaids, yellow, coral, powder blue,
Escorting Beauty's offering, and Love's,
Move altarward in rhythm, two by two
(Bonwit's ensemble, even to the gloves).
Phyllis McGinley 1905– : 'Epithalamion'

3 Flower girls, ring bearers, junior bridesmaids and the like
are relatives of the bride and groom who are too young to
serve any purpose in the ceremony but too hyperactive and
unruly to sit in the audience.
P. J. O'Rourke 1947– : *Modern Manners* (1984)

4 The bride usually has one friend who wanted to marry the
groom herself. This girl should be maid of honour so the
bride can rub it in.
P. J. O'Rourke 1947– : *Modern Manners* (1984)

5 And the bride-maidens whispered, ''Twere better by far,
  To have matched our fair cousin with young Lochinvar.'
  Sir Walter Scott 1771–1832: *Marmion* (1808)

Cars

1 The automobile changed our dress, manners, social
  customs, vacation habits, the shape of our cities, consumer
  purchasing patterns, common tastes and positions in
  intercourse.
  John Keats 1920– : *The Insolent Chariots* (1958)

2 Take up car maintenance and find the class is full of other
  thirty-something women like me, looking for a fella.
  Marian Keyes: 'Late Opening at the Last Chance Saloon' (1997)

3 Remarkable win today, old boy. Only evidence of adultery
  we had was a pair of footprints upside down on the
  dashboard of an Austin Seven parked in Hampstead Garden
  Suburb.
  Clifford Mortimer: John Mortimer *Clinging to the Wreckage* (1982)

4 There are two things no man will admit he can't do well—
  drive and make love.
  Stirling Moss 1929– : attributed

5 There are a number of mechanical devices which increase
  sexual arousal, particularly in women. Chief among these
  is the Mercedes-Benz 380SL convertible.
  P. J. O'Rourke 1947– : *Modern Manners* (1984)

6 Though the various scents of garages, showrooms, and racetracks have pleasing associations for me, I've yet to hear a woman say, 'Mmmmmmm, you smell like a car.'
P. J. O'Rourke 1947- : in *Automobile*, 1993

7 When a man opens the car door for his wife, it's either a new car or a new wife.
Prince Philip, Duke of Edinburgh 1921- : in *Today* 2 March 1988

Charm

1 Charm . . . it's a sort of bloom on a woman. If you have it, you don't need to have anything else; and if you don't have it, it doesn't much matter what else you have.
J. M. Barrie 1860–1937: *What Every Woman Knows* (1918)

2 Very often the only thing that comes between a charming man and a charming woman is the fact that they are married to each other.
Robert, Marquis de Flers 1872–1927 and **Arman de Caillavet** 1869–1915: *La Belle Aventure* (1914)

3 Oozing charm from every pore,
He oiled his way around the floor.
Alan Jay Lerner 1918–86: 'You Did It' (1956 song) from *My Fair Lady*

4 What is charm then? The free giving of a grace, the spending of something given by nature in her role of spendthrift . . . something extra, superfluous, unnecessary, essentially a power thrown away.
Doris Lessing 1919- : *Particularly Cats* (1967)

5 Falling out of love is chiefly a matter of *forgetting* how charming someone is.
Iris Murdoch 1919- : *A Severed Head* (1961)

6 The charms of a passing woman are generally in direct proportion to the swiftness of her passing.
Marcel Proust 1871–1922: *Within a Budding Grove* (1918)

Chastity see **Virtue and Chastity**

Children see **Pregnancy and Children**

Choosing

1 My dear fellow, buggers can't be choosers.
on being told he should not marry anyone as plain as his fiancée
Maurice Bowra 1898–1971: Hugh Lloyd-Jones *Maurice Bowra: a Celebration* (1974); possibly apocryphal

2 The people people choose for friends
Your common sense appal,
But the people people marry
Are the queerest ones of all.
Charlotte Perkins Gilman 1860–1935: 'Queer People'

3 I . . . chose my wife, as she did her wedding gown, not for a fine glossy surface, but such qualities as would wear well.
Oliver Goldsmith 1728–74: *The Vicar of Wakefield* (1766)

4 If you were the only girl in the world
And I were the only boy.
Clifford Grey 1887–1941: 'If You Were the Only Girl in the World' (1916 song)

5 How happy could I be with either,
Were t'other dear charmer away!
John Gay 1685–1732: *The Beggar's Opera* (1728)

6 She that denies me, I would have;
Who craves me, I despise:
Venus hath power to rule mine heart,
But not to please mine eyes.
Thomas Heywood c.1574–1641: 'She that denies me'

7 In my father's day a man married the first woman who allowed him to unclasp her brassiere. And a woman married the first man she met who had a job and didn't wipe his nose on his suit coat sleeve.
P. J. O'Rourke 1947– : *Age and Guile* (1995)

8 Nobody in their right minds would call me a nymphomaniac. I only sleep with good-looking men.
Fiona Pitt-Kethley 1954– : in *Listener* 17 November 1988

9 Like everybody who is not in love, he imagined that one chose the person whom one loved after endless deliberations and on the strength of various qualities and advantages.
Marcel Proust 1871–1922: *Cities of the Plain* (1922)

10 Nobody on this planet ever really chooses each other. I mean, it's all a question of quantum physics, molecular attraction and timing.
Ron Shelton 1945– : *Bull Durham* (1988 film)

11 O lovers true
And others too
Whose best is only better
Take my advice
Shun compromise
Forget him and forget her.
Stevie Smith 1902–71: 'To the Tune of the Coventry Carol'

12 In my day, I would only have sex with a man if I found him extremely attractive. These days, girls seem to choose them in much the same way as they might choose to suck on a boiled sweet.
Mary Wesley 1912– : in *Independent* 18 October 1997 'Quote Unquote'

13 Where one goes wrong when looking for the ideal girl is in making one's selection before walking the full length of the counter.
P. G. Wodehouse 1881–1975: *Much Obliged, Jeeves* (1971)

Clothes and Fashion see also Wedding Dresses

1 She had a womanly instinct that clothes possess an
   influence more powerful over many than the worth of
   character or the magic of manners.
   Louisa May Alcott 1832–88: *Little Women* (1868–9)

2 I never cared for fashion much. Amusing little seams and
   witty little pleats. It was the girls I liked.
   David Bailey 1938– : in *Independent* 5 November 1990

3 From the cradle to the grave, underwear first, last and all
   the time.
   Bertolt Brecht 1898–1956: *The Threepenny Opera* (1928)

4   She just wore
   Enough for modesty—no more.
   Robert Buchanan 1841–1901: 'White Rose and Red' (1873)

5 Clothes are our weapons, our challenges, our visible
   insults.
   Angela Carter 1940–92: *Nothing Sacred* (1982) 'Notes for a Theory of
   Sixties Style'

6 When I began, at least women dressed to please men. Now,
   they dress to astonish one another.
   Coco Chanel 1883–1971: attributed

7 Don't ever wear artistic jewellery; it wrecks a woman's
   reputation.
   Colette 1873–1954: *Gigi* (1944)

8 To teach thee, I am naked first: why then
   What need'st thou have more covering than a man.
   John Donne 1572–1631: *Elegies* 'To His Mistress Going to Bed' (c.1595)

9 It's amazing how much time and money can be saved in
   the world of dating by close attention to detail. A white
   sock here, a pair of red braces there, a grey slip-on shoe, a
   swastika, are as often as not all one needs to tell you
   there's no point writing down phone numbers and forking

out for expensive lunches because it's never going to be a
runner.
Helen Fielding 1958– : *Bridget Jones's Diary* (1996)

10 Here you could love human beings nearly as God loved
them, knowing the worst; you didn't love a pose, a pretty
dress, a sentiment artfully assumed.
Graham Greene 1904–91: *The Heart of the Matter* (1948)

11 The origins of clothing are not practical. They are mystical
and erotic. The primitive man in the wolf-pelt was not
keeping dry; he was saying: 'Look what I killed. Aren't I
the best?'
Katherine Hamnett 1948– : in *Independent on Sunday* 10 March 1991

12 A sweet disorder in the dress
Kindles in clothes a wantonness.
Robert Herrick 1591–1674: 'Delight in Disorder' (1648)

13 Whenas in silks my Julia goes,
Then, then (methinks) how sweetly flows
That liquefaction of her clothes.
Next, when I cast mine eyes and see
That brave vibration each way free;
O how that glittering taketh me!
Robert Herrick 1591–1674: 'Upon Julia's Clothes' (1648)

14 I do
And then again
She does
And then sometimes
Neither of us
Wears any trousers at all.
Maria Jastrzebska 1953– : 'Which of Us Wears the Trousers'

15 Robes loosely flowing, hair as free:
Such sweet neglect more taketh me,
Than all the adulteries of art;

They strike mine eyes, but not my heart.
Ben Jonson *c.*1573–1637: *Epicene* (1609)

16 There is no unhappier creature on earth than a fetishist
who yearns to embrace a woman's shoe and has to
embrace the whole woman.
Karl Kraus 1874–1936: *Aphorisms and More Aphorisms* (1909)

17 Where women are concerned, the rule is never to go out
with anyone better dressed than you.
John Malkovich 1953– : in *Independent on Sunday* 5 April 1992

18 Chanel No. 5.
on being asked what she wore in bed
Marilyn Monroe 1926–62: Pete Martin *Marilyn Monroe* (1956)

19 Sure, deck your lower limbs in pants;
Yours are the limbs, my sweeting.
You look divine as you advance—
Have you seen yourself retreating?
Ogden Nash 1902–71: 'What's the Use?' (1940)

20 Where's the man could ease a heart like a satin gown?
Dorothy Parker 1893–1967: 'The Satin Dress' (1937)

21 Brevity is the soul of lingerie, as the Petticoat said to the
Chemise.
Dorothy Parker 1893–1967: caption written for *Vogue* (1916); John Keats
You Might as well Live (1970)

22 In olden days a glimpse of stocking
Was looked on as something shocking
Now, heaven knows,
Anything goes.
Cole Porter 1891–1964: 'Anything Goes' (1934)

23 Beware of all enterprises that require new clothes.
Henry David Thoreau 1817–62: *Walden* (1854)

Clothes

24 Save your money, dress better and catch a better husband.
Evelyn Waugh 1903–66: to Nancy Mitford; Harold Acton *Nancy Mitford*
(1975)

25 What can you expect of a girl who was allowed to wear
black satin at her coming-out ball?
Edith Wharton 1862–1937: *The Age of Innocence* (1920)

26 If I were shabby no one would have me: a woman is asked
out as much for her clothes as for herself.
Edith Wharton 1862–1937: *The House of Mirth* (1905)

Compatibility see also Life Together

1 It is not time or opportunity that is to determine intimacy;
it is disposition alone. Seven years would be insufficient to
make some people acquainted with each other, and seven
days are more than enough for others.
Jane Austen 1775–1817: *Sense and Sensibility* (1811)

2 To be together is for us to be at once as free as in solitude,
as gay as in company. We talk, I believe, all day long: to
talk to each other is but a more animated and an audible
thinking.
Charlotte Brontë 1816–55: *Jane Eyre* (1847)

3 The most happy marriage I can picture or imagine to
myself would be the union of a deaf man to a blind woman.
Samuel Taylor Coleridge 1772–1834: Thomas Allsop *Letters, Conversations,
and Recollections of S. T. Coleridge* (1836)

4 You like potato and I like po-tah-to,
You like tomato and I like to-mah-to;
Potato, po-tah-to, tomato, to-mah-to—

Let's call the whole thing off!
Ira Gershwin 1896–1983: 'Let's Call the Whole Thing Off' (1937 song)

5   This was life, that two people, no matter how carefully chosen, could not be everything to each other.
Doris Lessing 1919– : *A Man and Two Women* (1963)

6   I love her too, but our neuroses just don't match.
Arthur Miller 1915– : *The Ride Down Mount Morgan* (1991)

7   I believe a little incompatibility is the spice of life, particularly if he has income and she is pattable.
Ogden Nash 1902–71: 'I Do, I Will, I Have' (1949)

8   To be happy with a man you must understand him a lot and love him a little. To be happy with a woman you must love her a lot and not try to understand her at all.
Helen Rowland 1875–1950: *A Guide to Men* (1922)

9   Those who have never known the deep intimacy and the intense companionship of happy mutual love have missed the best thing that life has to give; unconsciously, if not consciously, they feel this, and the resulting disappointment inclines them towards envy, oppression, and cruelty.
Bertrand Russell 1872–1970: *Marriage and Morals* (1929)

10   If I were a snob I wouldn't be living with Mrs Duffield, and Mrs Duffield has asked me to tell you that if I were a bore she wouldn't be living with me.
having been accused of being a snob and a bore
Jocelyn Stevens 1932– : in *Independent on Sunday* 15 November 1992

11   Love and sex can go together and sex and unlove can go together and love and unsex can go together. But personal love and personal sex is bad.
Andy Warhol 1927–87: *Philosophy of Andy Warhol (From A to B and Back Again)* (1975)

Compatibility

Cooking see Food and Cooking

Cosmetics

1 Most women are not so young as they are painted.
Max Beerbohm 1872–1956: *The Yellow Book* (1894)

2 I'm the female equivalent of a counterfeit $20 bill. Half of what you see is a pretty good reproduction, the rest is a fraud.
Cher 1946– : Doug McClelland *Star Speak: Hollywood on Everything* (1987)

3 What else do they want in life but to be as attractive as possible to men? Do not all their trimmings and cosmetics have this end in view, and all their baths, fittings, creams, scents, as well—and all those arts of making up, painting and fashioning the face, eyes and skin? Just so. And by what other sponsor are they better recommended to men than by folly?
Erasmus c.1469–1536: *In Praise of Folly* (1509)

4 Is it too much to ask that women be spared the daily struggle for superhuman beauty in order to offer it to the caresses of a subhumanly ugly mate?
Germaine Greer 1939– : *The Female Eunuch* (1970)

5 A girl whose cheeks are covered with paint
Has an advantage with me over one whose ain't.
Ogden Nash 1902–71: 'Biological Reflection' (1931)

6 Venus, take my votive glass:
Since I am not what I was;
What from this day I shall be,
Venus, let me never see.
Matthew Prior 1664–1721: 'The Lady who Offers her Looking-Glass to Venus'

7 In the factory we make cosmetics; in the store we sell hope.
Charles Revson 1906–75: A. Tobias *Fire and Ice* (1976)

8 The feminine vanity-case is the grave of masculine illusions.
Helen Rowland 1875–1950: *The Book of Diversion* (1925)

9 There are no ugly women, only lazy ones.
Helena Rubinstein 1882–1965: *My Life for Beauty* (1966)

10 I was tired of being a woman,
tired of the spoons and the pots,
tired of my mouth and my breasts
tired of the cosmetics and silks . . .
I was tired of the gender of things.
Anne Sexton 1928–74: 'Consorting with angels' (1967)

11 She wore far too much rouge last night and not quite enough clothes. That is always a sign of despair in a woman.
Oscar Wilde 1854–1900: *An Ideal Husband* (1895)

Courtship

1 Can you make me a cambric shirt,
Parsley, sage, rosemary, and thyme,
Without any seam or needlework?
And you shall be a true lover of mine.
Anonymous: traditional

2 There are very few of us who have heart enough to be really in love without encouragement. In nine cases out of ten, a woman had better show *more* affection than she feels.
Jane Austen 1775–1817: *Pride and Prejudice* (1813)

3 Woe betide the man who dares to pay a woman a compliment today . . . Forget the flowers, the chocolates, the soft word—rather woo her with a self-defence manual in one hand and a family planning leaflet in the other.
Alan Ayckbourn 1939– : *Round and Round the Garden* (1975)

4   Ten years of courtship is carrying celibacy to extremes.
    Alan Bennett 1934– : *Habeas Corpus* (1973)

5   Make love to every woman you meet. If you get five percent
    on your outlays it's a good investment.
    Arnold Bennett 1867–1931: Laurence J. Peter (ed.) *Quotations for our
    Time* (1977)

6   If you want to win her hand,
    Let the maiden understand
    That she's not the only pebble on the beach.
    Harry Braisted: 'You're Not the Only Pebble on the Beach' (1896 song)

7   For talk six times with the same single lady,
    And you may get the wedding dresses ready.
    Lord Byron 1788–1824: *Don Juan* (1819–24)

8   We have progressively improved into a less spiritual species
    of tenderness—but the seal is not yet fixed though the wax
    is preparing for the impression.
    of his relationship with Lady Frances Webster
    Lord Byron 1788–1824: letter to Lady Melbourne, 14 October 1813

9   I asked her to put me on a quest because she didn't believe
    me when I told her I wanted to marry her. And she made
    this list of almost impossible things to achieve. They were
    very creative things, which made me love her even more.
    Nicholas Cage 1964– : in *The Times* 17 June 1998

10 At the bottom of his heart, every decent man feels that his
    approach to the woman he loves is an approach to a
    shrine.
    Raymond Chandler 1888–1959: Tom Hiney *Raymond Chandler: A Biography*
    (1997)

11 Courtship to marriage, as a very witty prologue to a very
    dull play.
    William Congreve 1670–1729: *The Old Bachelor* (1693)

12 Everyone knows that dating in your thirties is not the happy-go-lucky free-for-all it was when you were twenty-two.
Helen Fielding 1958– : *Bridget Jones's Diary* (1996)

13 Holding hands at midnight
'Neath a starry sky . . .
Nice work if you can get it,
And you can get it if you try.
Ira Gershwin 1896–1983: 'Nice Work If You Can Get It' (1937 song)

14 I can't get no satisfaction
I can't get no girl reaction.
Mick Jagger 1943– and **Keith Richards** 1943– : '(I Can't Get No) Satisfaction' (1965 song)

15 So court a mistress, she denies you;
Let her alone, she will court you.
Ben Jonson c.1573–1637: 'That Women are but Men's Shadows' (1616)

16 She whom I love is hard to catch and conquer,
Hard, but O the glory of the winning were she won!
George Meredith 1828–1909: 'Love in the Valley'

17 Wooing, so tiring.
Nancy Mitford 1904–73: *The Pursuit of Love* (1945)

18 Dating is a social engagement with the threat of sex at its conclusion.
P. J. O'Rourke 1947– : *Modern Manners* (1984)

19 Come, woo me, woo me; for now I am in a holiday humour, and like enough to consent.
William Shakespeare 1564–1616: *As You Like It* (1599)

20 Was ever woman in this humour wooed?
Was ever woman in this humour won?
William Shakespeare 1564–1616: *Richard III* (1591)

Courtship

21 You think that you are Ann's suitor; that you are the
pursuer and she the pursued . . . Fool: it is you who are the
pursued, the marked down quarry, the destined prey.
George Bernard Shaw 1856–1950: *Man and Superman* (1903)

22 It is a woman's business to get married as soon as possible,
and a man's to keep unmarried as long as he can.
George Bernard Shaw 1856–1950: *Man and Superman* (1903)

23 Man is the hunter; woman is his game:
The sleek and shining creatures of the chase,
We hunt them for the beauty of their skins;
They love us for it, and we ride them down.
Alfred, Lord Tennyson 1809–92: *The Princess* (1847)

24 She knew how to allure by denying, and to make the gift
rich by delaying it.
Anthony Trollope 1815–82: *Phineas Finn* (1869)

25 We've got to have
We plot to have
For it's so dreary not to have
That certain thing called the Boy Friend.
Sandy Wilson 1924– : 'The Boyfriend' (1954 song)

26 Now she's losing interest, you can see it; she starts to
glance away, can't he see it? Fool!
Touch her! Reach across, just caress her with a finger on
her cheek: fool, fool—only touch her!
C. K. Williams 1936– : 'Love: Shyness'

27 LILL: He loves me. He's just waiting till the children are
settled.
VICTORIA: What in—sheltered housing?
Victoria Wood 1953– : *Mens Sana in Thingummy Doodah* (1990)

Dancing

1   Heaven—I'm in Heaven—And my heart beats so that I can
        hardly speak;
    And I seem to find the happiness I seek
    When we're out together dancing cheek-to-cheek.
    Irving Berlin 1888–1989: 'Cheek-to-Cheek' (1935 song)

2   There may be trouble ahead,
    But while there's moonlight and music and love and
        romance,
    Let's face the music and dance.
    Irving Berlin 1888–1989: 'Let's Face the Music and Dance' (1936 song)

3   This wondrous miracle did Love devise,
    For dancing is love's proper exercise.
    John Davies 1569–1626: 'Orchestra, or a Poem of Dancing' (1596)

4   I've danced with a man who's danced with a girl
    Who's danced with the Prince of Wales!
    Herbert Farjeon 1887–1945: 'I've danced with a man who's danced with a
    girl'; first written for Elsa Lanchester and sung at private parties; later sung
    on stage by Mimi Crawford (1928)

5   Dancing begets warmth, which is the parent of
    wantonness. It is, Sir, the great grandfather of cuckoldom.
    Henry Fielding 1707–54: *Love in Several Masques* (1728)

6   So gay the band,
    So giddy the sight,
    Full evening dress is a must,
    But the zest goes out of a beautiful waltz
    When you dance it bust to bust.
    Joyce Grenfell 1910–79: 'Stately as a Galleon' (1978 song)

7 Dancing is a wonderful training for girls, it's the first way you learn to guess what a man is going to do before he does it.
Christopher Morley 1890–1957: *Kitty Foyle* (1939)

8 Everyone else at the table had got up to dance, except him and me. There I was, trapped. Trapped like a trap in a trap.
Dorothy Parker 1893–1967: *After Such Pleasures* (1933)

9 And then, you waltz so like a Fay,
That round you envy rankles;
Your partner's head is turned, they say,
As surely as his ankles.
W. M. Praed 1802–39: 'Lines Written for a Blank Page of "The Keepsake"'

10 It occurred to me when I was thirteen and wearing gloves and Mary Janes and going to dancing school, that no one should have to dance backward all their lives.
Jill Ruckelshaus c.1937– : speech, 1973; Regina Barreca (ed.) *The Penguin Book of Women's Humour* (1996)

11 [Dancing is] a perpendicular expression of a horizontal desire.
George Bernard Shaw 1856–1950: in *New Statesman* 23 March 1962; attributed

12 Everyone knows that the real business of a ball is either to look out for a wife, to look after a wife, or to look after somebody else's wife.
R. S. Surtees 1805–64: *Mr Facey Romford's Hounds* (1865)

Death see also Epitaphs, Widows and Widowers

1 I would like my love to die
and the rain to be falling on the graveyard
and on me walking the streets
mourning she who sought to love me.
Samuel Beckett 1906–89: 'I would like my love to die'

2   All her hair
In one long yellow string I wound
Three times her little throat around,
And strangled her. No pain felt she;
I am quite sure she felt no pain.
Robert Browning 1812–89: 'Porphyria's Lover' (1842)

3 But, oh! fell Death's untimely frost,
That nipt my flower sae early!—
Now green's the sod, and cauld's the clay,
That wraps my Highland Mary!
Robert Burns 1759–96: 'Highland Mary'

4 The Bustle in a House
The Morning after Death
Is solemnest of industries
Enacted upon Earth—

The Sweeping up the Heart
And putting Love away
We shall not want to use again
Until Eternity.
Emily Dickinson 1830–86: 'The Bustle in a House' (c.1866)

5 When my grave is broke up again
Some second guest to entertain,
(For graves have learnt that woman-head
To be to more than one a bed)
And he that digs it, spies
A bracelet of bright hair about the bone,
Will he not let us alone?
John Donne 1572–1631: *Songs and Sonnets* 'The Relic'

6 Love is the only effective counter to death.
Maureen Duffy 1933– : *Wounds* (1969)

7 My thoughts are crowded with death
and it draws so oddly on the sexual
that I am confused
confused to be attracted

Death

by, in effect, my own annihilation.
Thom Gunn 1929– : 'In Time of Plague' (1992)

8 For my Embalming (Sweetest) there will be
No Spices wanting, when I'm laid by thee.
Robert Herrick 1591–1674: 'To Anthea: Now is the Time' (1648)

9 Bereavement is a universal and integral part of our
experience of love. It follows marriage as normally as
marriage follows courtship or as autumn follows summer.
C. S. Lewis 1898–1963: *A Grief Observed* (1961)

10 The grave's a fine and private place,
But none, I think, do there embrace.
Andrew Marvell 1621–78: 'To His Coy Mistress' (1681)

11 I thought of you tonight, *a leanbh*, lying there in your long
barrow,
colder and dumber than a fish by Francisco de Herrera.
Paul Muldoon 1951– : 'Incantata' (1994)

12 Forgive me.
If you are not living,
If you, beloved, my love,
If you have died
All the leaves will fall on my breast
It will rain on my soul, all night, all day
My feet will want to march to where you are sleeping
But I shall go on living.
Pablo Neruda 1904–73: 'The Dead Woman'

13 The pallor of girls' brows shall be their pall;
Their flowers the tenderness of patient minds,
And each slow dusk a drawing-down of blinds.
Wilfred Owen 1893–1918: 'Anthem for Doomed Youth' (written 1917)

14 Dig my grave for two, with a stone to show it,
And on the stone write my name:
If he never comes, I shall never know it,

But sleep on all the same.
Christina Rossetti 1830–94: 'Hoping against Hope'

15 If thou and nature can so gently part,
The stroke of death is as a lover's pinch,
Which hurts, and is desired.
William Shakespeare 1564–1616: *Antony and Cleopatra* (1606–7)

16 Though lovers be lost love shall not;
And death shall have no dominion.
Dylan Thomas 1914–53: 'And death shall have no dominion' (1936)

17 May I be looking at you when my last hour has come, and
dying may I hold you with my weakening hand.
Tibullus *c.*50–19 BC: *Elegies*

18 Beloved, come to me often in my dreams. No, not that. Live
in my dreams.
Marina Tsvetaeva 1892–1941: letter to Rainer Maria Rilke, 31 December
1926, after hearing of his death

19 Yet each man kills the thing he loves,
By each let this be heard,
Some do it with a bitter look,
Some with a flattering word.
The coward does it with a kiss,
The brave man with a sword!
Oscar Wilde 1854–1900: *The Ballad of Reading Gaol* (1898)

Deception see also Affairs, Trust and Betrayal

1 You know what man really desires? . . . One of two things:
to find someone who is so stupid that he can lie to her, or
to love someone so much that she can lie to him.
Djuna Barnes 1892–1982: *Nightwood* (1936)

2 Marriage always demands the finest arts of insincerity possible between two human beings.
Vicki Baum 1888-1960: *Results of an Accident* (1931)

3 I have somewhere suggested, I think, that when your fancy is taken by a young man of slender figure and pleasing profile, you should not disclose at too early a stage the true nature of your interest.
Sarah Caudwell 1939– : *The Shortest Way to Hades* (1984)

4 Where true love is, it showeth; it will not feign.
Christine de Pisan 1364–c.1430: 'The Epistle of Othea to Hector'

5 Love in her sunny eyes does basking play;
Love walks the pleasant mazes of her hair;
Love does on both her lips for ever stray;
And sows and reaps a thousand kisses there.
In all her outward parts Love's always seen;
But, oh, he never went within.
Abraham Cowley 1618-67: 'The Change' (1647)

6 It was the men I deceived the most that I loved the most.
Marguerite Duras 1914– : *Practicalities* (1990)

7 Sure men were born to lie, and women to believe them.
John Gay 1685-1732: *The Beggar's Opera* (1728)

8 Honesty in love, marquis! How can you think of that! Ah, you are a good man gone wrong.
Ninon de Lenclos 1616-1705: letter to the Marquis de Sévigné

9 CAMPASPE: Were women never so fair, men would be false.
APELLES: Were women never so false, men would be fond.
John Lyly c.1554-1606: *Campaspe* (1584)

10 If only one could tell true love from false love as one can tell mushrooms from toadstools.
Katherine Mansfield 1888-1923: *Journal of Katherine Mansfield* (1930) 1917

11 Never serious be, nor true,
And your wish will come to you—
And if that makes you happy, kid,
You'll be the first it ever did.
Dorothy Parker 1893–1967: 'The Lady's Reward'

12 'I saw you take his kiss!' ''Tis true.'
'O modesty!' ''Twas strictly kept:
He thought me asleep; at least, I knew
He thought I thought he thought I slept.'
Coventry Patmore 1823–96: *The Angel in the House* (1854–62) 'The Kiss'

13 Sigh no more, ladies, sigh no more,
Men were deceivers ever.
William Shakespeare 1564–1616: *Much Ado About Nothing* (1598–9)

14 There was altogether too much candour in married life; it
was an indelicate modern idea, and frequently led to upsets
in a household, if not divorce.
Muriel Spark 1918– : *Memento Mori* (1959)

15 Perhaps there is no position more perilous to a man's
honesty than that . . . of knowing himself to be quite loved
by a girl whom he almost loves himself.
Anthony Trollope 1815–82: *Phineas Finn* (1869)

16 The one charm of marriage is that it makes a life of
deception absolutely necessary for both parties.
Oscar Wilde 1854–1900: *The Picture of Dorian Gray* (1891)

Declarations see also Proposals

1 I love you
is all that you can't say.
Tracy Chapman 1964– : 'Baby Can I Hold You' (1988 song)

2 But love a womman that she woot it nought,
   And she wol quyte it that thow shalt nat fele;
   Unknowe, unkist, and lost, that is unsought.
   Geoffrey Chaucer *c.*1343–1400: *Troilus and Criseyde*

3 My heart has made its mind up
   And I'm afraid it's you.
   Wendy Cope 1945– : 'Valentine' (1992)

4 You know what I am going to say. I love you. What other
   men may mean when they use that expression, I cannot
   tell: what *I* mean is, that I am under the influence of some
   tremendous attraction which I have resisted in vain, and
   which overmasters me.
   Charles Dickens 1812–70: *Our Mutual Friend* (1865)

5 My soul is so knit to yours that it is but a divided life I live
   without you. And this moment, now you are with me, and
   I feel that our hearts are filled with the same love, I have a
   fullness of strength to bear and do our Heavenly Father's
   will, that I had lost before.
   George Eliot 1819–80: *Adam Bede* (1859)

6 I'd like to be your preference
   And hence
   I'd like to be around when you unhook.
   I'd like to be your only audience,
   The final name in your appointment book,
   Your future tense.
   John Fuller 1937– : 'Valentine'

7 We remain very married.
   full-page advertisement following rumours of their separation
   Richard Gere and Cindy Crawford: in *The Times* 6 May 1994

8 The moment I even say to a woman: I love you!—
   my love dies down considerably.
   D. H. Lawrence 1885–1930: 'The Mess of Love'

9 So many contradictions, so many contrary movements are
true, and can be explained in three words: *I love you.*
Julie de Lespinasse 1732–76: letter to the Comte de Guibert, 13
November 1774

10 'O tell me, when along the line
From my full heart the message flows,
What currents are induced in thine?
One click from thee will end my woes.'

Through many an Ohm the Weber flew,
And clicked the answer back to me,
'I am thy Farad, staunch and true,
Charged to a Volt with love for thee.'
*the early terms Weber and Farad have been replaced by ampere
and coulomb*
James Clerk Maxwell 1831–79: 'Valentine from a Telegraph Clerk [male] to
a Telegraph Clerk [female]

11 He either fears his fate too much,
Or his deserts are small,
That puts it not unto the touch
To win or lose it all.
James Graham, Marquess of Montrose 1612–50: 'My Dear and Only Love'
(written *c.*1642)

12 Yes, yours, my love, is the right human face.
I in my mind had waited for this long,
Seeing the false and searching for the true,
Then found you as a traveller finds a place
Of welcome suddenly amid the wrong
Valleys and rocks and twisting roads.
Edwin Muir 1887–1959: 'The Confirmation'

13 I did not know I loved you till I heard myself telling you
so—for one instant I thought 'Good God, what have I
said?' and then I knew it was the truth.
Bertrand Russell 1872–1970: letter to Ottoline Morrell, June 1912

Declarations

14 Dumb swans, not chattering pies, do lovers prove;
They love indeed who quake to say they love.
Philip Sidney 1554–86: *Astrophil and Stella* (1591)

15 If somebody says 'I love you,' to me, I feel as though I had
a pistol pointed at my head. What can anybody reply under
such conditions but that which the pistol-holder requires?
'I love you, *too*.'
Kurt Vonnegut 1922– : *Wampeters, Fama and Granfallons* (1974)

Desire see also Passion

1 Western wind, when will thou blow,
The small rain down can rain?
Christ, if my love were in my arms
And I in my bed again!
Anonymous: 'Western Wind' (written 16th century)

2 What is it men in women do require
The lineaments of gratified desire
What is it women do in men require
The lineaments of gratified desire.
William Blake 1757–1827: *MS Note-Book*

3   Only I discern—
Infinite passion, and the pain
Of finite hearts that yearn.
Robert Browning 1812–89: 'Two in the Campagna' (1855)

4 She . . . went on gazing at Leonidas with the expression of a
six-year-old contemplating a large slice of chocolate cake.
Sarah Caudwell 1939– : *The Shortest Way to Hades* (1984)

5 The man's desire is for the woman; but the woman's desire
is rarely other than for the desire of the man.
Samuel Taylor Coleridge 1772–1834: *Table Talk* (1835) 23 July 1827

6 O, she is the antidote to desire.
William Congreve 1670–1729: *The Way of the World* (1700)

7 Take me to you, imprison me, for I
Except you enthral me, never shall be free,
Nor ever chaste, except you ravish me.
John Donne 1572–1631: *Holy Sonnets* (after 1609) no. 10

8 What is commonly called love, namely the desire of
satisfying a voracious appetite with a certain quantity of
delicate white human flesh.
Henry Fielding 1707–54: *Tom Jones* (1749)

9 I've got you under my skin,
I've got you deep in the heart of me,
So deep in my heart, that you're really a part of me.
Cole Porter 1891–1964: 'I've Got You Under My Skin' (1936 song)

10 There is nothing like desire for preventing the things one
says from bearing any resemblance to what one has in
one's mind.
Marcel Proust 1871–1922: *The Guermantes Way* (1921)

11 On the brink of being satiated, desire still appears infinite.
Jean Rostand 1894–1977: *Journal d'un Caractère* (1931)

12 Is it not strange that desire should so many years outlive
performance?
William Shakespeare 1564–1616: *Henry IV, Part 2* (1597)

13 See! how she leans her cheek upon her hand:
O! that I were a glove upon that hand,
That I might touch that cheek.
William Shakespeare 1564–1616: *Romeo and Juliet* (1595)

14 The desire of the moth for the star,
Of the night for the morrow,
The devotion to something afar

Desire

From the sphere of our sorrow.
Percy Bysshe Shelley 1792–1822: 'To—: One word is too often profaned' (1824)

15 But what was the desire of the flesh beside the desire of the mind?
Helen Waddell 1889–1965: *Peter Abelard* (1933)

Difficulties see Opposition and Difficulties

Divorce

1 It was partially my fault that we got divorced . . . I tended to place my wife under a pedestal.
Woody Allen 1935– : night-club act in Chicago, March 1964

2 For a while we pondered whether to take a vacation or get a divorce. We decided that a trip to Bermuda is over in two weeks but a divorce is something you always have.
Woody Allen 1935– : in *Time* 3 July 1972

3 Divorce and suicide have many characteristics in common and one crucial difference: although both are devastatingly public admissions of failure, divorce, unlike suicide, has to be lived through.
Alfred Alvarez 1929– : *Life After Marriage* (1982)

4 A divorce is like an amputation; you survive, but there's less of you.
Margaret Atwood 1939– : in *Time*, 1973

5 Mention of divorce and avenues open up all round.
Alan Bennett 1934– : *Habeas Corpus* (1973)

6 DIVORCE. A resumption of diplomatic relations and rectification of boundaries.
Ambrose Bierce 1842–c.1914: *The Devil's Dictionary* (1911)

7 Divorce is the one human tragedy that reduces everything to cash.
Rita Mae Brown 1944– : *Sudden Death* (1983)

8 There is no fury like an ex-wife searching for a new lover.
Cyril Connolly 1903–74: *The Unquiet Grave* (1944)

9 The figure is unbelievable—just because she cooked a few meals now and again and wrote a few books.
on the £10 million divorce settlement awarded to Caroline Conran
Terence Conran 1931– : in *Mail on Sunday* 6 July 1997 'Quotes of the Week'

10 Reports of a divorce are totally false. There are no plans, nor have there been, for divorce. After 30 years, we now own 18,352 things: had there ever been plans for divorce, Europe would have spotted tea-chests stretching round the block.
Alan Coren 1938– : *A Bit on the Side* (1995)

11 So many persons think divorce a panacea for every ill, who find out, when they try it, that the remedy is worse than the disease.
Dorothy Dix 1861–1951: *Dorothy Dix, Her Book* (1926)

12 So that ends my first experience with matrimony, which I always thought a highly overrated performance.
on her divorce from the poet Sergei Yesenin
Isadora Duncan 1878–1927: in *New York Times*, 1923

13 He taught me housekeeping; when I divorce I keep the house.
of her fifth husband
Zsa Zsa Gabor 1919– : Ned Sherrin *Cutting Edge* (1984)

Divorce

D

14 There is a rhythm to the ending of a marriage just like the rhythm of a courtship—only backward. You try to start again but get into blaming over and over. Finally you are both worn out, exhausted, hopeless. Then the lawyers are called in to pick clean the corpses. The death has occurred much earlier.
Erica Jong 1942– : *How To Save Your Own Life* (1977)

15 Being divorced is like being hit by a Mack truck—if you survive you start looking very carefully to the right and left.
Jean Kerr 1923– : *Mary, Mary* (1963)

16 There are four stages to a marriage. First there's the affair, then the marriage, then children and finally the fourth stage, without which you cannot know a woman, the divorce.
Norman Mailer 1923– : in *Nova*, 1969

17 When a marriage ends, who is left to understand it?
Joyce Carol Oates 1938– : *The Wheel of Love and Other Stories* (1970) 'Unmailed, Unwritten Letters'

18 However often marriage is dissolved, it remains indissoluble. Real divorce, the divorce of heart and nerve and fibre, does not exist, since there is no divorce from memory.
Virgilia Peterson 1904–66: *A Matter of Life and Death* (1961)

19 Love the quest; marriage the conquest; divorce the inquest.
Helen Rowland 1875–1950: *Reflections of a Bachelor Girl* (1903)

20 A New York divorce is in itself a diploma of virtue.
Edith Wharton 1862–1937: *The Descent of Man* (1904)

21 I think it's a fresh, clean page. I think I go onwards and upwards.
the day before her divorce was made absolute
Sarah, Duchess of York 1959– : interview on *Sky News* 29 May 1996

Endearments

1   Two people who are in love are attached above all else to
    their names.
    Walter Benjamin 1892–1940: *One-Way Street* (1925–6)

2   MILLAMENT: I won't be called names after I'm married;
    positively, I won't be called names.
    MIRABELL: Names?
    MILLAMENT: Ay, as wife, spouse, my dear, joy, jewel, love,
    sweetheart, and the rest of that nauseous cant, in which
    men and their wives are so fulsomely familiar.
    William Congreve 1670–1729: *The Way of the World* (1700)

3   Mr. Sanders had often called her a 'duck', but never
    'chops', nor yet 'tomato sauce'. He was particularly fond of
    ducks. Perhaps if he had been as fond of chops and tomato
    sauce, he might have called her that, as a term of affection.
    Charles Dickens 1812–70: *Pickwick Papers* (1837)

4   Embrace me,
    My sweet embraceable you.
    Embrace me,
    You irreplaceable you.
    Ira Gershwin 1896–1983: 'Embraceable You' (1930 song)

5   If your husband ceases to call you 'Sugarfoot' or 'Candy
    Eyes' or 'Cutie Fudge Pie' during the first year of your
    marriage, it is not necessarily a sign that he has come to
    take you for granted or that he no longer cares.
    James Thurber 1894–1961: *Thurber Country* (1953)

6   Spoken love will palliate even spoken roughness. Had he
    once called her his own Lizzie, he might have scolded her
    as he pleased.
    Anthony Trollope 1815–82: *The Eustace Diamonds* (1873)

Engagements

1 An engaged woman is always more agreeable than a
   disengaged. She is satisfied with herself. Her cares are over,
   and she feels that she may exert all her powers of pleasing
   without suspicion.
   Jane Austen 1775–1817: *Mansfield Park* (1814)

2 A fate worse than marriage. A sort of eternal engagement.
   Alan Ayckbourn 1939– : *Living Together* (1975)

3 And the scent of her wrap, and the words never said,
   And the ominous, ominous dancing ahead.
   We sat in the car park till twenty to one
   And now I'm engaged to Miss Joan Hunter Dunn.
   John Betjeman 1906–84: 'A Subaltern's Love-Song' (1945)

4 I am to be married within these three days; married past
   redemption.
   John Dryden 1631–1700: *Marriage à la Mode* (1672)

5 Of all the stages in a woman's life, none is so dangerous as
   the period between her acknowledgment of a passion for a
   man, and the day set apart for her nuptials.
   Hugh Kelly 1739–77: *Memoirs of a Magdalen* (1767)

6 Kiss me Kate, we will be married o' Sunday.
   William Shakespeare 1564–1616: *The Taming of the Shrew* (1592)

Epitaphs

1 Here list my wife,
   Here lies she;
   Hallelujah!
   Hallelujee!
   Anonymous: epitaph, Leeds churchyard

2 Here lies Mary, the wife of John Ford,
   We hope her soul is gone to the Lord;
   But if for Hell she has changed this life
   She had better be there than be John Ford's wife.
   Anonymous: epitaph at Potterne, Wiltshire

3 She sleeps alone at last.
   *suggested epitaph for an unnamed movie queen whose love-life
   had been notorious*
   Robert Benchley 1889–1945: attributed

4 Here lies my wife,
   Susannah Prout;
   She was a shrew
   I don't misdoubt:
   Yet all I have
   I'd give, could she
   But for one hour
   Come back to me.
   Walter de la Mare 1873–1956: 'Susannah Prout'

5 Here lies my wife; here let her lie!
   Now she's at peace and so am I.
   John Dryden 1631–1700: epitaph; attributed but not traced in his works

6 Mine eyes wax heavy and ye day grows old.
   The dew falls thick, my beloved grows cold.
   Draw, draw ye closed curtains: and make room:
   My dear, my dearest dust; I come, I come.
   Catherine Dyer: 'Epitaph on the Monument of Sir William Dyer at
   Colmworth, 1641'

7 You may carve it on his tombstone, you may cut it on his
        card,
   That a young man married is a young man marred.
   Rudyard Kipling 1865–1936: *The Story of the Gadsbys* (1890);
   cf. **Bachelors 10**

8 Here lies the body of Patrick
Who served Aphrodite delightedly.
Even when quite geriatric
He still raised a nightie excitedly.
Patrick O'Shaughnessy: 'Endpiece' (1995)

9 Poor Hall caught his death standing under a spout
Expecting till midnight when Nan would come out
But fatal his patience as cruel the dame,
And curst was the rain that extinguisht this flame.
'Who e'er thou art that reads these moral lines
Make love at home, and go to bed betimes.'
Matthew Prior 1664–1721: 'Epigram'

10 When I die, my epitaph should read: *She Paid the Bills.*
That's the story of my private life.
Gloria Swanson 1899–1983: in *Saturday Evening Post* 22 July 1950

11 Love made me poet,
And this I writ;
My heart did do it,
And not my wit.
Elizabeth, Lady Tanfield c.1565–1628: epitaph for her husband, in Burford
Parish Church, Oxfordshire

Falling in Love

1 There is a lady sweet and kind,
Was never face so pleased my mind;
I did but see her passing by,
And yet I love her till I die.
Anonymous: found on the reverse of leaf 53 of 'Popish Kingdome or reigne
of Antichrist', in Latin verse by Thomas Naogeorgus, and Englished by
Barnabe Googe; printed in 1570; sometimes attributed to Thomas Forde

2 I cannot fix on the hour, or the spot, or the look, or the
words, which laid the foundation. It is too long ago. I was
in the middle before I knew I *had* begun.
Jane Austen 1775–1817: *Pride and Prejudice* (1813)

3 Love can find an entrance, not only into an open heart, but
also into a heart well fortified, if watch be not well kept.
Francis Bacon 1561–1626: *Essays* (1625) 'Of Love'

4 Oh, what a dear ravishing thing is the beginning of an
Amour!
Aphra Behn 1640–89: *The Emperor of the Moon* (1687)

5 They say that falling in love is wonderful,
It's wonderful, so they say.
Irving Berlin 1888–1989: 'They Say It's Wonderful' (1946 song) from *Annie Get Your Gun*

6 Yes . . . whatever that may mean.
when asked if he was 'in love', after the announcement of his engagement
Charles, Prince of Wales 1948– : interview, 24 February 1981

7 I never saw so sweet a face
As that I stood before
My heart has left its dwelling place
And can return no more.
John Clare 1793–1864: 'First Love'

8 On Waterloo Bridge I am trying to think:
This is nothing. You're high on the charm and the drink.
But the juke-box inside me is playing a song
That says something different. And when was it wrong?
Wendy Cope 1945– : 'After The Lunch' (1992)

9 I'm wild again,
Beguiled again,
A simpering, whimpering child again—
Bewitched, bothered and bewildered am I.
Lorenz Hart 1895–1943: 'Bewitched, Bothered and Bewildered' (1940 song)

Falling

10 O, there is nothing holier, in this life of ours, than the first consciousness of love,—the first fluttering of its silken wings.
Henry Wadsworth Longfellow 1807–82: *Hyperion* (1853)

11 Where both deliberate, the love is slight;
Who ever loved that loved not at first sight?
Christopher Marlowe 1564–93: *Hero and Leander* (1598)

12 Clang, clang, clang, went the trolley,
Ding, ding, ding, went the bell,
Zing, zing, zing, went my heart strings,
From the moment I saw him I fell.
Hugh Martin and Ralph Blane: 'The Trolley Song' (1944 song)

13 If I am pressed to say why I loved him, I feel it can only be explained by replying: 'Because it was he; because it was me.'
Montaigne 1533–92: *Essais* (1580)

14 Birds do it, bees do it,
Even educated fleas do it.
Let's do it, let's fall in love.
Cole Porter 1891–1964: 'Let's Do It' (1954 song; words added to the 1928 original)

15 Falling in love consists merely in uncorking the imagination and bottling the common sense.
Helen Rowland 1875–1950: *A Guide to Men* (1922)

16 She loved me for the dangers I had passed,
And I loved her that she did pity them.
William Shakespeare 1564–1616: *Othello* (1602–4)

17 Love sought is good, but giv'n unsought is better.
William Shakespeare 1564–1616: *Twelfth Night* (1601)

18 Werther had a love for Charlotte
Such as words could never utter;
Would you know how first he met her?

She was cutting bread and butter.
William Makepeace Thackeray 1811–63: 'Sorrows of Werther' (1855)

19 A man falls in love through his eyes, a woman through her ears.
Woodrow Wyatt 1918– : *To the Point* (1981)

The Family see also In-Laws

1 The business of her life was to get her daughters married; its solace was visiting and news.
Jane Austen 1775–1817: *Pride and Prejudice* (1813)

2 He that hath wife and children hath given hostages to fortune; for they are impediments to great enterprises, either of virtue or mischief.
Francis Bacon 1561–1626: *Essays* (1625) 'Of Marriage and the Single Life'

3 Never marry a man who hates his mother, because he'll end up hating you.
Jill Bennett 1931–90: in *Observer* 12 September 1982 'Sayings of the Week'

4 Beseech for me the indulgence of your father and mother, and ask your sister to love me. I feel so as if I had slipped down over the wall into somebody's garden.
to Robert Browning, shortly after their marriage
Elizabeth Barrett Browning 1806–61: letter, 14 September 1846

5 I want a girl (just like the girl that married dear old dad).
William Dillon: title of song (1911)

6 For men who want to flee Family Man America and never come back, there is a guaranteed solution: homosexuality is the new French Foreign Legion.
Florence King 1936– : *Reflections in a Jaundiced Eye* (1989)

7 Never praise a sister to a sister, in the hope of your
   compliments reaching the proper ears, and so preparing the
   way for you later on. Sisters are women first, and sisters
   afterwards.
   Rudyard Kipling 1865–1936: *Plain Tales from the Hills* (1888)

8 If only I hadn't had sisters
   How much more romantic I'd be
   But my sisters were such little blisters
   That all women are sisters to me.
   Justin Richardson 1900–75: 'Sisters' (1949)

9 It takes a woman twenty years to make a man of her son,
   and another woman twenty minutes to make a fool of him.
   Helen Rowland 1875–1950: *Reflections of a Bachelor Girl* (1903)

10 A girl who has a brother has a great advantage over one
   who hasn't; she gets a working knowledge of men without
   having to go through the matrimonial inquisition in order
   to acquire it.
   Helen Rowland 1875–1950: *Reflections of a Bachelor Girl* (1903)

11 I loved Ophelia: forty thousand brothers
   Could not, with all their quantity of love,
   Make up my sum.
   William Shakespeare 1564–1616: *Hamlet* (1601)

12 His biographers will tell how he helped the porter by
   drawing his own water, but no one will know that he
   never once thought to give his wife a moment's rest, or his
   sick child a drink of water. In 32 years he never once sat
   for five minutes by his sick child's bedside.
   on her husband Leo
   Sonya Tolstoy 1844–1919: William Shirer *Love and Hatred: The Stormy
   Marriage Of Leo and Sonya Tolstoy* (1994)

13 When one feels oneself smitten by love for a woman, one should say to oneself, 'Who are the people around her, What kind of a life has she led?' All one's future happiness lies in the answer.
Alfred de Vigny 1797–1863: *Journal d'un poète*

14 Every marriage is a battle between two families struggling to reproduce themselves.
Carl Whitaker d. 1995: in *New York Times* 25 April 1995

Fashion see Clothes and Fashion

Fear

1 The woman that deliberates is lost.
Joseph Addison 1672–1719: *Cato* (1713)

2 Faint heart never won fair lady.
Anonymous: proverb

3 There is no fear in love; but perfect love casteth out fear.
Bible: I John

4 None but the brave deserves the fair.
John Dryden 1631–1700: *Alexander's Feast* (1697)

5 Love, like fire, cannot survive without continual movement, and it ceases to live as soon as it ceases to hope or fear.
Duc de la Rochefoucauld 1613–80: *Maximes* (1678)

6 I tremble for what we are doing. Are you sure you will love me for ever? Shall we never repent?
Lady Mary Wortley Montagu 1689–1762: letter to Edward Wortley Montagu, 15 August 1712

7   Anxiety is love's greatest killer. It makes others feel as you
    might when a drowning man holds on to you. You want to
    save him, but you know he will strangle you with his
    panic.
    Anais Nin 1903–77: *The Diary of Anais Nin* vol. 4 (1944–7)

8   Of all forms of caution, caution in love is perhaps the most
    fatal to true happiness.
    Bertrand Russell 1872–1970: *The Conquest of Happiness* (1930)

9   For stony limits cannot hold love out,
    And what love can do that dares love attempt.
    William Shakespeare 1564–1616: *Romeo and Juliet* (1595)

10 Marriage is the only adventure open to the cowardly.
    Voltaire 1694–1778: *Thoughts of a Philosopher*

Fickleness see also Fidelity

1   I loved thee once, I'll love no more,
    Thine be the grief, as is the blame;
    Thou art not what thou wast before,
    What reason I should be the same?
    Robert Aytoun 1570–1638: 'To an Inconstant Mistress'

2   'Yes,' I answered you last night;
    'No,' this morning, sir, I say.
    Colours seen by candle-light
    Will not look the same by day.
    Elizabeth Barrett Browning 1806–61: 'The Lady's Yes' (1844)

3   Love is like linen often changed, the sweeter.
    Phineas Fletcher 1582–1650: *Sicelides* (1614)

4   An inconstant woman, tho' she has no chance to be very
    happy, can never be very unhappy.
    John Gay 1685–1732: 'Polly' (1729)

5 I can't fool you—and yet I would like to. I mean that I can
   never be absolutely loyal—it's not in me. I love women, or
   life, too much—which it is, I don't know.
   Henry Miller 1891–1980: letter to Anaïs Nin, 21 March 1932

6 But I kissed her little sister,
   And forgot my Clementine.
   Percy Montrose: 'Clementine' (1884 song)

7 It is easier to keep half a dozen lovers guessing than to keep
   one lover after he has stopped guessing.
   Helen Rowland 1875–1950: *Reflections of a Bachelor Girl* (1903)

8 O! how this spring of love resembleth
   The uncertain glory of an April day.
   William Shakespeare 1564–1616: *The Two Gentlemen of Verona* (1592)

9 The fickleness of the women I love is only equalled by the
   infernal constancy of the women who love me.
   George Bernard Shaw 1856–1950: *The Philanderer* (1898)

10 Once you admit that you can change the object of a
   strongly felt affection, you undermine the whole structure
   of love and marriage, the whole philosophy of
   Shakespeare's sonnet.
   Muriel Spark 1918– : *The Girls of Slender Means* (1963)

11 In matters of love men's eyes are always bigger than their
   bellies. They have violent appetites, 'tis true; but they have
   soon dined.
   John Vanbrugh 1664–1726: *The Relapse* (1696)

Fidelity see also **Fickleness, Trust and Betrayal**

1 Sexual fidelity is more important in a homosexual
   relationship than in any other. In other relationships there
   are a variety of ties. But here, fidelity is the only bond.
   W. H. Auden 1907–73: Nicholas Jenkins (ed.) *Table Talk of W. H. Auden*
   (1990) 20 October 1947

2 It is better to be unfaithful than faithful without wanting to be.
Brigitte Bardot 1934– : in *Observer* 18 February 1968

3 The highest level of sexual excitement is in a monogamous relationship.
Warren Beatty 1937– : in *Observer* 27 October 1991

4 Constancy . . . that small change of love, which people exact so rigidly, receive in such counterfeit coin, and repay in baser metal.
Lord Byron 1788–1824: letter to Thomas Moore, 17 November 1816

5 Translations (like wives) are seldom strictly faithful if they are in the least attractive.
Roy Campbell 1901–57: in *Poetry Review* June-July 1949

6 I'm not sitting here as some little woman standing by her man, like Tammy Wynette.
on her reasons for supporting her husband
Hillary Rodham Clinton 1947– : news conference, 1992; cf. **Fidelity 25**

7 You're . . . turning into a kind of serial monogamist.
Richard Curtis 1956– : *Four Weddings and a Funeral* (1994 film)

8 I have been faithful to thee, Cynara! in my fashion.
Ernest Dowson 1867–1900: 'Non Sum Qualis Eram' (1896) (also known as 'Cynara')

9 We only part to meet again.
Change, as ye list, ye winds: my heart shall be
The faithful compass that still points to thee.
John Gay 1685–1732: 'Sweet William's Farewell to Black-Eyed Susan' (1720)

10 As the holly groweth green
And never changeth hue,
So I am, ever hath been
Unto my lady true.
Henry VIII 1491–1547: J. Stevens (ed.) *Music at the Court of Henry VIII* (1973)

11 Will he always love me?
I cannot read his heart.
This morning my thoughts
Are as disordered
As my black hair.
Horikawa fl. 1135–65: Rexroth and Atsumi (eds.) *One Hundred Poems from the Japanese* (1964)

12 He cannot rate me very high if he thinks he is worth my fidelity!
Pierre Choderlos de Laclos 1741–1803: *Les Liaisons Dangereuses* (1782)

13 For men, infidelity is not inconstancy.
Pierre Choderlos de Laclos 1741–1803: *Les Liaisons Dangereuses* (1782)

14 And when, throughout all the wild orgasms of love
slowly a gem forms, in the ancient, once-more-molten
    rocks
of two human hearts, two ancient rocks, a man's heart and
    a woman's,
that is the crystal of peace, the slow hard jewel of trust,
the sapphire of fidelity.
D. H. Lawrence 1885–1930: 'Fidelity'

15 A father will have compassion on his son. A mother will never forget her child. A brother will cover the sin of his sister. But what husband ever forgave the faithlessness of his wife?
Marguerite d'Angoulême 1492–1549: *Mirror of the Sinful Soul* (1531)

16 My dear and only love, I pray
This noble world of thee,
Be governed by no other sway
But purest monarchy.
For if confusion have a part,
Which virtuous souls abhor,
And hold a synod in thy heart,
I'll never love thee more.
James Graham, Marquess of Montrose 1612–50: 'My Dear and Only Love' (written *c.*1642)

(F)

17 No, the heart that has truly loved never forgets,
But as truly loves on to the close,
As the sun-flower turns on her god, when he sets,
The same look which she turned when he rose.
Thomas Moore 1779–1852: 'Believe me, if all those endearing young charms' (1807)

18 But I'm always true to you, darlin', in my fashion.
Yes I'm always true to you, darlin', in my way.
Cole Porter 1891–1964: 'Always True to You in my Fashion' (1949 song) from *Kiss Me Kate*

19 Your idea of fidelity is not having more than one man in bed at the same time.
Frederic Raphael 1931– : *Darling* (1965)

20 I never was attached to that great sect,
Whose doctrine is that each one should select
Out of the crowd a mistress or a friend,
And all the rest, though fair and wise, commend
To cold oblivion.
Percy Bysshe Shelley 1792–1822: 'Epipsychidion' (1821)

21 My true love hath my heart and I have his,
By just exchange one for the other giv'n;
I hold his dear, and mine he cannot miss,
There never was a better bargain driv'n.
Philip Sidney 1554–86: *Arcadia* (1581)

22 Out upon it, I have loved
Three whole days together;
And am like to love three more,
If it prove fair weather.

Time shall moult away his wings,
Ere he shall discover
In the whole wide world again
Such a constant lover.
John Suckling 1609–42: 'A Poem with the Answer' (1659)

23 O tell her, Swallow, thou that knowest each,
That bright and fierce and fickle is the South,
And dark and true and tender is the North.
Alfred, Lord Tennyson 1809–92: *The Princess* (1847) song (added 1850)

24 No man worth having is true to his wife, or can be true to
his wife, or ever was, or ever will be so.
John Vanbrugh 1664–1726: *The Relapse* (1696)

25 Stand by your man.
Tammy Wynette 1942–98 and **Billy Sherrill**: title of song (1968)

First Love

1 The cure of a romantic first flame is a better surety to
subsequent discretion, than all the exhortations of all the
fathers, and mothers, and guardians, and maiden aunts in
the universe.
Fanny Burney 1752–1840: *Camilla* (1796)

2 In her first passion woman loves her lover,
In all the others all she loves is love.
Lord Byron 1788–1824: *Don Juan* (1819–24)

3 We love but once, for once only are we perfectly equipped
for loving.
Cyril Connolly 1903–74: *The Unquiet Grave* (1944)

4 The magic of first love is our ignorance that it can ever end.
Benjamin Disraeli 1804–81: *Henrietta Temple* (1837)

5 There are some things (like first love and one's reviews) at
which a woman in her middle years does not care to look
too closely.
Stella Gibbons 1902–89: *Cold Comfort Farm* (1932) foreword

6 What is a first love worth except to prepare for a second?
What does the second love bring? Only regret for the first.
John Milton Hay 1838–1905: 'Distich'

7 First love is only a little foolishness and a lot of curiosity.
   George Bernard Shaw 1856–1950: *John Bull's Other Island* (1907)

8 Deep as first love, and wild with all regret.
   Alfred, Lord Tennyson 1809–92: *The Princess* (1847), song (added 1850)

9 Men always want to be a woman's first love. That is their
   clumsy vanity. We women have a more subtle instinct
   about things. What we like is to be a man's last romance.
   Oscar Wilde 1854–1900: *A Woman of No Importance* (1893)

Flowers see also Gifts

1 O, my Luve's like a red, red rose
   That's newly sprung in June.
   Robert Burns 1759–96: 'A Red Red Rose' (1796); derived from various folk-
   songs

2 Then a sentimental passion of a vegetable fashion must
       excite your languid spleen,
   An attachment à la Plato for a bashful young potato, or a
       not too French French bean!
   Though the Philistines may jostle, you will rank as an
       apostle in the high aesthetic band,
   If you walk down Piccadilly with a poppy or a lily in your
       medieval hand.
   W. S. Gilbert 1836–1911: *Patience* (1881)

3 'Our couch shall be roses all spangled with dew'
   It would give me rheumatics, and so it would you.
   Walter Savage Landor 1775–1864: 'A Sensible Girl's Reply to Moore'; cf.
   Flowers 6; an original has not been found in Moore's works

4 Say it with flowers.
   Patrick O'Keefe 1872–1934: advertising slogan for Society of American
   Florists, 1917

5   Won't you come into the garden? I would like my roses to
    see you.
    to a young lady
    Richard Brinsley Sheridan 1751–1816: attributed

6   Vill you come to the bower I have shaded for you?
    Your bed shall be roses, all spangled with dew.
    Charles A. Somerset: *A Day After the Fair* (1828); cf. **Flowers 3**

7   From my experience of life I believe my personal motto
    should be 'Beware of men bearing flowers.'
    Muriel Spark 1918– : *Curriculum Vitae* (1992)

8   Come into the garden, Maud,
    For the black bat, night, has flown,
    Come into the garden, Maud,
    I am here at the gate alone;
    And the woodbine spices are wafted abroad,
    And the musk of the rose is blown.
    Alfred, Lord Tennyson 1809–92: *Maud* (1855)

9   Go, lovely rose!
    Tell her, that wastes her time and me,
    That now she knows,
    When I resemble her to thee,
    How sweet and fair she seems to be.
    Edmund Waller 1606–87: 'Go, lovely rose!' (1645)

10 The mulish short-sightedness of most Englishmen is such
    that they do not give women flowers, because they
    themselves can see no point to it—an attitude about as
    logical as refusing to bait a hook with a worm because you
    yourself are no worm-eater.
    Katharine Whitehorn 1928– : *Roundabout* (1962)

11 I never see a flower that pleases me, but I wish for you.
    William Wordsworth 1770–1850: letter to his wife, 1810

Folly

1 I am two fools, I know,
For loving, and for saying so
In whining poetry.
John Donne 1572–1631: 'The Triple Fool'

2 Love is the wisdom of the fool and the folly of the wise.
Samuel Johnson 1709–84: W. Cooke *Life of Samuel Johnson* (1805)

3 The silliest woman can manage a clever man; but it takes a
very clever woman to manage a fool.
Rudyard Kipling 1865–1936: *Plain Tales from the Hills* (1888)

4 A man may be a fool and not know it, but not if he is
married.
H. L. Mencken 1880–1956: Laurence J. Peter (ed.) *Quotations for our Time*
(1977)

5 There is nothing ridiculous in love.
Olive Schreiner 1855–1920: *Stories, Dreams, and Allegories* (1892) 'The
Buddhist Priest's Wife'

6 If thou remember'st not the slightest folly
That ever love did make thee run into,
Thou hast not loved.
William Shakespeare 1564–1616: *As You Like It* (1599)

7 Love is blind, and lovers cannot see
The pretty follies that themselves commit.
William Shakespeare 1564–1616: *The Merchant of Venice* (1596–8)

8 It is best to love wisely, no doubt: but to love foolishly is
better than not to be able to love at all.
William Makepeace Thackeray 1811–63: *Pendennis* (1848–50)

9 'Tis my maxim, he's a fool that marries, but he's a greater
that does not marry a fool.
William Wycherley c.1640–1716: *The Country Wife* (1675)

Food and Cooking

1   There are few virtues a man can possess more erotic than
    culinary skill. The first thing that attracted me to my
    husband was his incredible life story, but I actually fell in
    love with him several hours later as I was watching him
    prepare dinner for me.
    Isabel Allende 1942– : in *The Times* 25 April 1998

2   It has the perfume of a loved woman and the same
    hardness of heart, but it has the colour of the impassioned
    and scrawny lover.
    of the quince
    Anonymous: *Shafer ben Utman-al-Mustafi* (c.950)

3   Thousands have lived without love, not one without water.
    W. H. Auden 1907–73: 'First Things First'

4   Eat, drink, and love; the rest's not worth a fillip.
    Lord Byron 1788–1824: *Sardanapalus* (1821)

5   HERBERT BEERBOHM TREE: Let us give Shaw a beefsteak and
    put some red blood into him.
    MRS PATRICK CAMPBELL: For heaven's sake, don't. He is
    bad enough as it is; but if you give him meat no woman in
    London will be safe.
    of the vegetarian George Bernard Shaw
    Mrs Patrick Campbell 1865–1940: Frank Harris *Contemporary Portraits*
    (1919)

6   The right diet directs sexual energy into the parts that
    matter.
    Barbara Cartland 1901– : in *Observer* 11 January 1981

7   NANCY ASTOR: If I were your wife I would put poison in
    your coffee!
    CHURCHILL: And if I were your husband I would drink it.
    Winston Churchill 1874–1965: Consuelo Vanderbilt Balsan *Glitter and Gold*
    (1952)

8   Fool! Don't you see now that I could have poisoned you a
    hundred times had I been able to live without you!
    to Mark Antony
    Cleopatra 69–30 BC: attributed

9   It gives you a feeling of comfort. It's like having a pair of
    arms around you, but it's temporary.
    on food
    Diana, Princess of Wales 1961–97: interview on *Panorama*, BBC1 TV, 20
    November 1995

10 Dinner parties are for eating, not mating.
    on hostesses who only invite couples
    Edna Ferber 1887–1968: in *New York Times* 25 September 1984

11 Of soup and love, the first is the best.
    Thomas Fuller 1654–1732: *Gnomologia* (1732)

12 The fruit of love, marriage, fertility.
    of the quince
    Jane Grigson 1928–90: *Fruit Book* (1982)

13 The critical period in matrimony is breakfast-time.
    A. P. Herbert 1890–1971: *Uncommon Law* (1935)

14 Kissing don't last: cookery do!
    George Meredith 1828–1909: *The Ordeal of Richard Feverel* (1859)

15 There's only one secret to bachelor cooking—not caring
    how it tastes.
    P. J. O'Rourke 1947– : *The Bachelor Home Companion* (1987)

16 To the old saying that man built the house but woman
    made of it a 'home' might be added the modern supplement
    that woman accepted cooking as a chore but man has
    made of it a recreation.
    Emily Post 1873–1960: *Etiquette* (1922)

17 WIFE OF TWO YEARS' STANDING: Oh yes! I'm sure he's not
    so fond of me as at first. He's away so much, neglects me
    dreadfully, and he's so cross when he comes home. What
    shall I do?

WIDOW: Feed the brute!
Punch 1841–1992: vol. 89 (1885)

18 Cooking is like love. It should be entered into with abandon
or not at all.
Harriet Van Horne 1920– : in *Vogue* October 1996

19 My form, my friends observe with pain,
Is growing daily thinner.
Love only occupies the brain
That once could think of dinner.
P. G. Wodehouse 1881–1975: 'The Gourmet's Love Song'

20 There is no spectacle on earth more appealing than that of
a beautiful woman in the act of cooking dinner for
someone she loves.
Thomas Wolfe 1900–38: *The Web and the Rock* (1939)

21 I love to be envied, and would not marry a wife that I alone
could love; loving alone is as dull as eating alone.
William Wycherley *c.*1640–1716: *The Country Wife* (1675)

Forgiveness see Quarrels and Forgiveness

Friendship

1 *L'amour est aveugle; l'amitié ferme les yeux.*
Love is blind; friendship closes its eyes.
Anonymous: proverbial saying

2 Friendship is certainly the finest balm for the pangs of
disappointed love.
Jane Austen 1775–1817: *Northanger Abbey* (1818)

3 A crowd is not company, and faces are but a gallery of
pictures, and talk but a tinkling cymbal, where there is no
love.
Francis Bacon 1561–1626: *Essays* (1625) 'Of Friendship'

4 Love is like the wild rose-briar;
  Friendship like the holly-tree.
  The holly is dark when the rose-briar blooms,
  But which will bloom most constantly?
  Emily Brontë 1818–48: 'Love and Friendship' (1846)

5 A man's friendships are, like his will, invalidated by
  marriage—But they are also no less invalidated by the
  marriage of his friends.
  Samuel Butler 1835–1902: *The Way of All Flesh* (1903)

6 A mistress never is nor can be a friend. While you agree,
  you are lovers; and when it is over, anything but friends.
  Lord Byron 1788–1824: diary, 24 November 1813

7 A woman can become a man's friend only in the following
  stages—first an acquaintance, next a mistress, and only
  then a friend.
  Anton Chekhov 1860–1904: *Uncle Vanya* (1897)

8 No man can be friends with a woman he finds attractive.
  He always wants to have sex with her. Sex is always out
  there. Friendship is ultimately doomed and that is the end
  of the story.
  Nora Ephron 1941– : *When Harry Met Sally* (1989 film)

9 Friendship is a disinterested commerce between equals;
  love, an abject intercourse between tyrants and slaves.
  Oliver Goldsmith 1728–74: *The Good-Natured Man* (1768)

10 In a bad marriage, friends are the invisible glue. If we have
   enough friends, we may go on for years, intending to leave,
   talking about leaving—instead of actually getting up and
   leaving.
   Erica Jong 1942– : *How to Save Your Own Life* (1977)

11 Love begins with love, and the warmest friendship cannot
   change even to the coldest love.
   Jean de la Bruyère 1645–96: *Les Caractères ou les moeurs de ce siècle*
   (1688)

12 I've had the boyhood thing of being Elvis. Now I want to be with my best friend, and my best friend's my wife. Who could ask for anything more?
John Lennon 1940–80: interview RKO Radio New York, 8 December 1980

13 And much more am I sorrier for my good knights' loss than for the loss of my fair queen; for queens I might have enough, but such a fellowship of good knights shall never be together in no company.
Thomas Malory d. 1471: *Le Morte D'Arthur* (1485)

14 A woman may very well form a friendship with a man, but for this to endure, it must be assisted by a little physical antipathy.
Friedrich Nietzsche 1844–1900: *Human, All Too Human* (1878)

15 But for marriage 'tis good for nothing, but to make friends fall out.
Thomas Shadwell c.1642–92: *The Sullen Lovers* (1668)

16 Friendship is constant in all other things
Save in the office and affairs of love.
William Shakespeare 1564–1616: *Much Ado About Nothing* (1598–9)

17   Have you not heard
When a man marries, dies, or turns Hindoo,
His best friends hear no more of him?
Percy Bysshe Shelley 1792–1822: 'Letter to Maria Gisborne' (1820)

18 I have always detested the belief that sex is the chief bond between man and woman. Friendship is far more human.
Agnes Smedley c.1894–1950: *Battle Hymn of China* (1943)

19 All love that has not friendship for its base,
Is like a mansion built upon the sand.
Ella Wheeler Wilcox 1855–1919: 'Upon the Sand'

Gifts see also **Flowers**

1 I never hated a man enough to give him diamonds back.
Zsa Zsa Gabor 1919– : in *Observer* 25 August 1957

2 A diamond is forever.
Frances Gerety: advertising slogan for De Beers Consolidated Mines, 1940s
onwards

3 I know it's not much, but it's the best I can do,
My gift is my song and this one's for you.
Elton John 1947– and **Bernie Taupin** 1950– : 'Your Song' (1970 song)

4 I sent thee, late, a rosy wreath,
Not so much honouring thee,
As giving it a hope that there
It could not withered be.
Ben Jonson c.1573–1637: 'To Celia' (1616)

5 So I really think that American gentlemen are the best after
all, because kissing your hand may make you feel very very
good but a diamond and safire bracelet lasts forever.
Anita Loos 1893–1981: *Gentlemen Prefer Blondes* (1925); cf. **Gifts 8**

6 O June, fair June, what a month you are—
The costliest time in the calendar!
Filled, as a nettle is full of stings,
With sweet occasions for giving things.
Phyllis McGinley 1905– : 'Song for an Engraved Invitation'

7 Why is it no one ever sent me yet
One perfect limousine, do you suppose?
Ah no, it's always just my luck to get
One perfect rose.
Dorothy Parker 1893–1967: 'One Perfect Rose' (1937)

8 A kiss on the hand may be quite continental,
But diamonds are a girl's best friend.
Leo Robin 1900– : 'Diamonds are a Girl's Best Friend' (1949 song); from
the film *Gentlemen Prefer Blondes*; cf. **Gifts 5**

9 Win her with gifts if she respects not words.
Dumb jewels often in their silent kind
More than quick words do move a woman's mind.
William Shakespeare 1564–1616: *Much Ado About Nothing* (1598–9)

10 Item, I give unto my wife my second best bed, with the
furniture.
William Shakespeare 1564–1616: will, 1616

11 Men are always better at offering women things that men
like (Dr E. V. Rieu once even gave his wife a pair of fishing
boots *in his size*); and possibly one reason why women
value flowers so much is because they must have been
chosen simply to please her.
Katharine Whitehorn 1928– : *Roundabout* (1962)

12 But I, being poor, have only my dreams;
I have spread my dreams under your feet;
Tread softly because you tread on my dreams.
W. B. Yeats 1865–1939: 'He Wishes for the Cloths of Heaven' (1899)

God and Religion

1 St Catherine, St Catherine, O lend me thine aid,
And grant that I never may die an old maid.

A husband, St Catherine,
A good one, St Catherine;
But arn-a-one better than
Narn-a-one, St Catherine.
Anonymous: 'Prayer to St Catherine'

2 God is love—I dare say. But what a mischievous devil Love
is!
Samuel Butler 1835–1902: *Notebooks* (1912)

God

3 Christianity has done a great deal for love by making a sin of it.
Anatole France 1844–1924: *The Garden of Epicurus* (1894)

4 Marilyn has married a Protestant, a Catholic and a Jew, in that order, and divorced all of them, impartially, with the proper amount of tears. That's what I call brotherhood.
nominating Marilyn Monroe for his Interfaith Brotherhood Week Award
Harry Golden: in *Time* 17 March 1961

5 He for God only, she for God in him.
John Milton 1608–74: *Paradise Lost* (1667)

6 The orgasm has replaced the Cross as the focus of longing and the image of fulfilment.
Malcolm Muggeridge 1903–90: *Tread Softly* (1966)

7 King David and King Solomon
Led merry, merry lives,
With many, many lady friends,
And many, many wives;
But when old age crept over them—
With many, many qualms!—
King Solomon wrote the Proverbs
And King David wrote the Psalms.
James Ball Naylor 1860–1945: 'King David and King Solomon' (1935)

8 Christianity has ever been the enemy of human love.
Ouida 1839–1908: *Views and Opinions* (1895) 'The Failure of Christianity'

9 Liszt said to me today that God alone deserves to be loved. It may be true, but when one has loved a man it is very difficult to love God. It is so different.
George Sand 1804–76: Marie Jenny Howe *The Intimate Journal of George Sand* (1929) 1834

10 As the French say, there are three sexes—men, women, and clergymen.
Sydney Smith 1771–1845: Lady Holland *Memoir* (1855)

11 How can a bishop marry? How can he flirt? The most he
can say is, 'I will see you in the vestry after service.'
Sydney Smith 1771–1845: Lady Holland *Memoir* (1855)

12 The one certain way for a woman to hold a man is to leave
him for religion.
Muriel Spark 1918– : *The Comforters* (1957)

13 Of the delights of *this* world man cares *most* for sexual
intercourse. He will go to any lengths for it—risk fortune,
character, reputation, life itself. And what do you think he
has done? In a thousand years you would never guess—*He
has left it out of his heaven! Prayer takes its place.*
Mark Twain 1835–1910: *Notebooks* (1935)

Gossip

1 I make my boyfriends famous.
Naomi Campbell 1970– : attributed; in *Guardian* 25 June 1998

2 They come together like the Coroner's Inquest, to sit upon
the murdered reputations of the week.
William Congreve 1670–1729: *The Way of the World* (1700)

3 Love and scandal are the best sweeteners of tea.
Henry Fielding 1707–54: *Love in Several Masques* (1728)

4 Men have always detested women's gossip because they
suspect the truth: their measurements are being taken and
compared.
Erica Jong 1942– : *Fear of Flying* (1973)

5 As I grow older and older,
And totter towards the tomb,
I find that I care less and less
Who goes to bed with whom.
Dorothy L. Sayers 1893–1957: 'That's Why I Never Read Modern Novels'

6 Be thou as chaste as ice, as pure as snow, thou shalt not
escape calumny.
William Shakespeare 1564–1616: *Hamlet* (1601)

Hair

1 It was a blonde. A blonde to make a bishop kick a hole in a
stained glass window.
Raymond Chandler 1888–1959: *Farewell, My Lovely* (1940)

2 Being blonde is definitely a different state of mind. I can't
really put my finger on it, but the artifice of being blonde
has some incredible sort of sexual connotation.
Madonna 1959– : in *Rolling Stone* 23 March 1989

3 A chaste woman ought not to dye her hair yellow.
Menander 342–*c*.292 BC: *Fragments* no. 610

4 To Crystal, hair was the most important thing on earth.
She would never get married because you couldn't wear
curlers in bed.
Edna O'Brien 1936– : A. D. Maclean (ed.) *Winter's Tales 8* (1962) 'Come
into the Drawing Room, Doris'

5 Fair tresses man's imperial race insnare,
And beauty draws us with a single hair.
Alexander Pope 1688–1744: *The Rape of the Lock* (1714)

6 The tenderest spot in a man's make-up is sometimes the
bald spot on top of his head.
Helen Rowland 1875–1950: *Reflections of a Batchelor Girl* (1903)

7 Lord! I could not endure a husband with a beard on his
face: I had rather lie in the woollen.
William Shakespeare 1564–1616: *Much Ado About Nothing* (1598–9)

8 When I had curls
  I knew more girls.
  I do more reading
  Now my hair is receding.
  James Simmons 1933– : 'Epigrams'

9 In England and America a beard usually means that its
  owner would rather be considered venerable than virile; on
  the continent of Europe it often means that its owner
  makes a special claim to virility.
  Rebecca West 1892–1983: *The Thinking Reed* (1936)

10 Only God, my dear,
   Could love you for yourself alone
   And not your yellow hair.
   W. B. Yeats 1865–1939: 'Anne Gregory' (1932)

Happiness

1 Happiness in marriage is entirely a matter of chance.
  Jane Austen 1775–1817: *Pride and Prejudice* (1813)

2 People insist on confusing marriage and love on the one
  hand, and love and happiness on the other. But they have
  nothing in common. That is why, the absence of love being
  more frequent than love, there are happy marriages.
  Albert Camus 1913–60: *Carnets, 1942–51* (1964)

3 I couldn't stand a happiness that went on morning noon
  and night . . . I promise to be a splendid husband, but give
  me a wife who, like the moon, does not rise every night in
  my sky.
  Anton Chekhov 1860–1904: letter, 23 March 1895

4 It's afterwards you realize that the feeling of happiness you
  had with a man didn't necessarily prove that you loved
  him.
  Marguerite Duras 1914– : *Practicalities* (1990)

5 To be able to throw oneself away for the sake of a moment,
to be able to sacrifice years for a woman's smile—that is
happiness.
Hermann Hesse 1877–1962: *Diesseits*

6 Oh I loved too much, and by such, by such,
Is happiness thrown away.
Patrick Kavanagh 1904–67: 'On Raglan Road'

7 I'm the happiest I have ever been.
the star of Boyzone after his wedding to Yvonne Connolly
Ronan Keating 1977– : in *Irish Times* 9 May 1998

8 A man enjoys the happiness he feels, a woman the
happiness she gives.
Pierre Choderlos de Laclos 1741–1803: *Les Liaisons dangereuses* (1782)

9 *Quand il me prend dans ses bras,*
Il me parle tout bas,
Je vois la vie en rose!

When he takes me in his arms,
He speaks low,
Life takes on a rosy hue!
Edith Piaf 1915–63: 'La Vie en rose' (1946 song)

10 My heart is like a singing bird
Whose nest is in a watered shoot.
Christina Rossetti 1830–94: 'A Birthday' (1862)

11 There is only one happiness in life, to love and be loved.
George Sand 1804–76: letter to Lina Calamatta, 31 March 1862

12 I never knew what 'appiness was until I married Andy—
then it was too late.
Flo, the wife of cartoon character Andy Capp
Reg Smythe 1917–98: in *Daily Mirror*

(H)

Health see Sickness and Health

The Heart

1 The desires of the heart are as crooked as corkscrews.
W. H. Auden 1907–73: 'Death's Echo' (1937)

2 You should have a softer pillow than my heart.
to his wife, who had rested her head on his breast
Lord Byron 1788–1824: E. C. Mayne (ed.) *The Life and Letters of Anne
Isabella, Lady Noel Byron* (1929)

3 The world of the emotions that are so lightly called
physical.
Colette 1873–1954: *Le Blé en herbe* (1923)

4 The human heart likes a little disorder in its geometry.
Louis de Bernières 1954– : *Captain Corelli's Mandolin* (1994)

5 There are strings . . . in the human heart that had better
not be wibrated.
Charles Dickens 1812–70: *Barnaby Rudge* (1841)

6 The human heart, at whatever age, opens only to the heart
that opens in return.
Maria Edgeworth 1767–1849: *Letters to Literary Ladies* (1814)

7 We fluctuate long between love and hatred before we can
arrive at tranquillity.
Héloise c.1098–1164: first letter to Abelard, c.1122

8 What they call 'heart' lies much lower than the fourth
waistcoat button.
Georg Christoph Lichtenberg 1742–99: notebook (1776–79)

9 Pity me that the heart is slow to learn
What the swift mind beholds at every turn.
Edna St Vincent Millay 1892–1950: 'Pity Me Not' (1923)

10 The heart has its reasons which reason knows nothing of.
Blaise Pascal 1623–62: *Pensées* (1670)

11 We shall never learn to feel and respect our real calling and
destiny, unless we have taught ourselves to consider every
thing as moonshine, compared with the education of the
heart.
Sir Walter Scott 1771–1832: to J. G. Lockhart, August 1825

12 I am all for people having their heart in the right place; but
the right place for a heart is not inside the head.
Katharine Whitehorn 1928– : *Roundabout* (1962)

13 Now that my ladder's gone
I must lie down where all ladders start
In the foul rag and bone shop of the heart.
W. B. Yeats 1865–1939: 'The Circus Animals' Desertion' (1939)

Heartbreak see also **Sorrow**

1 Give me a dozen heart-breaks like that if you think it would
help me lose one pound.
Colette 1873–1954: *Chéri* (1920)

2 Unto a broken heart
No other one may go
Without the high prerogative
Itself hath suffered too.
Emily Dickinson 1830–86: 'Unto a broken heart'

3 Well since my baby left me
Well I found a new place to dwell
Well it's down at the end of lonely street
At Heartbreak Hotel.
Elvis Presley 1935–77, **Mae Boren Axton** 1907– , and **Tommy Durden**
1920– : 'Heartbreak Hotel' (1956 song)

4 There are various ways of mending a broken heart, but perhaps going to a learned conference is one of the more unusual.
Barbara Pym 1913–80: *No Fond Return of Love* (1961)

5 Don't waste time trying to break a man's heart; be satisfied if you can just manage to chip it in a brand new place.
Helen Rowland 1875–1950: *A Guide to Men* (1922)

6 Never worry for fear you have broken a man's heart; at the worst it is only sprained and a week's rest will put it in perfect working conditions again.
Helen Rowland 1875–1950: *Reflections of a Bachelor Girl* (1903)

7 Men have died from time to time, and worms have eaten them, but not for love.
William Shakespeare 1564–1616: *As You Like It* (1599)

8 A broken heart is a very pleasant complaint for a man in London if he has a comfortable income.
George Bernard Shaw 1856–1950: *Man and Superman* (1903)

9   Never morning wore
To evening, but some heart did break.
Alfred, Lord Tennyson 1809–92: *In Memoriam A. H. H.* (1850)

10 A lover forsaken
A new love may get,
But a neck when once broken
Can never be set.
William Walsh 1663–1708: 'The Despairing Lover'

The Home

1 Where marriage is concerned, CHEERFULNESS, SEXUAL ENTHUSIASM, AND GOOD COOKING are far nearer to Godliness than cleanliness about the house.
Jilly Cooper 1937– : *How to Stay Married* (1977)

2 It is the personality of the mistress that the home expresses.
  Men are forever guests in our homes, no matter how much
  happiness they may find there.
  Elsie de Wolfe 1865–1950: *The House in Good Taste* (1920)

3 What gadget's useful as a spouse?
  Considering that a minute,
  Confess that every proper house
  Should have a husband in it.
  Phyllis McGinley 1905– : 'Apology for Husbands'

4 How often does a house need to be cleaned, anyway? As a
  general rule, once every girlfriend.
  P. J. O'Rourke 1947– : *The Bachelor Home Companion* (1987)

5 Some dish more sharply spiced than this
  Milk-soup men call domestic bliss.
  Coventry Patmore 1823–96: 'Olympus'

6 Home is the girl's prison and the woman's workhouse.
  George Bernard Shaw 1856–1950: *Man and Superman* (1903)

7 So far as possible ensure that you allow your husband to
  come upon you only when there is delight in the meeting.
  Whenever the finances allow, the husband and wife should
  have separate bedrooms.
  Marie Stopes 1880–1958: *Married Love* (1918)

8 A man in the house is worth two in the street.
  Mae West 1892–1980: *Belle of the Nineties* (1934 film)

The Honeymoon

1 I think that most wearisome institution, the honeymoon,
  must have been inaugurated by a sworn foe to matrimony,
  some vile misogynist, who took to himself a wife in order to
  discover, by experience, the best mode of rendering married
  life a martyrdom.
  Mary Elizabeth Braddon 1837–1915: *Dead-Sea Fruit* (1868)

2 Our honeymoon will shine our life long: its beams will only fade over your grave or mine.
Charlotte Brontë 1816–55: *Jane Eyre* (1847)

3 When I was a young bride I never mentioned such things on my honeymoon . . . It was considered immodest to do anything but weep gently and ask for glasses of water.
Noël Coward 1899–1973: *Shadow Play* (1935)

4 Dear Mrs A.,
Hooray, hooray,
At last you are deflowered.
On this as every other day
I love you — Noel Coward.
telegram to Gertrude Lawrence, 5 July 1940 (the day after her wedding)
Noël Coward 1899–1973: Gertrude Lawrence *A Star Danced* (1945)

5 Nothing is to me more distasteful than that entire complacency and satisfaction which beam in the countenances of a new-married couple.
Charles Lamb 1775–1834: *Essays of Elia* (1823) 'A Bachelor's Complaint of the Behaviour of Married People'

6 I shall explain to them how hard on a man's health are the sulks and pouts and reconciliations of the honeymoon— that three months is long enough for any girl to remain a bride.
Phyllis McGinley 1905– : *Sixpence in Her Shoe* (1964)

7 ten milk bottles standing in the hall
ten milk bottles up against the wall
next door neighbour thinks we're dead
hasnt heard a sound he said
doesn't know we've been in bed
the ten whole days since we were wed
Roger McGough 1937– : *Summer With Monika* (1967)

8 These days the honeymoon is rehearsed much more often
than the wedding.
P. J. O'Rourke 1947– : *Modern Manners* (1984)

9 It doesn't much signify whom one marries, for one is sure
to find next morning that it was someone else.
Samuel Rogers 1763–1855: Alexander Dyce (ed.) *Table Talk of Samuel
Rogers* (1860)

10 My Lord Denbigh is going to marry a fortune, I forget her
name; my Lord Gover asked him how long the honeymoon
would last? He replied, 'don't tell me of the honeymoon; it
is the harvest moon with me.'
Horace Walpole 1717–97: letter to George Montague, 19 May 1756

11 When I first saw the falls I was disappointed in the outline.
Every American bride is taken there, and the sight must be
one of the earliest, if not the keenest, disappointments in
American married life.
of Niagara
Oscar Wilde 1854–1900: press interview in New York, 1882

Humour

1 She remembered that he had yet to learn to be laughed at.
Jane Austen 1775–1817: *Pride and Prejudice* (1813)

2 The ability to make love frivolously is the chief
characteristic which distinguishes human beings from
beasts.
Heywood Broun 1888–1939: Howard Teichman *George S. Kaufman* (1973)

3 Do you know why God withheld the sense of humour from
women? . . . That we may love you instead of laughing at
you.
Mrs Patrick Campbell 1865–1940: Margot Peters *Mrs Pat* (1984)

4 Marriage is the grave or tomb of wit.
Margaret Cavendish c.1624–74: *Nature's Three Daughters* (1662)

5 With your companions you make fun of me,
  Not thinking, Lady, what the reason is
  I cut so strange a figure in your eyes
  When, raising mine, your loveliness I see.
  Dante Alighieri 1265–1321: *La Vita Nuova*

6 A difference of taste in jokes is a great strain on the
  affections.
  George Eliot 1819–80: *Daniel Deronda* (1876)

7 It is well known that Beauty does not look with a good
  grace on the timid advances of Humour.
  W. Somerset Maugham 1874–1965: *Cakes and Ale* (1930)

8 Women liked me because I made them laugh. And what is
  an orgasm, except laughter of the loins?
  Mickey Rooney 1920– : *Life is Too Short* (1991)

9 Nothing spoils a romance so much as a sense of humour in
  the woman.
  Oscar Wilde 1854–1900: *A Woman of No Importance* (1893)

Husbands

1 Bigamy is having one husband too many. Monogamy is the
  same.
  Anonymous: Erica Jong *Fear of Flying* (1973) epigraph

2 I married beneath me, all women do.
  Nancy Astor 1879–1964: in *Dictionary of National Biography* (1917–)

3 His temper might perhaps be a little soured by finding, like
  many others of his sex, that through some unaccountable
  bias in favour of beauty, he was the husband of a very silly
  woman.
  Jane Austen 1775–1817: *Sense and Sensibility* (1811)

4 Women love scallywags, but some marry them and then
try to make them wear a blazer.
David Bailey 1938– : in *Mail on Sunday* 16 February 1997 'Quotes of the
Week'

5 A husband, like a government, never needs to admit a
fault.
Honoré de Balzac 1799–1850: *Physiology of Marriage* (1829)

6 A husband's first praise is a Friend and Protector:
Then change not these titles for Tyrant and Hector.
Mary Barber c.1690–1757: 'Conclusion of a Letter to the Revd Mr C—'
(1734)

7 You may marry the man of your dreams, ladies, but 14
years later you're married to a couch that burps.
Roseanne Barr 1952– : *Roseanne* (American TV series, 1988–)

8 Every man who is high up loves to think that he has done
it all himself; and the wife smiles, and lets it go at that. It's
our only joke. Every woman knows that.
J. M. Barrie 1860–1937: *What Every Woman Knows* (performed 1908,
published 1918)

9 Being a husband is a whole-time job. That is why so many
husbands fail. They cannot give their entire attention to it.
Arnold Bennett 1867–1931: *The Title* (1918)

10 My husbands have been very unlucky.
to her father after the murder of her second husband
Lucrezia Borgia 1480–1519: attributed; Rachel Erlanger *Lucrezia Borgia*
(1978)

11 Why should marriage bring only tears?
All I wanted was a man
With a single heart,
And we would stay together
As our hair turned white,
Not somebody always after wriggling fish
With his big bamboo rod.
Chuo Wen-chun c.179–117 BC: 'A Song of White Hair'

Husbands

12 I've never yet met a man who could look after me. I don't need a husband. What I need is a wife.
Joan Collins 1933– : in *Sunday Times* 27 December 1987

13 I never married because there was no need. I have three pets at home which answer the same purpose as a husband. I have a dog which growls every morning, a parrot which swears all the afternoon, and a cat that comes home late at night.
Marie Corelli 1855–1924: attributed

14 I revere the memory of Mr F. as an estimable man and most indulgent husband, only necessary to mention Asparagus and it appeared or to hint at any little delicate thing to drink and it came like magic in a pint bottle it was not ecstasy but it was comfort.
Charles Dickens 1812–70: *Little Dorrit* (1857)

15 Husbands are like fires. they go out when unattended.
Zsa Zsa Gabor 1919– : in *Newsweek* 28 March 1960

16 You mean apart from my own?
when asked how many husbands she had had
Zsa Zsa Gabor 1919– : K. Edwards *I Wish I'd Said That* (1976)

17 Marriage to a lover is fatal; lovers are not husbands. More important, husbands are not lovers. The compulsion to find a lover and a husband in a single person has doomed more women to misery than any other illusion.
Carolyn Heilbrun 1926– : attributed

18 I will allow only
My lord to possess my sacred
Lotus pond, and every night
You can make blossom in me

(H)

Flowers of fire.
Huang O 1498–1569: 'To the tune "Soaring Clouds" '

19 Marrying a man is like buying something you've been
  admiring for a long time in a shop window. You may love
  it when you get it home, but it doesn't always go with
  everything else in the house.
  Jean Kerr 1923– : *The Snake Has All the Lines* (1958)

20 One reproaches a lover, but can one reproach a husband,
  when his only fault is that he no longer loves?
  Madame de La Fayette 1634–93: *The Princess of Clèves* (1678)

21 I have known many single men I should have liked in my
  life (if it had suited them) for a husband: but very few
  husbands have I ever wished was mine.
  Mary Lamb 1764–1847: letter to Sarah Stoddart, 30 May–2 June 1806

22 The men that women marry,
  And why they marry them, will always be
  A marvel and a mystery to the world.
  Henry Wadsworth Longfellow 1807–82: *Michael Angelo* (1883)

23 He tells you when you've got on too much lipstick,
  And helps you with your girdle when your hips stick.
  Ogden Nash 1902–71: 'The Perfect Husband' (1949)

24 The kind of man that *men* like—not women—is the kind of
  man that makes the best husband.
  Frank Norris 1870–1902: *The Pit* (1903)

25 No matter how liberated she is every woman still wants a
  husband.
  P. J. O'Rourke 1947– : *Modern Manners* (1984)

26 A husband is what is left of a lover, after the nerve has
  been extracted.
  Helen Rowland 1875–1950: *A Guide to Men* (1922)

27 I shall change from a man with a future to a man with a past; I shall see in the greasy eyes of all the other husbands their relief at the arrival of a new prisoner to share their ignominy.
George Bernard Shaw 1856–1950: *Man and Superman* (1903)

28 Take care of him. And make him feel important. And if you can do that, you'll have a happy and wonderful marriage. Like two out of every ten couples.
Neil Simon 1927– : *Barefoot in the Park* (1964)

29 If you cannot have your dear husband for a comfort and a delight, for a breadwinner and a crosspatch, for a sofa, chair or a hot-water bottle, one can use him as a Cross to be Borne.
Stevie Smith 1902–71: *Novel on Yellow Paper* (1936)

30 He is dreadfully married. He's the most married man I ever saw in my life.
of the Mormon leader Brigham Young, who had more than 20 wives
Artemus Ward 1834–67: *Artemus Ward's Lecture* (1869) 'Brigham Young's Palace'

31 He looked home-made, as though his wife had self-consciously knitted or somehow contrived a husband when she sat alone at night.
Eudora Welty 1909– : *A Curtain of Green* (1941) 'The Key'

32 Chumps always make the best husbands. When you marry, Sally, grab a chump. Tap his forehead first, and if it rings solid, don't hesitate. All the unhappy marriages come from the husbands having brains.
P. G. Wodehouse 1881–1975: *The Adventures of Sally* (1920)

33 The *divine right* of husbands, like the divine right of kings, may, it is hoped, in this enlightened age, be contested without danger.
Mary Wollstonecraft 1759–97: *A Vindication of the Rights of Woman* (1792)

Husbands

Identity see Individuality and Identity

Imagination

1   A lady's imagination is very rapid; it jumps from
    admiration to love, from love to matrimony in a moment.
    Jane Austen 1775–1817: *Pride and Prejudice* (1813)

2   It would seem that love never seeks real perfection, and
    even fears it. It delights only in the perfection it has itself
    imagined.
    Nicolas-Sébastien Chamfort 1741–94: *Maximes et Pensées* (1796)

3   Dreaming is the poor retreat of the lazy, hopeless and
    imperfect lover.
    William Congreve 1670–1729: *Love for Love* (1695)

4   Were it not for imagination, Sir, a man would be as happy
    in the arms of a chambermaid as of a Duchess.
    Samuel Johnson 1709–84: James Boswell *Life of Johnson* (1791) 9 May
    1778

5   Picture yourself in a boat on a river with
    tangerine trees and marmalade skies.
    Somebody calls you, you answer quite slowly a
    girl with kaleidoscope eyes.
    John Lennon 1940–80 and **Paul McCartney** 1942– : 'Lucy in the Sky with
    Diamonds' (1966 song)

6   It is the terrible deception of love that it begins by engaging
    us in play not with a woman of the external world but with
    a doll fashioned in our brain—the only woman moreover
    that we have always at our disposal, the only one we shall
    ever possess.
    Marcel Proust 1871–1922: *The Guermantes Way* (1921)

7 Let us leave pretty women to men devoid of imagination.
Marcel Proust 1871–1922: *Remembrance of Things Past* ' The Sweet Cheat Gone'

8 The lunatic, the lover, and the poet,
Are of imagination all compact.
William Shakespeare 1564–1616: *A Midsummer Night's Dream* (1595–6)

9 Fantasy love is much better than reality love. Never doing it is very exciting. The most exciting attractions are between two opposites that never meet.
Andy Warhol 1927–87: *Philosophy of Andy Warhol (From A to B and Back Again)* (1975)

10 Sex is more exciting on the screen and between the pages than between the sheets.
Andy Warhol 1927–87: *Philosophy of Andy Warhol (From A to B and Back Again)* (1975)

11 If a bloke asks me the time of day often enough, after a while I only have to look at my watch to imagine myself saying 'I do' and driving a Volvo estate filled with children dressed in Baby Gap clothes.
Arabella Weir: *Does My Bum Look Big in This?* (1997)

12 If I had never met him I would have dreamed him into being.
Anzia Yezierska 1886–1970: *Red Ribbon on a White Horse* (1950)

Indifference

1 What strange creatures we are!—It seems as if your being secure of him (as you say yourself) had made you Indifferent.
Jane Austen 1775–1817: letter to Fanny Knight, 18 November 1814

2 If I love you, what does that matter to you!
Johann Wolfgang von Goethe 1749–1832: *Wilhelm Meister's Apprenticeship* (1795–6)

3 She's got a ticket to ride, but she don't care.
John Lennon 1940–80 and **Paul McCartney** 1942– : 'Ticket to Ride' (1965 song)

4 Ever since I came back from jail [in February 1990] not once has she ever entered my bedroom when I was awake.
of his wife Winnie Mandela during the hearing of their divorce
Nelson Mandela 1918– : in Johannesburg, 18 March 1996

5 I wish I could care what you do or where you go but I can't . . . My dear, I don't give a damn.
'Frankly, my dear, I don't give a damn!' in Sidney Howard's 1939 screenplay
Margaret Mitchell 1900–49: *Gone with the Wind* (1936)

Individuality and Identity see also Life Together

1 Oh, I hate a lover that can dare to think he draws a moment's air independent on the bounty of his mistress.
William Congreve 1670–1729: *The Way of the World* (1700)

2 PERSONALITY TITHE: A price paid for becoming a couple.
Douglas Coupland 1961– : *Generation X* (1991)

3 Sometimes I have wanted
to throw you off
like a heavy coat.

Sometimes I have said
you would not let me
breathe or move.
Vicki Feaver 1943– : 'Coat'

4 Most marriages don't add two people together. They subtract one from the other.
Ian Fleming 1908–64: *Diamonds are Forever* (1956)

5 It is easier to live through someone else than to become
complete yourself.
Betty Friedan 1921– : *The Feminine Mystique* (1963)

6 Love is often nothing but a favourable exchange between
two people who get the most out of what they can expect,
considering their value on the personality market.
Erich Fromm 1900–80: *The Sane Society* (1955)

7 No human relation gives one possession in another—every
two souls are absolutely different. In friendship or in love,
the two side by side raise hands together to find what one
cannot reach alone.
Kahlil Gibran 1883–1931: *Beloved Prophet: the love letters of Kahlil Gibran
and Mary Haskell and her private journal* (1972)

8 You shall be together when the white wings of death
    scatter your days.
Ay, you shall be together even in the silent memory of God.
But let there be spaces in your togetherness,
And let the winds of the heavens dance between you.
Kahlil Gibran 1883–1931: *The Prophet* (1923) 'On Marriage'

9 What love is, if thou wouldst be taught,
Thy heart must teach alone—
Two souls with but a single thought,
Two hearts that beat as one.
Friedrich Halm 1806–71: *Der Sohn der Wildnis* (1842)

10 Love is mutually feeding each other, not one living on
another like a ghoul.
Bessie Head 1937–86: *A Question of Power* (1973)

11 He loved her and she loved him
His kisses sucked out her whole past and future or tried to
He had no other appetite
She bit him she gnawed him she sucked
She wanted him complete inside her
Safe and Sure forever and ever.
Ted Hughes 1930–98: 'Lovesong'

Individuality

12 Let us form, as Freud said, 'a group of two'.
You are the best thing this world can offer—
He said so.
Randall Jarrell 1914–65: 'Woman' (1966)

13 The meeting of two personalities is like the contact of two
chemical substances: if there is any reaction, both are
transformed.
Carl Gustav Jung 1875–1961: *Modern Man in Search of a Soul* (1933)

14 We love in another's soul
whatever of ourselves
we can deposit in it;
the greater the deposit;
the greater the love.
Irving Layton 1912– : 'Aphs' (1969)

15 Come
leh we hug up
and brace-up
and sweet one another up

But then
leh we break free
yes, leh we break free

And keep to de motion
of we own person/ality.
Grace Nichols 1950– : 'Even Tho' (1984)

16 All we have to do is just admire each other and love each
other 24 hours a day until we vanish . . . The rest is just
foreplay to get to that.
Yoko Ono 1933– : attributed, 1973

17 We need in love to practise only this:
letting each other go. For holding on
comes easily; we do not need to learn it.
Rainer Maria Rilke 1875–1926: 'Requiem for a Friend'

18 I cannot abide the Mr and Mrs Noah attitude towards
marriage; the animals went in two by two, forever stuck
together with glue.
Vita Sackville-West 1892–1962: *No Signposts in the Sea* (1961)

In-Laws

1 Oh, your sister-in-law is a dangerous thing!
The daily comparisons, too, she will bring!
Wife—curl-papered, slip-shod, unwashed and undressed;
She—ringleted, booted, and 'fixed' in her best;
Wife—sulky, or storming, or preaching, or prating;
She—merrily singing, or laughing, or chatting.
Anonymous: 'Sisters-in-Law' (*c.*1850)

2 There are some things the parents of the groom-to-be don't
want to see and the bride's nipples are two of them.
*on the transparent dress worn by Emma Noble, fiancée of James
Major, to the Bafta awards*
Anonymous: in *Sun* May 1998

3 She is the kind of girl who will not go anywhere without
her mother. And her mother will go everywhere.
of his ex-wife Elaine
John Barrymore 1882–1942: in *Stage* January 1941

4 Nye loved telling people that he had to marry Jennie to get
his mother-in-law.
Aneurin Bevan 1897–1960: Michael Foot *Aneurin Bevan* (1962)

5 I should, many a good day, have blown my brains out, but
for the recollection that it would have given pleasure to my
mother-in-law; and, even *then*, if I could have been certain
to haunt her . . .
Lord Byron 1788–1824: letter 28 January 1817

6 Well, Betjeman, if you're going to be my son-in-law you
   needn't go on calling me 'Sir'. Call me 'Field Marshal'.
   to John Betjeman
   Lord Chetwode 1869–1950: in *Observer* 8 February 1959

7 The ideal is to marry an orphan.
   Jilly Cooper 1937– : *How to Stay Married* (1977)

8 When she introduces me to her parents
   back straightened, hair finally combed, strangled by a tie,
   should I sit knees together on their 3rd degree sofa
   and not ask Where's the bathroom?
   Gregory Corso 1930– : 'Marriage' (1960)

9 The awe and dread with which the untutored savage
   contemplates his mother-in-law are amongst the most
   familiar facts of anthropology.
   James George Frazer 1854–1941: *The Golden Bough* (2nd ed., 1900)

10 I was a post-war, utility son-in-law!
   Not quite the Frog-Prince. Maybe the Swineherd.
   Ted Hughes 1930–98: *Birthday Letters* (1998) 'A Pink Wool Knitted Dress'

11 Two mothers-in-law.
   *reply when asked by a lady what was the maximum
   punishment for bigamy*
   Lord Russell of Killowen 1832–1900: Edward Abinger *Forty Years at the
   Bar* (1930)

Intelligence and the Mind

1 It's very hard to get your heart and head together in life. In
  my case, they're not even friendly.
  Woody Allen 1935– : *Husbands and Wives* (1992 film)

2 Miss Buss and Miss Beale
  Cupid's darts do not feel.
  How different from us,

Miss Beale and Miss Buss.
*of the Headmistress of the North London Collegiate School and
the Principal of the Ladies' College, Cheltenham*
Anonymous: *c.*1884

3 To the man-in-the-street, who, I'm sorry to say,
Is a keen observer of life,
The word 'Intellectual' suggests straight away
A man who's untrue to his wife.
W. H. Auden 1907–73: *New Year Letter* (1941)

4 Where people wish to attach, they should always be
ignorant. To come with a well-informed mind, is to come
with an inability of administering to the vanity of others,
which a sensible person would always wish to avoid. A
woman especially, if she have the misfortune of knowing
any thing, should conceal it as well as she can.
Jane Austen 1775–1817: *Northanger Abbey* (1818)

5 Whoso loves
Believes the impossible.
Elizabeth Barrett Browning 1806–61: *Aurora Leigh* (1857)

6 In love, everything is true, everything is false; and it is the
one subject on which one cannot express an absurdity.
Nicolas-Sébastien Chamfort 1741–94: *Maximes et Pensées* (1796)

7 There is a road from the eye to the heart that does not go
through the intellect.
G. K. Chesterton 1874–1936: *The Defendant* (1901)

8 It has been said that love robs those who have it of their
wit, and gives it to those who have none.
Denis Diderot 1713–84: *Paradoxe sur le comédien*

9 And love's the noblest frailty of the mind.
John Dryden 1631–1700: *The Indian Emperor* (1665)

Intelligence

10   Well, love is insanity. The ancient Greeks knew that. It is
     the taking over of a rational and lucid mind by delusion
     and self-destruction. You lose yourself, you have no power
     over yourself, you can't even think straight.
     Marilyn French 1929– : *The Women's Room* (1977)

11   There's nothing so nice as a new marriage. No psychoses
     yet, no aggressions, no guilt complexes.
     Ben Hecht 1894–1964: *Spellbound* (1945 film)

12   Men know that women are an over-match for them, and
     therefore they choose the weakest or most ignorant. If they
     did not think so, they never could be afraid of women
     knowing as much as themselves.
     Samuel Johnson 1709–84: James Boswell *Journal of a Tour to the Hebrides*
     (1785) 19 September 1773

13   A man is in general better pleased when he has a good
     dinner upon his table, than when his wife talks Greek.
     Samuel Johnson 1709–84: John Hawkins (ed.) *The Works of Samuel
     Johnson* (1787)

14   In Britain, an attractive woman is somehow suspect. If
     there is talent as well it is overshadowed. Beauty and
     brains just can't be entertained; someone has been too
     extravagant.
     Vivien Leigh 1913–67: Gwen Robyns *Light of a Star* (1967)

15   Any scientist who has ever been in love knows that he may
     understand everything about sex hormones but the actual
     experience is something quite different.
     Kathleen Lonsdale 1903–71: in *Universities Quarterly* 1963

16   So this gentleman said a girl with brains ought to do
     something with them besides think.
     Anita Loos 1893–1981: *Gentlemen Prefer Blondes* (1925)

17   I have every reason to love you. What I lack is the
     unreason.
     Robert Mallet 1915– : *Apostilles*

Intelligence

18 If intelligence were taken out of my life, it would only be more or less reduced. If I had no one to love, it would be ruined.
Henry de Montherlant 1896–1972: 'Explicit Mysterium' (1931)

19 When a woman becomes a scholar there is usually something wrong with her sexual organs.
Friedrich Nietzsche 1844–1900: Leonard Louis Levinson *Bartlett's Unfamiliar Quotations* (1900)

20 In general all curvaceousness strikes men as incompatible with the life of the mind.
Françoise Parturier 1919– : *Open Letter to Men* (1968)

21 A Bachelor of Arts is one who makes love to a lot of women, and yet has the art to remain a bachelor.
Helen Rowland 1875–1950: *A Guide to Men* (1922)

22 It is as easy to count atomies as to resolve the propositions of a lover.
William Shakespeare 1564–1616: *As You Like It* (1599)

23   To be wise, and love,
Exceeds man's might.
William Shakespeare 1564–1616: *Troilus and Cressida* (1602)

24 Do you think it pleases a man when he looks into a woman's eyes and sees a reflection of the British Museum Reading Room?
Muriel Spark 1918– : L. and M. Cowan *The Wit of Women* (1969)

25 I was always interested in books as a girl and would come home with lots of prizes only to be told by my mother, 'I couldn't care less, you have gravy on your clothes and your hair is a mess'.
on men's attitude to 'clever gels'
Raine, Countess Spencer 1929– : in *The Times* 5 May 1998

26 What is a highbrow? He is a man who has found something more interesting than women.
Edgar Wallace 1875–1932: in *New York Times* 24 January 1932

27 The right education of the female sex, as it is in a manner
everywhere neglected, so it ought to be generally lamented.
Most in this depraved later age think a woman learned and
wise enough if she can distinguish her husband's bed from
another's.
Hannah Woolley 1623–75: 'On Female Education'

Jealousy

1 No man is offended by another man's admiration of the
woman he loves; it is the woman only who can make it a
torment.
Jane Austen 1775–1817: *Northanger Abbey* (1818)

2 The ear of Jealousy heareth all things.
Bible: Wisdom of Solomon

3 Jealousy is no more than feeling alone against smiling
enemies.
Elizabeth Bowen 1899–1973: *The House in Paris* (1935)

4 The French are jealous of their mistresses, but never of
their wives.
Jacques Casanova 1725–98: *Memoirs*

5 As we all know from witnessing the consuming jealousy of
husbands who are never faithful, people do not confine
themselves to the emotions to which they are entitled.
Quentin Crisp 1908– : *The Naked Civil Servant* (1968)

6 People may go on talking for ever of the jealousies of pretty
women; but for real genuine hard-working envy, there is
nothing like an ugly woman with a taste for admiration.
Emily Eden 1797–1869: *The Semi-Attached Couple* (1830)

7 Anger and jealousy can no more bear to lose sight of their
objects than love.
George Eliot 1819–80: *The Mill on the Floss* (1860)

8 Jealousy is never satisfied with anything short of an
omniscience that would detect the subtlest fold of the heart.
George Eliot 1819–80: *The Mill on the Floss* (1860)

9 Jealousy, that dragon which slays love under the pretence
of keeping it alive.
Havelock Ellis 1859–1939: *On Life and Sex: Essays of Love and Virtue*
(1937)

10 Jealousy is all the fun you *think* they had.
Erica Jong 1942– : *How to Save Your Own Life* (1977)

11 Though jealousy be produced by love, as ashes are by fire,
yet jealousy extinguishes love as ashes smother the flame.
Marguerite d'Angoulême 1492–1549: *The Heptameron, or Novels of the
Queen of Navarre* 'Novel XLVIII, the Fifth Day' (1558)

12 To jealousy, nothing is more frightful than laughter.
Françoise Sagan 1935– : *La Chamade* (1965)

13 Oh! how bitter a thing it is to look into happiness through
another man's eyes.
William Shakespeare 1564–1616: *As You Like It* (1599)

14   Trifles light as air
Are to the jealous confirmations strong
As proofs of holy writ.
William Shakespeare 1564–1616: *Othello* (1602–4)

15   O! beware, my lord, of jealousy;
It is the green-eyed monster which doth mock
The meat it feeds on.
William Shakespeare 1564–1616: *Othello* (1602)

16 Inquisitiveness as seldom cures jealousy, as drinking in a
fever quenches the thirst.
William Wycherley c.1640–1716: *Love in a Wood* (1672)

Kissing

1 I still remember the chewing gum, tobacco, and beer taste
of my first kiss, exactly 40 years ago, although I have
completely forgotten the face of the American sailor who
kissed me.
Isabel Allende 1942– : in *The Times* 25 April 1998

2 When the gorse is out of bloom, kissing's out of fashion.
Anonymous: proverb

3 Let him kiss me with the kisses of his mouth: for thy love is
better than wine.
Bible: Song of Solomon

4 The moth's kiss, first!
Kiss me as if you made believe
You were not sure, this eve,
How my face, your flower, had pursed
Its petals up . . .
The bee's kiss, now!
Kiss me as if you entered gay
My heart at some noonday.
Robert Browning 1812–89: 'In a Gondola' (1842)

5 What of soul was left, I wonder, when the kissing had to
stop?
Robert Browning 1812–89: 'A Toccata of Galuppi's' (1855)

6 Gin a body meet a body
Comin thro' the rye,
Gin a body kiss a body
Need a body cry?
Robert Burns 1759–96: 'Comin thro' the rye' (1796)

7 *Da mi basia mille, deinde centum,*
Dein mille altera, dein secunda centum,
Deinde usque altera mille, deinde centum.

Give me a thousand kisses, then a hundred, then another
thousand, then a second hundred, then yet another
thousand, then a hundred.
Catullus *c*.84–*c*.54 BC: *Carmina*

8 It's like kissing Hitler.
when asked what it was like to kiss Marilyn Monroe
Tony Curtis 1925– : A. Hunter *Tony Curtis* (1985)

9 These poor half-kisses kill me quite.
Michael Drayton 1563–1631: 'To His Coy Love' (1619)

10 A fine romance with no kisses.
A fine romance, my friend, this is.
Dorothy Fields 1905–74: 'A Fine Romance' (1936 song)

11 But his kiss was so sweet, and so closely he pressed,
That I languished and pined till I granted the rest.
John Gay 1685–1732: *The Beggar's Opera* (1728)

12 Oh, innocent victims of Cupid,
Remember this terse little verse;
To let a fool kiss you is stupid,
To let a kiss fool you is worse.
E. Y. Harburg 1898–1981: 'Inscriptions on a Lipstick' (1965)

13 Where do the noses go? I always wondered where the
noses would go.
Ernest Hemingway 1899–1961: *For Whom the Bell Tolls* (1940)

Kissing

(K)

14 What is a kiss? Why this, as some approve:
The sure, sweet cement, glue and lime of love.
Robert Herrick 1591–1674: 'Kiss'

15 Those lips please me which are placed
Close but not too strictly laced:
Yielding I would have them; yet
Not a wimbling tongue admit.
Robert Herrick 1591–1674: 'Kisses Loathsome' (1648)

16 Jenny kissed me when we met,
Jumping from the chair she sat in;
Time, you thief, who love to get
Sweets into your list, put that in:
Say I'm weary, say I'm sad,
Say that health and wealth have missed me,
Say I'm growing old, but add,
Jenny kissed me.
Leigh Hunt 1784–1859: 'Rondeau' (1838)

17 You must remember this, a kiss is still a kiss,
A sigh is just a sigh;
The fundamental things apply,
As time goes by.
Herman Hupfeld 1894–1951: 'As Time Goes By' (1931 song)

18 Being kissed by a man who *didn't* wax his moustache
was—like eating an egg without salt.
Rudyard Kipling 1865–1936: *The Story of the Gadsbys* (1889)

19 If love is the best thing in life, then the best part of love is
the kiss.
Thomas Mann 1875–1955: *Lotte in Weimar* (1939)

20 Her lips suck forth my soul: see, where it flies!
Come Helen, come give me my soul again.
Here will I dwell, for heaven be in these lips.
Christopher Marlowe 1564–93: *Doctor Faustus* (1604)

21 I wasn't kissing her, I was just whispering in her mouth.
on being discovered by his wife with a chorus girl
Chico Marx 1891–1961: Groucho Marx and Richard J. Anobile *Marx Brothers Scrapbook* (1973)

22 A kiss can be a comma, a question mark or an exclamation point. That's basic spelling that every woman ought to know.
Mistinguette 1875–1956: in *Theatre Arts* December 1955

23 But kiss: one kiss! Rubies unparagoned,
How dearly they do't!
William Shakespeare 1564–1616: *Cymbeline* (1609–10)

24 I kissed thee ere I killed thee, no way but this,
Killing myself to die upon a kiss.
William Shakespeare 1564–1616: *Othello* (1602–4)

25 And the sunlight clasps the earth,
And the moonbeams kiss the sea—
What are all these kissings worth,
If thou kiss not me?
Percy Bysshe Shelley 1792–1822: 'Love's Philosophy' (written 1819)

26 O Love, O fire! once he drew
With one long kiss my whole soul through
My lips, as sunlight drinketh dew.
Alfred, Lord Tennyson 1809–92: 'Fatima' (1832)

27 A man had given all other bliss,
And all his worldly worth for this,
To waste his whole heart in one kiss
Upon her perfect lips.
Alfred, Lord Tennyson 1809–92: 'Sir Launcelot and Queen Guinevere' (1842)

28 I smoked my first cigarette and kissed my first woman on the same day. I have never had time for tobacco since.
Arturo Toscanini 1867–1957: in *Observer* 30 June 1946

Kissing

Lasting Love see also **Transience**

1 Love me little, love me long,
Is the burden of my song.
Anonymous: 'Love me little, love me long' (1569–70)

2 I'll love you, dear, I'll love you
Till China and Africa meet
And the river jumps over the mountain
And the salmon sing in the street.
W. H. Auden 1907–73: 'As I Walked Out One Evening' (1940)

3 'I will love You for ever,' swears the poet. I find this easy to
swear too. *I will love You at 4.15 p.m. next Tuesday*: is that
still as easy?
W. H. Auden 1907–73: attributed

4 Many waters cannot quench love, neither can the floods
drown it.
Bible: Song of Solomon

5 So sweet love seemed that April morn,
When first we kissed beside the thorn,
So strangely sweet, it was not strange
We thought that love could never change.
Robert Bridges 1844–1930: 'So Sweet Love Seemed'

6 If all else perished, and he remained, I should still continue
to be; and if all else remained, and he were annihilated, the
universe would turn to a mighty stranger: I should not
seem a part of it. My love for Linton is like the foliage in the
woods; time will change it, I'm well aware, as winter
changes the trees—My love for Heathcliff resembles the
eternal rocks beneath:—a source of little visible delight, but
necessary.
Emily Brontë 1818–48: *Wuthering Heights* (1847)

7 But love me for love's sake, that evermore
  Thou may'st love on through love's eternity.
  Elizabeth Barrett Browning 1806–61: *Sonnets from the Portuguese* (1850)
  no. 14

8 As fair art thou, my bonie lass,
  So deep in luve am I,
  And I will luve thee still, my dear,
  Till a' the seas gang dry.
  Robert Burns 1759–96: 'A Red Red Rose' (1796), derived from various folk-
  songs

9 When we are not in love too much, we are not in love
  enough.
  Comte de Bussy-Rabutin 1618–93: *Histoire Amoureuse des Gaules:
  Maximes d'Amour* (1665)

10 All other things, to their destruction draw,
   Only our love hath no decay;
   This, no tomorrow hath, nor yesterday,
   Running it never runs from us away,
   But truly keeps his first, last, everlasting day.
   John Donne 1572–1631: 'The Anniversary'

11 If yet I have not all thy love,
   Dear, I shall never have it all.
   John Donne 1572–1631: 'Lovers' Infiniteness'

12 Love me tender, love me sweet,
   Never let me go.
   Elvis Presley 1935–77 and **Vera Matson**: 'Love Me Tender' (1956 song)

13 But true love is a durable fire,
   In the mind ever burning,
   Never sick, never old, never dead,
   From itself never turning.
   Walter Ralegh *c.*1552–1618: 'Walsinghame'

14 Love was a terrible thing. You poisoned it and stabbed at it
and knocked it down into the mud—well down—and it got
up and staggered on, bleeding and muddy and awful.
Like—like Rasputin.
Jean Rhys c.1890–1979: *Quartet* (1928)

15 ANTONY: There's beggary in the love that can be reckoned.
CLEOPATRA: I'll set a bourn how far to be beloved.
ANTONY: Then must thou needs find out new heaven, new
earth.
William Shakespeare 1564–1616: *Antony and Cleopatra* (1606–7)

16 My bounty is as boundless as the sea,
My love as deep; the more I give to thee,
The more I have, for both are infinite.
William Shakespeare 1564–1616: *Romeo and Juliet* (1595)

17 Let me not to the marriage of true minds
Admit impediments. Love is not love
Which alters when it alteration finds,
Or bends with the remover to remove:
O, no! it is an ever-fixèd mark,
That looks on tempests and is never shaken.
William Shakespeare 1564–1616: sonnet 116

Letters

1 You bid me burn your letters. But I must forget you first.
John Adams 1735–1826: letter to Abigail Adams, 28 April 1776

2 That will do very nicely, Nurse . . . write it in triplicate, will
you . . . one for Nellie, and one for Jessie and one for
Margaret.
*an injured sergeant during World War I, after asking Agatha
Christie to write a love letter for him*
Anonymous: Agatha Christie *Autobiography* (1977)

3 A woman is not to marry a man merely because she is asked, or because he is attached to her, and can write a tolerable letter.
Jane Austen 1775–1817: *Emma* (1816)

4 If I had had a notion of it, I would not have joked her about it for all my money. But . . . I made sure of its being nothing but a common love letter, and you know young people like to be laughed at about them.
Jane Austen 1775–1817: *Sense and Sensibility* (1811)

5 But indeed, dear, these kisses on paper are scarce worth keeping. You gave me one on my neck that night you were in such good-humour, and one on my lips on some forgotten occasion, that I would not part with for a hundred thousand paper ones.
Jane Carlyle 1801–66: letter to Thomas Carlyle, 3 October 1826

6 Indeed, Mr Scott, I am by no means pleased with all this writing. I have told you how much I dislike it, and yet you still persist in asking me to write, and that by return of post.
Charlotte Carpenter b. 1777: letter to Sir Walter Scott, October 1797

7 WITWOUD: Madam, do you pin up your hair with all your letters?
MILLAMANT: Only with those in verse, Mr Witwoud. I never pin up my hair with prose.
William Congreve 1670–1729: *The Way of the World* (1700)

8 She'll vish there wos more, and that's the great art o' letter writin'.
Charles Dickens 1812–70: *Pickwick Papers* (1837-8)

9 Sir, more than kisses, letters mingle souls.
John Donne 1572–1631: 'To Sir Henry Wotton' (1597)

10 It's very dangerous if you keep love letters from someone who is not now your husband.
Diana Dors 1931–84: in *Observer* 28 December 1980 'Sayings of the Year'

Letters

11 A woman's best love letters are always written to the man she is betraying.
Lawrence Durrell 1912–90: *Clea* (1960)

12   But I cannot think
The life and blood of love is ink.
William Hammond 1828–1900: 'On the Infrequency of Celia's Letters'

13 I'd like to shame her . . . 'twould be good as a play to read her love-letters, the proud piece of silk and wax-work!
Thomas Hardy 1840–1928: *The Mayor of Casterbridge* (1886)

14 How many times did I not wish to write to you! But I felt the reason of your silence, and I feared to be importunate by a letter. Yours has been a balm for me.
Joséphine, Empress of France 1763–1814: letter to Napoleon Bonaparte, April 1810

15 Why it should be such an effort to write to the people one loves I can't imagine. It's none at all to write to those who don't really count.
Katherine Mansfield 1888–1923: *Journal of Katherine Mansfield* (1930)

16 It was the first love letter he had ever written, and he was conscious of its tameness; he felt he should say all sorts of vehement things, how he thought of her every minute of the day and how he longed to kiss her beautiful hands and how he trembled at the thought of her red lips, but . . . instead he told her of his new rooms and office.
W. Somerset Maugham 1874–1965: *Of Human Bondage* (1915)

17 The very touch of the letter was as if you had taken me all into your arms.
Anais Nin 1903–77: letter to Henry Miller, 6 August 1932

18 I am *in extremis*, and the only thing that can save me is a few lines from your incomparable hand. If I had the good fortune to behold them I should forthwith be healed.
Sophia Dorothea of Hanover 1666–1727: letter to her lover Count Philip von Königsmarck

19 Barney . . . always looks as if he didn't know whether it
was a love letter or an order to go to Botany Bay. If he saw
the inside of them, how short they are, I don't think he'd
think much of you as a lover.
Anthony Trollope 1815–82: *Phineas Finn* (1869)

20 I obey an emotion of my heart, which made me think of
wishing thee, my love, good night! before I go to rest, with
more tenderness than I can tomorrow, when writing a
hasty line or two under Colonel —'s eye.
Mary Wollstonecraft 1759–97: letter to Gilbert Imlay, August 1793

21 It was a very very nice letter you wrote by the light of the
stars at midnight. Always write then, for your heart
requires moonlight to deliquesce it.
Virginia Woolf 1882–1941: letter to Vita Sackville-West

22 It is not in my power to tell thee how I have been affected
by this dearest of all letters—it was so unexpected—so new
a thing to see the breathing of thy inmost heart upon
paper.
Mary Wordsworth 1782–1859: letter to William Wordsworth, 1 August
1810

Life

1 There is love of course. And then there's life, its enemy.
Jean Anouilh 1910–87: *Ardèle* (1949)

2 To live is like to love—all reason is against it, and all
healthy instinct for it.
Samuel Butler 1835–1902: *Notebooks* (1912)

3 I cannot live with you—
It would be life—
And life is over there—
Behind the shelf.
Emily Dickinson 1830–86: poem no. 640

4 I don't want to live—I want to love first, and live
   incidentally.
   Zelda Fitzgerald 1900–48: Nancy Mitford *Zelda* (1970)

5 All that matters is love and work.
   Sigmund Freud 1856–1939: attributed

6 I see in life nothing but the certainty of your love—
   convince me of it my sweetheart. If I am not somehow
   convinced I shall die of agony.
   John Keats 1795–1821: letter to Fanny Brawne

7 Oh, life is a glorious cycle of song,
   A medley of extemporanea;
   And love is a thing that can never go wrong;
   And I am Marie of Roumania.
   Dorothy Parker 1893–1967: 'Comment' (1937)

8 Love . . .
   That cordial drop heaven in our cup has thrown
   To make the nauseous draught of life go down.
   Lord Rochester 1647–80: 'Letter from Artemisia in the Town to Chloe in
   the Country' (1679)

Life Together see also Compatibility,
                       Individuality and Identity

1 'You have no compassion on my poor nerves.'
    'You mistake me, my dear. I have a high respect for your
   nerves. They are my old friends. I have heard you mention
   them with consideration these twenty years at least.'
   Jane Austen 1775–1817: *Pride and Prejudice* (1813)

2 It is better to know as little as possible of the defects of the
   person with whom you are to pass your life.
   Jane Austen 1775–1817: *Pride and Prejudice* (1813)

3 When I look back on the paint of sex, the love like a wild
   fox so ready to bite, the antagonism that sits like a twin
   beside love, and contrast it with affection, so deeply
   unrepeatable, of two people who have lived a life together
   (and of whom one must die), it's the affection I find richer.
   It's that I would have again. Not all those doubtful rainbow
   colours. (But then she's old, one must say.)
   Enid Bagnold 1889–1981: *Autobiography* (1969)

4 Constant togetherness is fine—but only for Siamese twins.
   Victoria Billings 1945– : *The Womansbook* (1974)

5 Grow old along with me!
   The best is yet to be,
   The last of life, for which the first was made.
   Robert Browning 1812–89: 'Rabbi Ben Ezra' (1864)

6 One of those looks which only a quarter-century of wedlock
   can adequately marinate.
   Alan Coren 1938– : *Seems Like Old Times* (1989)

7 In the beginning of all relationships you are out there
   bungee jumping every weekend but after six months you
   are renting videos and buying corn chips just like everyone
   else—and the next day you can't even remember what
   video you rented.
   Douglas Coupland 1961– : *Life After God* (1994)

8 It destroys one's nerves to be amiable every day to the same
   human being.
   Benjamin Disraeli 1804–81: *The Young Duke* (1831)

9 It seemed to me that the desire to get married—which, I
   regret to say, I believe is basic and primal in women—is
   followed almost immediately by an equally basic and
   primal urge—which is to be single again.
   Nora Ephron 1941– : attributed

10 You yawn at one another,
You treat him like a brother!
He treats you like his mother!
When there's no doubt the fire's out
A lady needs a change!
Dorothy Fields 1905–74: 'The Lady Needs a Change' (1939)

11 Do you think your mother and I should have lived
comfortably so long together, if ever we had been married?
John Gay 1685–1732: *The Beggar's Opera* (1728)

12 Imagine signing a lease together;
And hanging a Matisse together;
Being alone and baking bread together.
Reading the *New Yorker* in bed together!
Starting a family tree together!
Voting for the GOP together!
Ira Gershwin 1896–1983: 'There's Nothing Like Marriage for People' (1946)

13 I've grown accustomed to the trace
Of something in the air;
Accustomed to her face.
Alan Jay Lerner 1918–86: 'I've Grown Accustomed to her Face' (1956
song) from *My Fair Lady*

14 Love doesn't just sit there, like a stone, it has to be made,
like bread; remade all the time, made new.
Ursula K. Le Guin 1929– : *The Lathe of Heaven* (1971)

15 We've got this gift of love, but love is like a precious plant.
You can't just accept it and leave it in the cupboard or just
think it's going to get on by itself. You've got to keep
watering it. You've got to really look after it and nurture it.
John Lennon 1940–80: television interview, 30 December 1969

16 Between husband and wife there should be no MEUM and
TUUM. All things should be in common between them,
without any distinction or means of distinguishing.
Martin Luther 1483–1546: *Table Talk* (1569)

17 Like cautious partners in a marriage, we improved but did
not try to re-form.
Phyllis McGinley 1905– : *Sixpence in Her Shoe* (1964)

18 So they were married—to be the more together—
And found they were never again so much together,
Divided by the morning tea,
By the evening paper,
By children and tradesmen's bills.
Louis MacNeice 1907–63: 'Les Sylphides' (1941)

19 When people are tied for life, tis their mutual interest not to
grow weary of one another.
Lady Mary Wortley Montagu 1689–1762: letter to Edward Wortley
Montagu, 25 April 1710

20 They were intimate. They had found out so much about
each other that everything had got cancelled out by
something else. That was why the sex between them could
seem so shamefaced, merely and drearily lustful, like sex
between siblings.
Alice Munro 1931– : *The Progress of Love* (1986)

21 The great secret of a successful marriage is to treat all
disasters as incidents and none of the incidents as disasters.
Harold Nicolson 1886–1968: attributed

22 Tolerance is the one essential ingredient . . . You can take it
from me that the Queen has the quality of tolerance in
abundance.
*his recipe for a successful marriage, during celebrations for their
golden wedding anniversary*
Prince Philip, Duke of Edinburgh 1921– : in *The Times* 20 November 1997

23 Men are April when they woo, December when they wed:
maids are May when they are maids, but the sky changes
when they are wives.
William Shakespeare 1564–1616: *As You Like It* (1599)

24 The concerts you enjoy together
Neighbours you annoy together
Children you destroy together,
That keep marriage intact.
Stephen Sondheim 1930– : 'The Little Things You Do Together' (1970 song)

25 Like two convicts hating each other and chained together, poisoning one another's lives and trying not to see it. I did not know that 99% of married people live in a similar hell to the one I was in.
Leo Tolstoy 1828–1910: William Shirer *Love and Hatred: The Stormy Marriage Of Leo and Sonya Tolstoy* (1994)

26 Familiarity breeds contempt—and children.
Mark Twain 1835–1910: *Notebooks* (1935)

27 In married life three is company and two none.
Oscar Wilde 1854–1900: *The Importance of Being Earnest* (1895)

Literature see Books and Literature

Loneliness see Solitude and Loneliness

Loss see also Breaking Up, Sorrow

1 I wonder who's kissing her now.
Frank Adams and **Will M. Hough**: title of song (1909)

2 Alas, my love, you do me wrong,
To cast me off discourteously:
And I have loved you so long
Delighting in your company.

Greensleeves was all my joy,
Greensleeves was my delight,

Greensleeves was my heart of gold,
And who but Lady Greensleeves?
Anonymous: 'A new Courtly Sonnet of the Lady Greensleeves' (1584)

3 He was my North, my South, my East and West,
My working week and my Sunday rest,
My noon, my midnight, my talk, my song;
I thought that love would last for ever: I was wrong.
W. H. Auden 1907–73: 'Funeral Blues' (1936)

4 No other song has lightened up my heaven;
No other star has ever shone for me:
All my life's bliss from thy dear life was given—
All my life's bliss is in the grave with thee.
Emily Brontë 1818–48: 'R. Alcona to J. Brenzaida'

5 First I lost weight, then I lost my voice, and now I've lost
Onassis.
Maria Callas 1923–77: Barbara McDowell and Hana Umlauf *Woman's
Almanac* (1977)

6 Say what you will, 'tis better to be left than never to have
been loved.
William Congreve 1670–1729: *The Way of the World* (1700)

7 The day he moved out was terrible—
That evening she went through hell.
His absence wasn't a problem
But the corkscrew had gone as well.
Wendy Cope 1945– : 'Loss' (1992)

8 And I am desolate and sick of an old passion,
Yea hungry for the lips of my desire:
I have been faithful to thee, Cynara! in my fashion.
Ernest Dowson 1867–1900: 'Non Sum Qualis Eram' (1896) (also known as
'Cynara')

9 I feel the loss more than I had thought I should . . .
Without my wishing it she chose to lose herself in me, and
the result was she became truly my better half.
on the death of his wife Kasturba
Mahatma Gandhi 1869–1948: Arun Gandhi *Daughter of Midnight: The Child
Bride of Gandhi* (1998)

10 Woman much missed, how you call to me, call to me.
Saying that now you are not as you were
When you had changed from the one who was all to me,
But as at first, when our day was fair.
Thomas Hardy 1840–1928: 'The Voice' (1914)

11 Pale hands I loved beside the Shalimar,
Where are you now? Who lies beneath your spell?
Laurence Hope (Adela Florence Nicolson) 1865–1904: *The Garden of
Kama* (1901) 'Kashmiri Song'

12 I cannot say what loves have come and gone;
I only know that summer sang in me
A little while, that in me sings no more.
Edna St Vincent Millay 1892–1950: 'What lips my lips have kissed' (1923)

13 Oh, my darling, oh my darling, oh my darling Clementine!
Thou art lost and gone for ever, dreadful sorry, Clementine.
Percy Montrose: 'Clementine' (1884 song)

14 Silently and hopelessly I loved you,
At times too jealous and at times too shy.
God grant you find another who will love you
As tenderly and truthfully as I.
Alexander Pushkin 1799–1837: 'I Loved You' (1829)

15 Oh my grief, I've lost him surely. I've lost the only Playboy
of the Western World.
John Millington Synge 1871–1909: *The Playboy of the Western World*
(1907)

16 'Tis better to have loved and lost
Than never to have loved at all.
Alfred, Lord Tennyson 1809–92: *In Memoriam A. H. H.* (1850)

17 O that 'twere possible,
After long grief and pain,
To find the arms of my true-love
Round me once again!
Alfred, Lord Tennyson 1809–92: *Maud* (1855)

18 Peculiar mathematics . . . apply to many cases of desertion.
A woman who loses her husband or her lover seems to lose
more by his absence than she ever gained by his presence.
Rebecca West 1892–1983: in *Times Literary Supplement* 26 July 1974

Love

1 We do not easily expect evil of those whom we love most.
Peter Abelard 1079–1142: *The Story of My Misfortunes*

2 In real love you want the other person's good. In romantic
love you want the other person.
Margaret Anderson 1893–1973: *The Fiery Fountains* (1969)

3 You know very well that love is, above all, the gift of
oneself!
Jean Anouilh 1910–87: *Ardèle* (1949)

4 Is it prickly to touch as a hedge is,
Or soft as eiderdown fluff?
Is it sharp or quite smooth at the edges?
O tell me the truth about love.
W. H. Auden 1907–73: 'Oh Tell Me the Truth about Love' (1938)

5 Nuptial love maketh mankind; friendly love perfecteth it;
but wanton love corrupteth and embaseth it.
Francis Bacon 1561–1626: *Essays* (1625) 'Of Love'

6 Love has its own instinct. It knows how to find the road to
the heart just as the weakest insect moves towards its
flower by an irresistible will which fears nothing.
Honoré de Balzac 1799–1850: *La Femme de trente ans* (1832)

7 Love is just a system for getting someone to call you darling after sex.
Julian Barnes 1946– : *Talking It Over* (1991)

8 The fate of love is that it always seems too little or too much.
Amelia E. Barr 1831–1919: *The Belle of Bolling Green* (1904)

9 'With people like you, love only means one thing.' 'No,' he replied. 'It means twenty things, but it doesn't mean nineteen.'
Arnold Bennett 1867–1931: diary, 20 November 1904

10 Love is patient and kind; love is not jealous or boastful; it is not arrogant or rude.
Love does not insist on its own way; it is not irritable or resentful;
It does not rejoice at wrong, but rejoices in the right.
Love bears all things, believes all things, hopes all things, endures all things.
Bible: I Corinthians

11 Love seeketh not itself to please,
Nor for itself hath any care;
But for another gives its ease,
And builds a Heaven in Hell's despair.
William Blake 1757–1827: 'The Clod and the Pebble' (1794)

12 Real love is a pilgrimage. It happens when there is no strategy, but it is very rare because most people are strategists.
Anita Brookner 1938– : Olga Kenyon (ed.) *Women Writers Talk* (1989)

13 If thou must love me, let it be for nought
Except for love's sake only.
Elizabeth Barrett Browning 1806–61: *Sonnets from the Portuguese* (1850) no. 14

14 How do I love thee? Let me count the ways.
Elizabeth Barrett Browning 1806–61: *Sonnets from the Portuguese* (1850) no. 43

Love

15 I love thee with the breath,
Smiles, tears, of all my life!—and if God choose,
I shall but love thee better after death.
Elizabeth Barrett Browning 1806–61: *Sonnets from the Portuguese* (1850)
no. 43

16 Such was ever love's way; to rise, it stoops.
Robert Browning 1812–89: 'A Death in the Desert' (1864)

17 O lyric Love, half-angel and half-bird
And all a wonder and a wild desire.
Robert Browning 1812–89: *The Ring and the Book* (1868–9)

18 Love, in the form in which it exists in society, is nothing
but the exchange of two fantasies and the superficial
contact of two bodies.
Nicolas-Sébastien Chamfort 1741–94: *Maximes et Pensées* (1796)

19 All thoughts, all passions, all delights,
Whatever stirs this mortal frame,
All are but ministers of Love,
And feed his sacred flame.
Samuel Taylor Coleridge 1772–1834: 'Love' (1800)

20 love is more thicker than forget
more thinner than recall
more seldom than a wave is met
more frequent than to fail.
e. e. cummings 1894–1962: 'love is more thicker than forget'

21 Love is anterior to life,
Posterior to death,
Initial of creation, and
The exponent of breath.
Emily Dickinson 1830–86: 'Love is anterior to life'

22 Love is a growing or full constant light;
And his first minute, after noon, is night.
John Donne 1572–1631: 'A Lecture in the Shadow'

Love

23 Whoever loves, if he do not propose
The right true end of love, he's one that goes
To sea for nothing but to make him sick.
John Donne 1572–1631: 'Love's Progress' (*c.*1600)

24 Whatever 'in love' means,
true love is talented.
Someone vividly gifted in love has gone.
on the death of Diana, Princess of Wales
Carol Ann Duffy 1965– : 'September, 1997' (1997); cf. **Falling in Love 6**

25 We don't believe in rheumatism and love until after the
first attack.
Marie von Ebner-Eschenbach 1830–1916: *Aphorisms* (1905)

26 Love is the bright foreigner, the foreign self.
Ralph Waldo Emerson 1803–82: *Essays* (1841) 'Compensation'

27 Don't you know that to love excessively brings bad luck to
lover and beloved? It's like over-fondled children: they died
young.
Gustave Flaubert 1821–80: letter to Louise Colet, 9 August 1846

28 Immature love says: 'I love you because I need you.'
Mature love says: 'I need you because I love you.'
Erich Fromm 1900–80: *The Art of Loving* (1956)

29 What is deep, as love is deep, I'll have
Deeply. What is good, as love is good,
I'll have as well. Then if time and space
Have any purpose, I shall belong to it.
Christopher Fry 1907– : *The Lady's not for Burning* (1949)

30 Love is a universal migraine.
A bright stain on the vision
Blotting out reason.
Robert Graves 1895–1985: 'Symptoms of Love'

31 Grass-green and aspen-green,
Laurel-green and sea-green,
Fine-emerald-green,

And many another hue:
As green commands the variables of green
So love my loves of you.
Robert Graves 1895–1985: 'Variables of Green'

32 Love, love, love—all the wretched cant of it, masking
egotism, lust, masochism, fantasy under a mythology of
sentimental postures, a welter of self-induced miseries and
joys, blinding and masking the essential personalities in the
frozen gestures of courtship, in the kissing and the dating
and the desire, the compliments and the quarrels which
vivify its barrenness.
Germaine Greer 1939– : *The Female Eunuch* (1970)

33 Love bade me welcome: yet my soul drew back,
Guilty of dust and sin.
But quick-eyed Love, observing me grow slack
From my first entrance in,
Drew nearer to me, sweetly questioning,
If I lacked any thing.
George Herbert 1593–1633: 'Love: Love bade me welcome' (1633)

34 Do you want me to tell you something really subversive?
Love *is* everything it's cracked up to be. That's why people
are so cynical about it. . . . It really *is* worth fighting for.
And the trouble is, if you don't risk anything, you risk even
more.
Erica Jong 1942– : *How To Save Your Own Life* (1977)

35 True love is like ghosts, which everyone talks about but few
have seen.
Duc de la Rochefoucauld 1613–80: *Maximes* (1678)

36 Yet we reiterate love! love! love!
as if it were coin with a fixed value
instead of a flower that dies, and opens a different bud.
D. H. Lawrence 1885–1930: 'Lies About Love'

37 All you need is love.
John Lennon 1940–80 and **Paul McCartney** 1942– : title of song (1967)

38 Love in my bosom like a bee
   Doth suck his sweet;
   Now with his wings he plays with me,
   Now with his feet.
   Thomas Lodge 1558–1625: 'Love in my bosom like a bee' (1590)

39 Love is a wound within the body
   That has no outward sign.
   Marie de France fl. 1160–70: 'Love is a wound within the body'

40 To us love says humming that the heart's stalled motor has
   begun working again.
   Vladimir Mayakovsky 1893–1930: 'Letter from Paris to Comrade Kostorov
   on the Nature of Love' (1928)

41 The art of writing, like the art of love, runs all the way
   from a kind of routine hard to distinguish from piling bricks
   to a kind of frenzy closely related to delirium tremens.
   H. L. Mencken 1880–1956: *Minority Report* (1956)

42 Love is not all: it is not meat nor drink
   Nor slumber nor a roof against the rain;
   Nor yet a floating spar to men that sink.
   Edna St Vincent Millay 1892–1950: 'Love is Not All' (1931)

43 Love is the extremely difficult realisation that something
   other than oneself is real. Love, and so art and morals, is
   the discovery of reality.
   Iris Murdoch 1919– : 'The Sublime and the Good' in *Chicago Review* 13
   (1959)

44 In love there are two things: bodies and words.
   Joyce Carol Oates 1938– : in *Mademoiselle* February 1970 'What is the
   Connection Between Men and Women?'

45 Four be the things I'd been better without:
   Love, curiosity, freckles, and doubt.
   Dorothy Parker 1893–1967: 'Inventory' (1937)

46 Most people experience love, without noticing that there is anything remarkable about it.
Boris Pasternak 1890–1960: *Doctor Zhivago* (1958)

47 Love is an attempt at penetrating another being, but it can only succeed if the surrender is mutual.
Octavio Paz 1914–98: attributed

48 What thing is love for (well I wot) love is a thing.
It is a prick, it is a sting,
It is a pretty, pretty thing;
It is a fire, it is a coal
Whose flame creeps in at every hole.
George Peele c.1556–96: *The Hunting of Cupid* (c.1591)

49 Love is so simple.
Jacques Prévert 1900–77: *Les Enfants du Paradis* (1945 film)

50 Love is something far more than desire for sexual intercourse; it is the principal means of escape from the loneliness which afflicts most men and women throughout the greater part of their lives. There is a deep-seated fear, in most people, of the cold world and the possible cruelty of the herd.
Bertrand Russell 1872–1970: *Marriage and Morals* (1929)

51 Life has taught us that love does not consist in gazing at each other but in looking together in the same direction.
Antoine de Saint-Exupéry 1900–44: *Wind, Sand and Stars* (1939)

52 Love looks not with the eyes, but with the mind,
And therefore is winged Cupid painted blind.
William Shakespeare 1564–1616: *A Midsummer Night's Dream* (1595–6)

53 Love is a spirit all compact of fire,
Not gross to sink, but light, and will aspire.
William Shakespeare 1564–1616: *Venus and Adonis* (1593)

54 Love comforteth like sunshine after rain.
William Shakespeare 1564–1616: *Venus and Adonis* (1593)

55 To say a man is fallen in love,—or that he is deeply in love,—or up to the ears in love,—and sometimes even over head and ears in it,—carries an idiomatical kind of implication, that love is a thing below a man.
Laurence Sterne 1713–68: *Tristram Shandy* (1759–67)

56 If love is the answer, could you rephrase the question?
Lily Tomlin 1939– : attributed; David Housham and John Frank-Keyes *Funny Business* (1992)

57 I thought love would adapt itself
to my needs.
But needs grow too fast;
they come up like weeds.
Through cracks in the conversation.
Through silences in the dark.
Through everything you thought was concrete.
Alice Walker 1944– : 'Did This Happen to Your Mother? Did Your Sister Throw Up a Lot?' (1979)

58 Love is a many-splendoured thing . . .
Love is nature's way of giving a reason to be living,
The golden crown that makes a man a king..
Paul Francis Webster: 'Love is a Many-Splendoured Thing' (1955 song)

59 However it is debased or misinterpreted, love is a redemptive feature. To focus on one individual so that their desires become superior to yours is a very cleansing experience.
Jeanette Winterson 1959– : in *The Times* 26 August 1992

60 Love, a child, is ever crying:
Please him and he straight is flying,
Give him, he the more is craving,
Never satisfied with having.
Lady Mary Wroth c.1586–c.1652: 'Love, a child, is ever crying' (1621)

61 A woman can be proud and stiff
When on love intent;
But Love has pitched his mansion in

The place of excrement;
For nothing can be sole or whole
That has not been rent.
W. B. Yeats 1865–1939: 'Crazy Jane Talks with the Bishop' (1932)

62 A pity beyond all telling,
Is hid in the heart of love.
W. B. Yeats 1865–1939: 'The Pity of Love' (1893)

Lovers

1 In love there is always one who kisses and one who offers
the cheek.
Anonymous: French proverb

2 It seemed to them that fate itself had meant them for one
another, and they could not understand why he had a wife
and she a husband; and it was as though they were a pair
of birds of passage, caught and forced to live in different
cages.
Anton Chekhov 1860–1904: 'The Lady with the Dog'

3 All mankind love a lover.
Ralph Waldo Emerson 1803–82: *Essays* 'Love'

4 Our days will be so ecstatic
Our nights will be so exotic
For I'm a neurotic erratic
And you're an erratic erotic.
E. Y. Harburg 1898–1981: 'Courtship in Greenwich Village' (1965)

5 When a pair of magpies fly together
They do not envy the pair of phoenixes.
Lady Ho fl. 300 BC: 'A Song of Magpies'

6 It's the same old story,
A fight for love and glory,
A case of do or die!
The world will always welcome lovers

As time goes by.
Herman Hupfeld 1894–1951: 'As Time Goes By' (1931 song)

7 Lovers never get tired of each other, because they are
always talking about themselves.
Duc de la Rochefoucauld 1613–80: *Maximes* (1678)

8 Lovers. Not a soft word, as people thought, but cruel and
tearing.
Alice Munro 1931– : *Something I've Been Meaning to Tell You* (1974)

9 Every lover is a warrior, and Cupid has his camps.
Ovid 43 BC– AD c.17: *Amores*

10 Scratch a lover, and find a foe.
Dorothy Parker 1893–1967: 'Ballade of a Great Weariness' (1937)

11   And then the lover,
Sighing like furnace, with a woful ballad
Made to his mistress' eyebrow.
William Shakespeare 1564–1616: *As You Like It* (1599)

12 A lover's eyes will gaze an eagle blind;
A lover's ears will hear the lowest sound.
William Shakespeare 1564–1616: *Love's Labour's Lost* (1595)

13 And you have only to look these happy couples in the face,
to see that they have never been in love, or in hate, or in
any other high passion all their days.
Robert Louis Stevenson 1850–94: *Virginibus Puerisque* (1881)

14 No matter how much of a gargoyle someone is, if they are
in love they have that spring in their step, accompanied by
that infuriating I'm-in-an-exclusive-secret-special-club-and-
you-don't-know-the-password smugness.
Arabella Weir: *Does My Bum Look Big in This?* (1997)

Marriage see also **Arranged Marriages, Divorce, Engagements, The Honeymoon, Life Together, Weddings**

1 Like everything which is not the involuntary result of fleeting emotion but the creation of time and will, any marriage, happy or unhappy, is infinitely more interesting than any romance, however passionate.
W. H. Auden 1907–73: *A Certain World* (1970)

2 There is not one in a hundred of either sex who is not taken in when they marry. Look where I will, I see that it *is* so; and I feel that it *must* be so, when I consider that it is, of all transactions, the one in which people expect most from others, and are least honest themselves.
Jane Austen 1775–1817: *Mansfield Park* (1814)

3 Is that how you've seen us for five years? A legal contract? Some marriage. No confetti please—just throw sealing wax and red tape. Do you take this woman, hereinafter called the licensee of the first party . . .
Alan Ayckbourn 1939– : *Table Manners* (1975)

4 Marriage should always combat the monster that devours everything: habit.
Honoré de Balzac 1799–1850: *Physiology of Marriage* (1829)

5 Therefore shall a man leave his father and his mother, and shall cleave unto his wife: and they shall be one flesh.
Bible: Genesis

6 It is better to marry than to burn.
Bible: I Corinthians

7 MARRIAGE, *n.* The state or condition of a community consisting of a master, a mistress and two slaves, making in all, two.
Ambrose Bierce 1842–c.1914: *Devil's Dictionary* (1911)

8 I *N.* take thee *M.* to my wedded husband, to have and to hold from this day forward, for better for worse, for richer for poorer, in sickness and in health, to love, cherish, and to obey, till death us do part.
The Book of Common Prayer 1662: *Solemnization of Matrimony* Betrothal

9 One was never married, and that's his hell: another is, and that's his plague.
Robert Burton 1577–1640: *The Anatomy of Melancholy* (1621–51)

10 Still I can't contradict, what so oft has been said,
'Though women are angels, yet wedlock's the devil.'
Lord Byron 1788–1824: 'To Eliza' (1806)

11 Love and marriage, love and marriage,
Go together like a horse and carriage,
This I tell ya, brother,
Ya can't have one without the other.
Sammy Cahn 1913–93: 'Love and Marriage' (1955 song)

12 The deep, deep peace of the double-bed after the hurly-burly of the chaise-longue.
Mrs Patrick Campbell 1865–1940: A. Woollcott *While Rome Burns* (1934)

13 I learnt a long time ago that the only people who count in any marriage are the two that are in it.
Hillary Rodham Clinton 1947– : television interview with NBC, 27 January 1998

14 Marriage is a feast where the grace is sometimes better than the dinner.
Charles Caleb Colton 1780–1832: *Lacon* (1822)

15 Tho' marriage makes man and wife one flesh, it leaves 'em still two fools.
William Congreve 1670–1729: *The Double Dealer* (1694)

16 Marriage is a wonderful invention; but, then again, so is a bicycle repair kit.
Billy Connolly 1942– : Duncan Campbell *Billy Connolly* (1976)

17 The heart of marriage is memories.
Bill Cosby 1937– : *Love and Marriage* (1989)

18 So basically you're saying marriage is just a way of getting out of an embarrassing pause in conversation.
Richard Curtis 1956– : *Four Weddings and a Funeral* (1994 film)

19 Ven you're a married man, Samivel, you'll understand a good many things as you don't understand now; but vether it's worth while goin' through so much to learn so little, as the charity-boy said ven he got to the end of the alphabet, is a matter o' taste.
Charles Dickens 1812–70: *Pickwick Papers* (1837)

20 The chains of marriage are so heavy that it takes two to bear them, and sometimes three.
Alexandre Dumas 1824–95: Léon Treich *L'Esprit d'Alexandre Dumas*

21 Having once embarked upon your marital voyage, it is impossible not to be aware that you make no way and that the sea is not within sight—that in fact, you are exploring a closed basin.
George Eliot 1819–80: *Middlemarch* (1871–2)

22 Love is temporary and ends with marriage. Marriage is the perfection which love aimed at, ignorant of what it sought.
Ralph Waldo Emerson 1803–82: journal, 1850

23 A picnic without the wasps.
of his early married life
Terence Frisby: in *Daily Telegraph* 5 June 1998

24 By god, D. H. Lawrence was right when he had said there must be a dumb, dark, dull, bitter belly-tension between a man and a woman, and how else could this be achieved save in the long monotony of marriage?
Stella Gibbons 1902–89: *Cold Comfort Farm* (1932)

Marriage

(M)

25 When a woman gets married it is like jumping into a hole
    in the ice in the middle of winter; you do it once and you
    remember it the rest of your days.
    Maxim Gorky 1868–1936: *The Lower Depths* (1903)

26 The married are those who have taken the terrible risk of
    intimacy and, having taken it, know life without intimacy
    to be impossible.
    Carolyn Heilbrun 1926– : in *Ms* August 1974

27 I am your clay.
    You are my clay.
    In life we share a single quilt.
    In death we will share one coffin.
    Kuan Tao-sheng 1262–1319: 'Married Love'

28 There are good marriages, but no delightful ones.
    Duc de la Rochefoucauld 1613–80: *Maximes* (1678)

29 Love is blind, but marriage restores its sight.
    Georg Christoph Lichtenberg 1742–99: *Aphorisms*

30 A party is like a marriage . . . making itself up while
    seeming to follow precedent, running on steel rails into
    uncharted wilderness while the promises shiver and wobble
    on the armrests like crystal stemware.
    Jay McInerney 1955– : *Brightness Falls* (1992)

31 Prostitution. Selling one's body to keep one's soul . . . one
    might say of most marriages that they were selling one's
    soul to keep one's body.
    Compton Mackenzie 1883–1972: *The Adventures of Sylvia Scarlett* (1918)

32 The trouble with marriage is that it ends every night after
    making love, and it must be rebuilt every morning before
    breakfast.
    Gabriel Garcia Marquez 1928– : *Love in the Time of Cholera* (1985)

33 There once was an old man of Lyme
    Who married three wives at a time,
    When asked 'Why a third?'

He replied, 'One's absurd!
And bigamy, Sir, is a crime!'
William Cosmo Monkhouse 1840–1901: *Nonsense Rhymes* (1902)

34 We cannot do without it, and yet we disgrace and vilify the
same. It may be compared to a cage, the birds without
despair to get in, and those within despair to get out.
on marriage
Montaigne 1533–92: *Essays* (1588) 'Upon Some Verses by Virgil'

35 One doesn't have to get anywhere in a marriage. It's not a
public conveyance.
Iris Murdoch 1919– : *A Severed Head* (1961)

36 That is why marriage is so much more interesting than
divorce,
Because it's the only known example of the happy meeting
of the immovable object and the irresistible force.
Ogden Nash 1902–71: 'I Do, I Will, I Have'

37 Staying married may have long-term benefits. You can
elicit much more sympathy from friends over a bad
marriage than you ever can from a good divorce.
P. J. O'Rourke 1947– : *Modern Manners* (1984)

38 They dream in courtship, but in wedlock wake.
Alexander Pope 1688–1744: *Translations from Chaucer* (1714)

39 When two people are under the influence of the most
violent, most insane, most delusive, and most transient of
passions, they are required to swear that they will remain
in that excited, abnormal, and exhausting condition
continuously until death do them part.
George Bernard Shaw 1856–1950: preface to *Getting Married* (1911)

40 Marriage is popular because it combines the maximum of
temptation with the maximum of opportunity.
George Bernard Shaw 1856–1950: *Man and Superman* (1903)

41 'Tis safest in matrimony to begin with a little aversion.
Richard Brinsley Sheridan 1751–1816: *The Rivals* (1775)

Marriage

42 Chains do not hold a marriage together. It is threads, hundreds of tiny threads which sew people together through the years. That is what makes a marriage last—more than passion or even sex!
Simone Signoret 1921–85: in *Daily Mail* 4 July 1978

43 Marriage I think
For women
Is the best of opiates.
It kills the thoughts
That think about the thoughts,
It is the best of opiates.
Stevie Smith 1902–71: 'Marriage I Think'

44 My definition of marriage . . . it resembles a pair of shears, so joined that they cannot be separated; often moving in opposite directions, yet always punishing anyone who comes between them.
Sydney Smith 1771–1845: Lady Holland *Memoir* (1855)

45 Marriage is like life in this—that it is a field of battle, and not a bed of roses.
Robert Louis Stevenson 1850–94: *Virginibus Puerisque* (1881)

46 To marry is to domesticate the Recording Angel. Once you are married, there is nothing left for you, not even suicide, but to be good.
Robert Louis Stevenson 1850–94: *Virginibus Puerisque* (1881)

47 Marriage! That feeble institution! Child, it will pass away with priestcraft from the pulpit into the crypt, into the abyss. For does not Nature herself teach us that marriage is against nature. Look at the birds—they pair for the season and part; but how merrily they sing! While marrying is like chaining two dogs together by the collar. They snarl and bite each other because there is no hope of parting.
Alfred, Lord Tennyson 1809–92: *The Promise of May* (1882)

48 So, now I am in for Hobbes's voyage, a great leap in the dark.
on marriage
John Vanbrugh 1664–1726: *The Provoked Wife* (1697)

49 Marriage isn't a word . . . it's a *sentence*!
King Vidor 1895–1982: *The Crowd* (1928)

50 Marriage is the waste-paper basket of the emotions.
Sidney Webb 1859–1947: Bertrand Russell *Autobiography* (1967)

51 'You got to get married, ' said Uncle Penstemon. 'That's the way of it. I done it long before I was your age. It's nat'ral—like poaching, or drinking, or wind on the stummick. You can't 'elp it, and there you are!'
H. G. Wells 1866–1946: *The History of Mr Polly* (1909)

52 Marriage is a great institution, but I'm not ready for an institution yet.
Mae West 1892–1980: attributed

53 I wonder, among all the tangles of this mortal coil, which one contains tighter knots to undo, and consequently suggests more tugging, and pain, and diversified elements of misery, than the marriage tie.
Edith Wharton 1862–1937: letter, 12 February 1909

54 The world has grown suspicious of anything that looks like a happily married life.
Oscar Wilde 1854–1900: *Lady Windermere's Fan* (1892)

55 There's nothing in the world like the devotion of a married woman. It's a thing no married man knows anything about.
Oscar Wilde 1854–1900: *Lady Windermere's Fan* (1892)

56 Marriage is a bribe to make a housekeeper think she's a householder.
Thornton Wilder 1897–1975: *The Merchant of Yonkers* (1939)

Marriage

57 I feel I must give you everything; and if I can't, marriage
    would only be second-best for you as well as for me.
    Virginia Woolf 1882–1941: letter to Leonard Woolf, 1 May 1912

Meeting see also **Assignations, Parting**

1 A tap at the pane, the quick sharp scratch
   And blue spurt of a lighted match,
   And a voice less loud, through its joys and fears,
   Than the two hearts beating each to each!
   Robert Browning 1812–89: 'Meeting at Night' (1845)

2 O whistle, an' I'll come to you, my lad:
   O whistle, an' I'll come to you, my lad:
   Tho' father and mither should baith gae mad,
   O whistle, and I'll come to you, my lad.
   Robert Burns 1759–96: 'O Whistle, an' I'll come to you, my Lad' (1788)

3 If I should meet thee
   After long years,
   How should I greet thee?—
   With silence and tears.
   Lord Byron 1788–1824: 'When we two parted' (1816)

4   *Men che dramma*
   Di sangue m'è rimaso, che no tremi;
   Conosco i segni dell' antica fiamma.

   Less than a drop of blood remains in me that does not
   tremble; I recognize the signals of the ancient flame.
   on meeting Beatrice in the Earthly Paradise
   Dante Alighieri 1265–1321: *Divina Commedia* 'Purgatorio'

5 Of all the gin joints in all the towns in all the world, she
   walks into mine.
   Julius J. Epstein 1909– , **Philip G. Epstein** 1909–52, and **Howard Koch**
   1902– : *Casablanca* (1942 film); spoken by Humphrey Bogart

6 Harris, I am not well; pray get me a glass of brandy.
on first seeing Caroline of Brunswick, his future wife
George IV 1762–1830: Earl of Malmesbury *Diaries and Correspondence*
(1844) 5 April 1795

7 Some enchanted evening,
You may see a stranger,
You may see a stranger,
Across a crowded room.
Oscar Hammerstein II 1895–1960: 'Some Enchanted Evening' (1949 song)

8 I found my love by the gasworks crofts
Dreamed a dream by the old canal
Kissed my girl by the factory wall
Dirty old town, dirty old town.
Ewen MacColl 1915–89: 'Dirty Old Town' (1950 song)

9 We'll meet again, don't know where,
Don't know when,
But I know we'll meet again some sunny day.
Ross Parker 1914–74 and **Hugh Charles** 1907– : 'We'll Meet Again' (1939
song)

10 My heart is gladder than all these
Because my love is come to me.
Christina Rossetti 1830–94: 'A Birthday' (1862)

11 I wish I could remember the first day,
First hour, first moment of your meeting me,
If bright or dim the season, it might be
Summer or winter for aught I can say.
So unrecorded did it slip away.
Christina Rossetti 1830–94: 'The First Day'

12 Ill met by moonlight, proud Titania.
William Shakespeare 1564–1616: *A Midsummer Night's Dream* (1595–6)

13 Their meetings made December June,
Their every parting was to die.
Alfred, Lord Tennyson 1809–92: *In Memoriam A. H. H.* (1850)

Meeting

14 Now folds the lily all her sweetness up,
And slips into the bosom of the lake:
So fold thyself, my dearest, thou, and slip
Into my bosom and be lost in me.
Alfred, Lord Tennyson 1809–92: *The Princess* (1847) song (added 1850)

15 It was with some emotion . . . that I beheld Albert—who is
beautiful.
of her first meeting with Prince Albert, c.1838
Queen Victoria 1819–1901: attributed; Stanley Weintraub *Albert: Uncrowned King* (1997)

16 Is that a gun in your pocket, or are you just glad to see me?
usually quoted as 'Is that a pistol in your pocket . . . '
Mae West 1892–1980: Joseph Weintraub *Peel Me a Grape* (1975)

Memories

1 Body, remember not only how much you were loved,
not only the beds you lay on,
but also those desires glowing openly
in eyes that looked at you,
trembling for you in voices.
Constantine Cavafy 1863–1933: 'Body, Remember'

2 Love makes up for the lack of long memories by a sort of
magic. All other affections need a past: love creates a past
which envelopes us, as if by enchantment.
Benjamin Constant 1767–1834: *Adolphe* (1816)

3 I have forgot much, Cynara! gone with the wind,
Flung roses, roses, riotously, with the throng,
Dancing, to put thy pale, lost lilies out of mind.
Ernest Dowson 1867–1900: 'Non Sum Qualis Eram' (1896)

4 There should be an invention that bottles up a memory like
a perfume, and it never faded, never got stale, and
whenever I wanted to I could uncork the bottle, and live
the memory all over again.
Daphne Du Maurier 1907–89: *Rebecca* (1938)

5 H: We met at nine
G: We met at eight
H: I was on time
G: No, you were late
H: Ah yes! I remember it well.
Alan Jay Lerner 1918–86: 'I Remember It Well' (1957 song)

6 A cigarette that bears a lipstick's traces,
An airline ticket to romantic places;
And still my heart has wings
These foolish things
Remind me of you.
Holt Marvell 1901–69: 'These Foolish Things Remind Me of You' (1935
song)

7 I must not think of thee; and, tired yet strong,
I shun the thought that lurks in all delight—
The thought of thee—and in the blue heaven's height,
And in the sweetest passage of a song.
Alice Meynell 1847–1922: 'Renouncement'

8 And entering with relief some quiet place
Where never fell his foot or shone his face
I say, 'There is no memory of him here!'
And so stand stricken, so remembering him.
Edna St Vincent Millay 1892–1950: 'Time does not bring relief'

9 When I am sad and weary,
When I think all hope has gone,
When I walk along High Holborn
I think of you with nothing on.
Adrian Mitchell 1932– : 'Celia, Celia'

10 The memories of long love gather like drifting snow,
poignant as the mandarin ducks who float side by side in
sleep.
Murasaki Shikibu *c.*978–*c.*1031: *The Tale of Genji*

11 Remember me when I am gone away,
Gone far away into the silent land;
When you can no more hold me by the hand,
Nor I half turn to go yet turning stay.
Christina Rossetti 1830–94: 'Remember' (1862)

12 Better by far you should forget and smile
Than that you should remember and be sad.
Christina Rossetti 1830–94: 'Remember' (1862)

13 There's rosemary, that's for remembrance; pray, love,
remember.
William Shakespeare 1564–1616: *Hamlet* (1601)

14 Haply I think on thee,—and then my state,
Like to the lark at break of day arising
From sullen earth, sings hymns at heaven's gate;
For thy sweet love remembered such wealth brings
That then I scorn to change my state with kings.
William Shakespeare 1564–1616: sonnet 29

15 When the lamp is shattered
The light in the dust lies dead—
When the cloud is scattered
The rainbow's glory is shed.
When the lute is broken,
Sweet tones are remembered not;
When the lips have spoken,
Loved accents are soon forgot.
Percy Bysshe Shelley 1792–1822: 'Lines: When the lamp' (1824)

16 Rose leaves, when the rose is dead,
Are heaped for the belovèd's bed;
And so thy thoughts, when thou art gone,

Love itself shall slumber on.
Percy Bysshe Shelley 1792–1822: 'To—: Music, when soft voices die'
(1824)

17 And the best and the worst of this is
That neither is most to blame,
If you have forgotten my kisses
And I have forgotten your name.
Algernon Charles Swinburne 1837–1909: 'An Interlude' (1866)

18 Friends,
you are lucky you can talk
about what you did as lovers:
the tricks, laughter, the words, the ecstasy.
After my darling put his hand on the knot of my dress,
I swear I remember nothing.
Vidya fl. *c.*700–1050: Aliki and Willis Barnstone eds. *A Book of Women
Poets* (1980)

Men see also Bachelors, Husbands

1 Nobody ever, unless he is very wicked, deliberately tries to
hurt anybody. It's just that men cannot help not loving you
or behaving badly.
Beryl Bainbridge 1933– : interview in *Daily Telegraph* 10 September 1996

2 Women were brought up to believe that men were the
answer. They weren't. They weren't even one of the
questions.
Julian Barnes 1946– : *Staring at the Sun* (1986)

3 God be thanked, the meanest of his creatures
Boasts two soul-sides, one to face the world with,
One to show a woman when he loves her!
Robert Browning 1812–89: 'One Word More' (1855)

4 A man when he is making up to anybody can be cordial
and gallant and full of little attentions and altogether
charming. But when a man is really in love he can't help
looking like a sheep.
Agatha Christie 1890–1976: *The Mystery of the Blue Train* (1928)

5 My mother wanted me to be a nice boy. I didn't let her
down. I don't smoke, drink or mess around with women.
Julian Clary 1959– : in *Independent* 2 March 1996 'Quote Unquote'

6 Bloody men are like bloody buses—
You wait for about a year
And as soon as one approaches your stop
Two or three others appear.
Wendy Cope 1945– : 'Bloody Men' (1992)

7 What makes men so tedious
Is the need to show off and compete.
They'll bore you to death for hours and hours
Before they'll admit defeat.
Wendy Cope 1945– : 'Men and their boring arguments' (1988)

8 Mad about the boy,
It's pretty funny but I'm mad about the boy.
He has a gay appeal
That makes me feel
There may be something sad about the boy.
Noël Coward 1899–1973: 'Mad about the Boy' (1932 song)

9 Beware of men who cry. It's true that men who cry are
sensitive to and in touch with feelings, but the only feelings
they tend to be sensitive to and in touch with are their
own.
Nora Ephron 1941– : attributed

10 Whatever they may be in public life, whatever their
relations with men, in their relations with women, all men
are rapists, and that's all they are. They rape us with their
eyes, their laws, and their codes.
Marilyn French 1929– : *The Women's Room* (1977)

11 It was the promise of men, that around each corner there
    was yet another man, more wonderful than the last, that
    sustained me. You see, I had men confused with life . . .
    You can't get what I wanted from a man, not in this life.
    Nancy Friday 1937– : *My Mother, My Self* (1977)

12 Why can't a woman be more like a man?
    Men are so honest, so thoroughly square;
    Eternally noble, historically fair;
    Who, when you win, will always give your back a pat.
    Why can't a woman be like that?
    Alan Jay Lerner 1918–86: 'A Hymn to Him' (1956 song) from *My Fair Lady*

13 Those creatures with two legs and eight hands.
    Jayne Mansfield 1932–67: Sally Feldman (ed.) *Woman's Hour Book of
    Humour* (1993)

14 There is nothing about which men lie so much as about
    their sexual powers. In this at least every man is, what in
    his heart he would like to be, a Casanova.
    W. Somerset Maugham 1874–1965: *A Writer's Notebook* (1949)

15 The true man wants two things: danger and play. For that
    reason he wants woman as the most dangerous plaything.
    Friedrich Nietzsche 1844–1900: *Thus Spake Zarathustra* (1883)

16 No woman has to prove herself a woman in the grim way a
    man has to prove himself a man. He must perform, or the
    show does not go on. Social convention is irrelevant. A flop
    is a flop.
    Camille Paglia 1947– : *Sexual Personae* (1990)

17 Some men break your heart in two,
    Some men fawn and flatter,
    Some men never look at you;
    And that cleans up the matter.
    Dorothy Parker 1893–1967: 'Experience'

18 Most gentlemen don't like love,
    They just like to kick it around.
    Cole Porter 1891–1964: 'Most Gentlemen don't like Love' (1938 song)

Men

19 I like men to behave like men—strong and childish.
Françoise Sagan 1935– : attributed

20 Immodest creature, you do not want a woman who will
accept your faults, you want one who pretends that you
are faultless—one who will caress the hand that strikes her
and kiss the lips that lie to her.
George Sand 1804–76: *Intimate Journal* (1926) 13 June 1837

21   There is no woman's sides
Can bide the beating of so strong a passion
As love doth give my heart; no woman's heart
So big, to hold so much.
William Shakespeare 1564–1616: *Twelfth Night* (1601)

22 A woman despises a man for loving her, unless she returns
his love.
Elizabeth Stoddard 1823–1902: *Two Men* (1888)

23 It's not the men in my life that counts—it's the life in my
men.
Mae West 1892–1980: *I'm No Angel* (1933)

24 Give a man a free hand and he'll try to put it all over you.
Mae West 1892–1980: *Klondike Annie* (1936 film)

25 A hard man is good to find.
Mae West 1892–1980: attributed

26 There is, of course, no reason for the existence of the male
sex except that sometimes one needs help with moving the
piano.
Rebecca West 1892–1983: in *Sunday Telegraph* 28 June 1970

Men and Women

1 Women are really much nicer than men:
No wonder we like them.
Kingsley Amis 1922–95: 'A Bookshop Idyll' (1956)

2 Women are programmed to love completely, and men are
  programmed to spread it around.
  Beryl Bainbridge 1933– : interview in *Daily Telegraph* 10 September 1996

3 Once you know what women are like, men get kind of
  boring. I'm not trying to put them down, I mean I like
  them sometimes as people, but sexually they're dull.
  Rita Mae Brown 1944– : attributed

4 Auld nature swears, the lovely dears
  Her noblest work she classes, O;
  Her prentice han' she tried on man,
  An' then she made the lasses, O.
  Robert Burns 1759–96: 'Green Grow the Rashes' (1787)

5 Man's love is of man's life a thing apart,
  'Tis woman's whole existence.
  Lord Byron 1788–1824: *Don Juan* (1819–24)

6 Women deprived of the company of men pine, men
  deprived of the company of women become stupid.
  Anton Chekhov 1860–1904: *Notebooks* (1921)

7 There is more difference within the sexes than between
  them.
  Ivy Compton-Burnett 1884–1969: *Mother and Son* (1955)

8 In the sex-war thoughtlessness is the weapon of the male,
  vindictiveness of the female.
  Cyril Connolly 1903–74: *Unquiet Grave* (1944)

9 Most women set out to change a man and when they have
  changed him they do not like him.
  Marlene Dietrich 1901–92: in *Observer* 30 December 1956 'Sayings of the
  Year'

10 I have always thought that every woman should marry,
   and no man.
   Benjamin Disraeli 1804–81: *Lothair* (1870)

11   Just such disparity
As is 'twixt air and angels' purity,
'Twixt women's love, and men's will ever be.
John Donne 1572–1631: 'Air and Angels'

12 It is only rarely that one can see in a little boy the promise
of a man, but one can almost always see in a little girl the
threat of a woman.
Alexandre Dumas 1824–95: attributed remark, 1895

13 Here's how men think. Sex, work—and those are
reversible, depending on age—sex, work, food, sports and
lastly, begrudgingly, relationships. And here's how women
think. Relationships, relationships, relationships, work, sex,
shopping, weight, food.
Carrie Fisher 1956– : *Surrender the Pink* (1990)

14 Where young boys plan for what they will achieve and
attain, young girls plan for whom they will achieve and
attain.
Charlotte Perkins Gilman 1860–1935: *Women and Economics* (1898)

15 Men are from Mars, women are from Venus.
John Gray 1951– : title of book (1992)

16 Man has his will,—but woman has her way.
Oliver Wendell Holmes 1809–94: *The Autocrat of the Breakfast-Table*
(1858)

17 Hogamus, higamous
Man is polygamous
Higamus, hogamous
Woman monogamous.
William James 1842–1910: in *Oxford Book of Marriage* (1990)

18 Men are what they do, women are what they are.
Randall Jarrell 1914–65: 'In Nature There is Neither Right nor Left nor
Wrong'

19 Men have a much better time of it than women. For one
thing, they marry later. For another thing, they die earlier.
H. L. Mencken 1880–1956: *Chrestomathy* (1949)

20 A man who loves like a woman becomes a slave; but a
woman who loves like a woman becomes a *more perfect*
woman.
Friedrich Nietzsche 1844–1900: *The Gay Science* (1882)

21 Woman lives but in her lord;
Count to ten, and man is bored.
With this the gist and sum of it,
What earthly good can come of it?
Dorothy Parker 1893–1967: 'General Review of the Sex Situation' (1937)

22 Then give me health, wealth, mirth, and wine,
And if busy Love entrenches,
There's a sweet soft page of mine,
Does the trick worth forty wenches.
Lord Rochester 1647–80: 'Song'

23 What is most beautiful in virile men is something feminine;
what is most beautiful in feminine women is something
masculine.
Susan Sontag 1933– : *Against Interpretation* (1966)

24 We are becoming the men we wanted to marry.
Gloria Steinem 1934– : in *Ms* July/August 1982

25 Man dreams of fame while woman wakes to love.
Alfred, Lord Tennyson 1809–92: *Idylls of the King* 'Merlin and Vivien'
(1859)

26 'Tis strange what a man may do, and a woman yet think
him an angel.
William Makepeace Thackeray 1811–63: *The History of Henry Esmond*
(1852)

Men and Women

27 Me Tarzan, you Jane.
summing up his role in Tarzan, the Ape Man (*1932 film*)
Johnny Weissmuller 1904–84: in *Photoplay Magazine* June 1932; the
words occur neither in the film nor the original novel, by Edgar Rice
Burroughs

28 Women represent the triumph of matter over mind, just as
men represent the triumph of mind over morals.
Oscar Wilde 1854–1900: *The Picture of Dorian Gray* (1891)

29 The only time a woman really succeeds in changing a man
is when he is a baby.
Natalie Wood 1938–81: attributed

The Mind see Intelligence and the Mind

Mistakes

1 Had I said that, had I done this,
So might I gain, so might I miss.
Might she have loved me? just as well
She might have hated, who can tell!
Robert Browning 1812–89: 'The Last Ride Together' (1855)

2 Many a man has fallen in love with a girl in a light so dim
he would not have chosen a suit by it.
Maurice Chevalier 1888–1972: attributed, 1955

3 SHARPER: Thus grief still treads upon the heels of pleasure:
Married in haste, we may repent at leisure.
SETTER: Some by experience find those words mis-placed:
At leisure married, they repent in haste.
William Congreve 1670–1729: *The Old Bachelor* (1693)

4 There are so many kinds of awful men—
One can't avoid them all. She often said
She'd never make the same mistake again:

She always made a new mistake instead.
Wendy Cope 1945– : 'Rondeau Redoublé' (1986)

5 CONGRESSMAN: I've always thought of women as kissable,
cuddly, and smelling good.
FENWICK: That's what I feel about men. I only hope you
haven't been disappointed as often as I have.
discussing women's rights legislation
Millicent Fenwick 1910– : *Ned Sherrin in his Anecdotage* (1993)

6 Spontaneous and honest love admits errors, hesitations,
and human failings; it can be tested and repaired. Idealized
love ties us because we already intuit that it is unreal and
are afraid to face this truth.
Nancy Friday 1937– : *My Mother, My Self* (1977)

7 Many years ago I chased a woman for almost two years,
only to discover that her tastes were exactly like mine: we
both were crazy about girls.
Groucho Marx 1895–1977: letter 28 March 1955

8 All our failures are ultimately failures in love.
Iris Murdoch 1919– : *The Bell* (1958)

9 And then I go and spoil it all, by saying somethin' stupid
Like 'I love you.'
C. Carson Parks: 'Somethin' Stupid' (1967 song)

10 To think that I've wasted years of my life, that I've longed
to die, that I've experienced my greatest love for a woman
who didn't appeal to me, who wasn't even my type!
Marcel Proust 1871–1922: *Swann's Way* (1913)

11 A woman has got to love a bad man once or twice in her
life, to be thankful for a good one.
Marjorie Kinnan Rawlings 1896–1953: *The Yearling* (1938)

12   Then, must you speak
Of one that loved not wisely but too well.
William Shakespeare 1564–1616: *Othello* (1602–4)

Mistakes

13 He is all fault who hath no fault at all:
For who loves me must have a touch of earth.
Alfred, Lord Tennyson 1809–92: *Idylls of the King* 'Lancelot and Elaine'
(1859)

14 GERRY: We can't get married at all . . . I'm a man.
OSGOOD: Well, nobody's perfect.
Billy Wilder 1906– and **I. A. L. Diamond** 1915–88: *Some Like It Hot*
(1959 film); closing words

Money see also Wealth and Poverty

1 What is the difference in matrimonial affairs, between the
mercenary and the prudent move? Where does discretion
end, and avarice begin?
Jane Austen 1775–1817: *Pride and Prejudice* (1813)

2 Money, it turned out, was exactly like sex, you thought of
nothing else if you didn't have it and thought of other
things if you did.
James Baldwin 1924–87: in *Esquire* May 1961

3 Buy old masters. They fetch a better price than old
mistresses.
Lord Beaverbrook 1879–1964: attributed

4 Those who have some means think that the most
important thing in the world is love. The poor know that it
is money.
Gerald Brenan 1894–1987: *Thoughts in a Dry Season* (1978)

5 For money has a power above
The stars and fate, to manage love.
Samuel Butler 1612–80: *Hudibras* pt. 3 (1680)

6 Nothing to be done without a bribe I find, in love as well as
law.
Susanna Centlivre *c.*1669–1723: *The Perjured Husband* (1700)

7 I am not against hasty marriages where a mutual flame is fanned by an adequate income.
Wilkie Collins 1824–89: *No Name* (1862)

8 Money is the sinews of love, as of war.
George Farquhar 1678–1707: *Love and a Bottle* (1698)

9 His designs were strictly honourable, as the phrase is; that is, to rob a lady of her fortune by way of marriage.
Henry Fielding 1707–54: *Tom Jones* (1749)

10 Of all the icy blasts that blow on love, a request for money is the most chilling and havoc-wreaking.
Gustave Flaubert 1821–80: *Madame Bovary* (1857)

11 A lifelong devotion is measured after the fact; and meanwhile it is customary in these cases to give few material securities. What are yours?
Henry James 1843–1916: *Washington Square* (1881)

12 Positively no money refunded after the curtain has risen.
notice on a playbill sent to her former lover, the Duke of Clarence, refusing repayment of her allowance
Mrs Jordan 1762–1816: Duke of Windsor 'My Hanoverian Ancestors' (unpublished reminiscences); Elizabeth Longford (ed.) *The Oxford Book of Royal Anecdotes* (1989)

13 For I don't care too much for money,
For money can't buy me love.
John Lennon 1940–80 and **Paul McCartney** 1942– : 'Can't Buy Me Love' (1964 song)

14 And you can say it was a real love match. We married for money.
S. J. Perelman 1904–79 and **Will Johnstone**: *Monkey Business* (1931 film)

15 The only way for a woman to provide for herself decently is for her to be good to some man that can afford to be good to her.
George Bernard Shaw 1856–1950: *Mrs Warren's Profession* (1898)

16 And all for love, and nothing for reward.
Edmund Spenser c.1552-99: *The Faerie Queen* (1596)

17 Doänt thou marry for munny, but goä wheer munny is!
Alfred, Lord Tennyson 1809-92: 'Northern Farmer. New Style' (1869)

18 Love is not to be bought, in any sense of the word; its silken wings are instantly shrivelled up when any thing beside a return in kind is sought.
Mary Wollstonecraft 1759-97: *A Vindication of the Rights of Woman* (1792)

Music

1 If music be the breakfast food of love, kindly do not disturb until lunch time.
James Agee 1909-55: *Agee on Film* (1963)

2 We all fell in love, fell out of love, and fell in love again to the sound of his voice.
of Frank Sinatra
Tony Bennett 1926- : at Sinatra's funeral, Beverley Hills, 20 May 1998

3 Consort not with a female musician lest thou be taken in by her snares.
Ben Sira c.190 BC: *The Book of Wisdom*

4 Our young women and wives, they that being maids took so much pains to sing, play and dance, with such cost and charge to their parents to get these graceful qualities, now being married will scarce touch an instrument, they care not for it.
Robert Burton 1577-1640: *The Anatomy of Melancholy* (1621-51)

5 Extraordinary how potent cheap music is.
Noël Coward 1899-1973: *Private Lives* (1930)

6 I conclude that musical notes and rhythms were first acquired by the male or female progenitors of mankind for the sake of charming the opposite sex.
Charles Darwin 1809–82: *The Descent of Man* (1871)

7 No artist should ever marry . . . if ever you do have to marry, marry a girl who is more in love with your art than with you.
Frederick Delius 1862–1934: Eric Fenby *Delius as I Knew Him* (1936)

8 When lovely woman stoops to folly and
Paces about her room again, alone,
She smoothes her hair with automatic hand,
And puts a record on the gramophone.
T. S. Eliot 1888–1965: *The Waste Land* (1922)

9 Maybe the most that you can expect from a relationship that goes bad is to come out of it with a few good songs.
Marianne Faithfull 1946– : *Faithfull* (1994)

10 Most people get into bands for three very simple rock and roll reasons: to get laid, to get fame, and to get rich.
Bob Geldof 1954– : in *Melody Maker* 27 August 1977

11 Excluding two-letter prepositions and 'an', I imagine *me* is the most used two-letter word in Songdom. 'I' (leaving out indefinite article 'a') is doubtless the most used one-letter word (and everywhere else, for that matter). 'You' (if definite article 'the' bows out) is the most frequent three-letter word. 'Love' probably gets the four-letter nod (referring strictly to songs that can be heard in the home). In the five-letter stakes I would wager that 'heart' and 'dream' photo-finish in a dead heat. As for words of more than five letters, you're on your own.
Ira Gershwin 1896–1983: *Lyrics on Several Occasions: A Brief Concordance* (1977)

12 'Bed,' as the Italian proverb succinctly puts it, 'is the poor man's opera.'
Aldous Huxley 1894–1963: *Heaven and Hell* (1956)

13 Tenors get women by the score.
James Joyce 1882–1941: *Ulysses* (1922)

14 Ballads and babies. That's what happened to me.
Paul McCartney 1942– : in *Time* 8 June 1992

15 I always thought music was more important than sex—then I thought if I don't hear a concert for a year-and-a-half it doesn't bother me.
Jackie Mason 1931– : in *Guardian* 17 February 1989

16 I love, you love, we all love, why do we love, how much do we love, where do we love, why did you stop loving me?
on themes of popular songs
Mitch Miller: attributed, 1954

17 It might not be a bad idea for some teenagers, when they are being 'sent' by a piece of jazz, to ask themselves where the music stopped and the sex began.
Beverley Nichols 1898–1983: remark, 1960s; Edward Lee *Music of the People* (1970)

18 Music and women I cannot but give way to, whatever my business is.
Samuel Pepys 1633–1703: diary 9 March 1666

19 The man who is not thrilled to the bone by the sight of a woman playing the flute, blowing a clarinet or struggling with the intricacies of a trombone is no man.
Malcolm Sargent 1895–1967: Charles Gattey *Peacocks on the Podium* (1982)

20 Give me some music—music, moody food
Of us that trade in love.
William Shakespeare 1564–1616: *Antony and Cleopatra* (1606–7)

21 If music be the food of love, play on;
    Give me excess of it, that, surfeiting,
    The appetite may sicken, and so die.
    William Shakespeare 1564–1616: *Twelfth Night* (1601)

22 I think no woman I have had ever gave me so sweet a
    moment, or at so light a price, as the moment I owe to a
    newly heard musical phrase.
    Stendhal 1783–1842: letter to his sister Pauline, 29 October 1808

23 All my life I was having trouble with women . . . Then,
    after I quit having trouble with them, I could feel in my
    heart that somebody would always have trouble with
    them, so I kept writing those blues.
    Muddy Waters 1915–83: Tony Palmer *All You Need is Love* (1976)

Night see also The Skies

1 I've known for years our marriage has been a mockery. My
   body lying there night after night in the wasted moonlight.
   I know now how the Taj Mahal must feel.
   Alan Bennett 1934– : *Habeas Corpus* (1973)

2   For the night
   Shows stars and women in a better light.
   Lord Byron 1788–1824: *Don Juan* (1819–24)

3 Though the night was made for loving,
   And the day returns too soon,
   Yet we'll go no more a-roving
   By the light of the moon.
   Lord Byron 1788–1824: 'So we'll go no more a-roving' (written 1817)

Night

4 Wild nights! Wild nights!
Were I with thee,
Wild nights should be
Our luxury!
Emily Dickinson 1830–86: 'Wild nights! Wild nights!'

5 Night and day, you are the one,
Only you beneath the moon and under the sun.
Cole Porter 1891–1964: 'Night and Day' (1932 song)

6 *Trois allumettes une à une allumées dans la nuit*
La première pour voir ton visage tout entier
La seconde pour voir tes yeux
La dernière pour voir ta bouche
Et l'obscurité tout entière pour me rappeler tout cela
En te serrant dans mes bras.

Three matches in the night lit one by one.
The first to see your whole face.
The second to see your eyes.
The last to see your mouth.
And then deep darkness to let me remember it all
As I hold you in my arms.
Jacques Prévert 1900–77: 'Paris at Night' (1949); translated by A. J.
Tessimond

7 Midnight,
                              a hotel bedroom, open window,
sibilant tyres on rain-washed asphalt streets
whispering a repetitious *finish, finish.*
You stroke your lover comprehensively,
who purrs contentment, clings to your neck and sobs.
Peter Reading 1946– : 'Midnight' (1994)

8 Now lies the Earth all Danaë to the stars,
And all thy heart lies open unto me.
Alfred, Lord Tennyson 1809–92: *The Princess* (1847), song (added 1850)

Old Age see also Age

1 You'll have to ask somebody older than me.
when asked at what age the sex drive goes, at the age of ninety-seven
Eubie Blake 1883–1983: in *Ned Sherrin in his Anecdotage* (1993)

2 Every woman should marry an archaeologist because she grows increasingly attractive to him as she grows increasingly to resemble a ruin.
Agatha Christie 1890–1976: Russell H. Fitzgibbon *The Agatha Christie Companion* (1980); attributed, perhaps apocryphal

3 Oh, to be seventy again!
on seeing a pretty girl on his eightieth birthday
Georges Clemenceau 1841–1929: James Agate, diary, 19 April 1938

4 There are three classes into which all the women past seventy that ever I knew were to be divided: 1. That dear old soul; 2. That old woman; 3. That old witch.
Samuel Taylor Coleridge 1772–1834: *Table Talk* (1835)

5 No spring, nor summer beauty hath such grace,
As I have seen in one autumnal face.
John Donne 1572–1631: 'The Autumnal' (*c.*1600)

6 They that marry ancient people merely in expectation to bury them, hang themselves, in hope that one will come and cut the halter.
Thomas Fuller 1608–61: *The Holy State and the Profane State*

7 You, that are going to be married, think things can never be done too fast; but we, that are old, and know what we are about, must elope methodically, madam.
Oliver Goldsmith 1728–74: *The Good-Natured Man* (1768)

8 There is no point in growing old unless you can become a
witch.
Germaine Greer 1939– : attributed; Sally Feldman (ed.) *Woman's Hour
Book of Humour* (1993)

9 The love of old men is not worth a lot,
Desperate and dry even when it is hot.
You cannot tell what is enthusiasm
And what involuntary clawing spasm.
Thom Gunn 1929– : 'Lines for My 55th Birthday'

10 A woman would rather visit her own grave than the place
where she has been young and beautiful after she is aged
and ugly.
Corra May Harris 1869–1935: *Eve's Second Husband* (1910)

11 Love's like the measles—all the worse when it comes late in
life.
Douglas Jerrold 1803–57: *The Wit and Opinions of Douglas Jerrold* (1859)
'Love'

12 There are few things that we so unwillingly give up, even
in advanced age, as the supposition that we still have the
power of ingratiating ourselves with the fair sex.
Samuel Johnson 1709–84: George Birkbeck Hill (ed.) *Johnsonian
Miscellanies* (1897)

13 Will you still need me, will you still feed me,
When I'm sixty four?
John Lennon 1940–80 and **Paul McCartney** 1942– : 'When I'm Sixty Four'
(1967 song)

14 Coquettes with doctors; hoards her breath
For blandishments; fluffs out her hair;
And keeps her stubborn suitor, Death,
Moping upon the stair.
Phyllis McGinley 1905– : 'The Old Beauty'

15 Darling, I am growing old,
Silver threads among the gold.
Eben E. Rexford 1848–1916: 'Silver Threads Among the Gold' (1873 song)

16 *Quand vous serez bien vieille, au soir, à la chandelle,*
    Assise auprès du feu, dévidant et filant,
    Direz, chantant mes vers, en vous émerveillant,
    Ronsard me célébrait du temps que j'étais belle.

When you are very old, and sit in the candle-light at
evening spinning by the fire, you will say, as you murmur
my verses, a wonder in your eyes, 'Ronsard sang of me in
the days when I was fair.'
Pierre de Ronsard 1524–85: *Sonnets pour Hélène* (1578)

17 When you are old and grey and full of sleep,
    And nodding by the fire, take down this book
    And slowly read and dream of the soft look
    Your eyes had once, and of their shadows deep.
    W. B. Yeats 1865–1939: 'When You Are Old' (1893)

Opposition and Difficulties

1 From this day you must be a stranger to one of your
   parents.—Your mother will never see you again if you do
   not marry Mr Collins, and I will never see you again if you
   do.
   Jane Austen 1775–1817: *Pride and Prejudice* (1813)

2 Love laughs at locksmiths.
   George Colman, the Younger 1762–1836: title of play (1808)

3 John Donne, Anne Donne, Un-done.
   *in a letter to his wife, on being dismissed from the service of his
   father-in-law, George More*
   John Donne 1572–1631: Izaak Walton *Life of Dr Donne* (1640)

4 The path of true love isn't smooth,
   the ruffled feathers sex can soothe
   ruffle again—for couples never
   spend all their lives in bed together.
   Gavin Ewart 1916–95: '24th March 1986' (1987)

5 Of all actions of a man's life, his marriage does least
   concern other people; yet of all actions of our life, 'tis the
   most meddled with by other people.
   John Selden 1584–1654: *Table Talk* (1689)

6 The course of true love never did run smooth.
   William Shakespeare 1564–1616: *A Midsummer Night's Dream* (1595–6)

7 From forth the fatal loins of these two foes
   A pair of star-crossed lovers take their life.
   William Shakespeare 1564–1616: *Romeo and Juliet* (1595)

Pain and Suffering see also **Heartbreak,**
Sorrow

1 I've always had this penchant for what I call kamikaze
   women. I call them kamikaze because they crash their
   plane. They're self-destructive—but they crash it into you,
   taking you with them.
   Woody Allen 1935– : *Husbands and Wives* (1992 film)

2 Those have most power to hurt us that we love.
   Francis Beaumont 1584–1616 and **John Fletcher** 1579–1625: *The Maid's
   Tragedy* (written 1610–11)

3 When people say, 'You're breaking my heart,' they do in
   fact usually mean that you're breaking their genitals.
   Jeffrey Bernard 1932–97: in *The Spectator* 31 May 1986

4 Love is a boy, by poets styled,
   Then spare the rod, and spoil the child.
   Samuel Butler 1612–80: *Hudibras* pt. 2 (1664)

5 It was very good of God to let Carlyle and Mrs Carlyle
marry one another and so make only two people miserable
instead of four.
Samuel Butler 1835–1902: letter to Miss E. M. A. Savage, 21 November
1884

6 Great loves too must be endured.
Coco Chanel 1883–1971: Marcel Haedrich *Coco Chanel, Her Life, Her Secrets*
(1971)

7 They say that men suffer,
As badly, as long.
I worry, I worry,
In case they are wrong.
Wendy Cope 1945– : 'I Worry' (1992)

8 Love's passives are his activ'st part.
The wounded is the wounding heart.
Richard Crashaw c.1612–49: 'The Flaming Heart upon the Book of Saint
Teresa' (1652)

9 Love is a sickness full of woes,
All remedies refusing;
A plant that with most cutting grows,
Most barren with best using.
Samuel Daniel 1563–1619: 'Love'

10 In the past, in old novels, the price of love was death, a
price which virtuous women paid in childbirth, and the
wicked, like Nana, with the pox. Nowadays it is paid in
thrombosis or neurosis: one can take one's pick.
Margaret Drabble 1939– : *The Waterfall* (1969)

11 The pain of love is the pain of being alive. It's a perpetual
wound.
Maureen Duffy 1933– : *Wounds* (1969)

Pain

12 The struggle is over and I have found peace. I think today I could let you marry another without losing it—for I know the spiritual union between us will outlive this life, even if we never see each other in this world again.
Maud Gonne 1867–1953: letter to W. B. Yeats, December 1908

13 Desire may be dead
and still a man can be
a meeting place for sun and rain, wonder outwaiting pain
as in a wintry tree.
D. H. Lawrence 1885–1930: 'Desire is Dead'

14 How alike are the groans of love to those of the dying.
Malcolm Lowry 1909–57: *Under the Volcano* (1947)

15 *Plaisir d'amour ne dure qu'un moment,*
Chagrin d'amour dure toute la vie.

Love's pleasure lasts but a moment; love's sorrow lasts all through life.
Jean-Pierre Claris de Florian 1755–94: *Célestine* (1784)

16 One does not kill oneself for love of *a* woman, but because love—any love—reveals us in our nakedness, our misery, our vulnerability, our nothingness.
Cesare Pavese 1908–50: diary, 25 March 1950

17 O! many a shaft, at random sent,
Finds mark the archer little meant!
And many a word, at random spoken,
May soothe or wound a heart that's broken.
Sir Walter Scott 1771–1832: *The Lord of the Isles* (1813)

18 An oyster may be crossed in love!
Richard Brinsley Sheridan 1751–1816: *The Critic* (1779)

19 When evening falls so hard,
I will comfort you.
I'll take your part.
When darkness comes
And pain is all around,

Like a bridge over troubled water
I will lay me down.
Paul Simon 1942– : 'Bridge Over Troubled Water' (1970 song)

20 Love is the fart
Of every heart:
It pains a man when 'tis kept close,
And others doth offend, when 'tis let loose.
John Suckling 1609–42: 'Love's Offence' (1646)

21 No thorns go as deep as a rose's,
And love is more cruel than lust.
Algernon Charles Swinburne 1837–1909: 'Dolores' (1866)

22 Love hurt you once, you said, too much.
You said you'd have no more of such
Hot heartbreak and long loneliness.
You said you'd give and ask for less
Than love, that daemon without pity.
A. J. Tessimond 1902–62: 'The Bargain'

23 There are some meannesses which are too mean even for
man—woman, lovely woman alone, can venture to
commit them.
William Makepeace Thackeray 1811–63: *A Shabby Genteel Story* (1840)

24 A man goes through earthquakes, epidemics, the horror of
disease, and all sorts of spiritual torments, but the most
agonizing tragedy he ever knows always has been, and
always will be, the tragedy of the bedroom.
Leo Tolstoy 1828–1910: remark to Gorky; Maxim Gorky *On Literature*

25 Those who have courage to love should have courage to
suffer.
Anthony Trollope 1815–82: *The Bertrams* (1859)

26 Crying is the refuge of plain women but the ruin of pretty
ones.
Oscar Wilde 1854–1900: *Lady Windermere's Fan* (1892)

Pain

Parting see also Absence, Loss

1 Ae fond kiss, and then we sever;
   Ae fareweel, and then for ever!
   Robert Burns 1759–96: 'Ae fond Kiss' (1792)

2 How long ago Hector took off his plume,
   Not wanting that his little son should cry,
   Then kissed his sad Andromache goodbye —
   And now we three in Euston waiting-room.
   Frances Cornford 1886–1960: 'Parting in Wartime' (1948)

3 Farewell sweet kisses, pigeon-wise,
   With lip and tongue, farewell again
   The secret sports betwixt us twain.
   Diane de Poitiers 1499–1566: 'To Henry II Upon His Leaving for a Trip'
   (*c.*1552)

4 Parting is all we know of heaven,
   And all we need of hell.
   Emily Dickinson 1830–86: 'My life closed twice before its close'

5 When I died last, and, dear, I die
   As often as from thee I go,
   Though it be but an hour ago,
   And lovers' hours be full eternity.
   John Donne 1572–1631: 'The Legacy'

6 Since there's no help, come let us kiss and part,
   Nay, I have done: you get no more of me.
   Michael Drayton 1563–1631: sonnet (1619)

7 You and I, when our days are done, must say
   Without exactly saying it, good-bye.
   John Fuller 1937– : 'Pyrosymphonie' (1996)

8 He would not stay for me; and who can wonder?
   He would not stay for me to stand and gaze.
   I shook his hand and tore my heart in sunder

And went with half my life about my ways.
A. E. Housman 1859–1936: 'He would not stay for me; and who can wonder'

9 We're drinking my friend,
To the end of a brief episode,
Make it one for my baby
And one more for the road.
Johnny Mercer 1909–76: 'One For My Baby' (1943 song)

10 How can I live without thee, how forgo
Thy sweet converse and love so dearly joined,
To live again in these wild woods forlorn?
John Milton 1608–74: *Paradise Lost* (1667)

11 Our parting now will dampen
Rumours we have not denied.
This gown will rot away
From tears of intense longing.
Lady Nijō: letter to Iinuma, 1289

12 Oh, seek, my love, your newer way;
I'll not be left in sorrow.
So long as I have yesterday,
Go take your damned tomorrow!
Dorothy Parker 1893–1967: 'Godspeed'

13 There's no love song finer,
But how strange the change from major to minor
Every time we say goodbye.
Cole Porter 1891–1964: 'Every Time We Say Goodbye' (1944 song)

14 A man never knows how to say goodbye; a woman never
knows when to say it.
Helen Rowland 1875–1950: *Reflections of a Bachelor Girl* (1903)

15 Good-night, good-night! parting is such sweet sorrow
That I shall say good-night till it be morrow.
William Shakespeare 1564–1616: *Romeo and Juliet* (1595)

Parting

16 Farewell! thou art too dear for my possessing.
William Shakespeare 1564–1616: sonnet 87

17 Good-night? ah! no; the hour is ill
Which severs those it should unite;
Let us remain together still,
Then it will be *good* night.
Percy Bysshe Shelley 1792–1822: 'Good Night' (1822)

18 When we were a soft amoeba, in ages past and gone,
Ere you were Queen of Sheba, or I King Solomon,
Alone and undivided, we lived a life of sloth,
Whatever you did, I did; one dinner served for both.
Anon came separation, by fission and divorce,
A lonely pseudopodium I wandered on my course.
Arthur Shipley 1861–1927: 'Ere you were Queen of Sheba' (1923)

19 I remember the way we parted,
The day and the way we met;
You hoped we were both broken-hearted,
And knew we should both forget.
Algernon Charles Swinburne 1837–1909: 'An Interlude' (1866)

Passion see also Desire

1 How little of permanent happiness could belong to a couple
who were only brought together because their passions
were stronger than their virtue.
Jane Austen 1775–1817: *Pride and Prejudice* (1813)

2 One mad magenta moment and I have paid for it all my
life.
Alan Bennett 1934– : *Habeas Corpus* (1973)

3 Repentance must come. It is the after-taste of passion.
Mary Elizabeth Braddon 1837–1915: attributed

4   Ah, Sweet—
The moment eternal—just that and no more—
When ecstasy's utmost we clutch at the core
While cheeks burn, arms open, eyes shut and lips meet!
Robert Browning 1812–89: 'Now'

5 Give me more love or more disdain;
The torrid or the frozen zone:
Bring equal ease unto my pain;
The temperate affords me none.
Thomas Carew c.1595–1640: 'Mediocrity in Love Rejected' (1640)

6 Passion always goes, and boredom stays.
Coco Chanel 1883–1971: Frances Kennett *Coco: the Life and Loves of Gabrielle Chanel* (1989)

7 A passionate nature always loves women, but one who loves women is not necessarily a passionate nature.
Chang Ch'ao fl. c.1650: *Sweet Dream Shadows*

8 To me, passionate love has always been like a tight shoe rubbing blisters on my Achilles heel . . . I resent it and love it and wallow and recover . . . and I wish to God I could handle it, but I never have and I know I never will.
Noël Coward 1899–1973: diary 1 December 1957

9 My heart's just a mush this evening. I'm consumed by passion for you and it couldn't be more painful. This has been brewing all day and it came down on me like a tornado in the streets of Douarnenez, where I broke into sobs.
Simone de Beauvoir 1908–86: letter to Jean-Paul Sartre, 25 September 1939

10 Passion should believe itself irresistible. It should forget civility and consideration and all the other curses of a refined nature. Above all, it should never ask for leave where there is a right of way.
E. M. Forster 1879–1970: *A Room with a View* (1908)

11 Passion makes the world go round. Love just makes it a
safer place.
Ice-T 1958– : *The Ice Opinion* (1994)

12 A man who has not passed through the inferno of his
passions has never overcome them.
Carl Gustav Jung 1875–1961: *Memories, Dreams, Reflections* (1962)

13 And down his mouth comes to my mouth! and down
His bright dark eyes come over me, like a hood
Upon my mind! his lips meet mine, and a flood
Of sweet fire sweeps across me, so I drown
Against him, die, and find death good.
D. H. Lawrence 1885–1930: 'Love on the Farm'

14 It is with our passions as it is with fire and water, they are
good servants, but bad masters.
Roger L'Estrange 1616–1704: *Aesop's Fables*

15 Here I am back and still smouldering with passion, like
wine smoking. Not a passion any longer for flesh, but a
complete hunger for you, a devouring hunger.
Henry Miller 1891–1980: letter to Anais Nin, 14 August 1932

16 *Ce n'est plus une ardeur dans mes veines cachée:*
C'est Vénus tout entière à sa proie attachée.

It's no longer a burning within my veins: it's Venus entire
latched onto her prey.
Jean Racine 1639–99: *Phèdre* (1677)

17 A continual atmosphere of hectic passion is very trying if
you haven't got any of your own.
Dorothy L. Sayers 1893–1957: *The Unpleasantness at the Bellona Club*
(1928)

18 So I triumphed ere my passion, sweeping thro' me, left me
dry,
Left me with the palsied heart, and left me with the
jaundiced eye.
Alfred, Lord Tennyson 1809–92: 'Locksley Hall' (1842)

19 Strange fits of passion have I known:
And I will dare to tell,
But in the lover's ear alone,
What once to me befell.
William Wordsworth 1770–1850: 'Strange Fits of Passion'

Places and Peoples see also Travel

1 Every American woman has two souls to call her own, the other being her husband's.
James Agate 1877–1947: diary 15 May 1937

2 A Canadian is somebody who knows how to make love in a canoe.
Pierre Berton 1920– : in *The Canadian* 22 December 1973

3 I like the English. They have the most rigid code of immorality in the world.
Malcolm Bradbury 1932– : *Eating People is Wrong* (1959)

4 The isles of Greece, the isles of Greece!
Where burning Sappho loved and sung.
Lord Byron 1788–1824: *Don Juan* (1819–24)

5 Love in this part of the world is no sinecure.
Lord Byron 1788–1824: letter to John Murray from Venice, 27 December 1816

6 France is the only place where you can make love in the afternoon without people hammering on your door.
Barbara Cartland 1901– : in *Guardian* 24 December 1984

7 Kent, sir—everybody knows Kent—apples, cherries, hops, and women.
Charles Dickens 1812–70: *Pickwick Papers* (1837)

8 Sex. In America an obsession. In other parts of the world a fact.
Marlene Dietrich 1901–92: *Marlene Dietrich's ABC* (1962)

9 Latins are tenderly enthusiastic. In Brazil they throw
flowers at you. In Argentina they throw themselves.
Marlene Dietrich 1901–92: in *Newsweek* 24 August 1959

10 Get yourself a Geisha. The flower of Asia,
She's one with whom to take up.
At night your bed she'll make up,
And she'll be there when you wake up.
Howard Dietz 1896–1983: 'Get Yourself a Geisha' (1935)

11 The average Hollywood film star's ambition is to be
admired by an American, courted by an Italian, married to
an Englishman, and have a French boyfriend.
Katharine Hepburn 1909– : in *New York Journal-American* 22 February
1954

12 It's true the French have a certain obsession with sex, but
it's a particularly adult obsession. France is the thriftiest of
all nations; to a Frenchman sex provides the most
economical way to have fun. The French are a logical race.
Anita Loos 1893–1981: *Kiss Hollywood Good-Bye* (1978)

13 In no country, I believe, are the marriage laws so
iniquitous as in England, and the conjugal relation, in
consequence, so impaired.
Harriet Martineau 1802–76: *Society in America* (1837)

14 Continental people have sex life; the English have hot-
water bottles.
George Mikes 1912– : *How to be an Alien* (1946)

15 One becomes aware in France, after having lived in
America, that sex pervades the air. It's there all around
you, like a fluid.
Henry Miller 1891–1980: George Plimpton (ed.) *Writers at Work* (1963)

16 Do you know what 'le vice Anglais'—the English vice—
really is? Not flagellation, not pederasty—whatever the
French believe it to be. It's our refusal to admit our
emotions. We think they demean us, I suppose.
Terence Rattigan 1911–77: *In Praise of Love* (1973)

17 I was so cold I almost got married.
of England
Shelley Winters 1922– : in *New York Times* 25 April 1956

18 The Irish men are reckoned terrible heart stealers—but I do not find them so very formidable.
Mary Wollstonecraft 1759–97: letter, 11 May 1787

Pleasure

1 I'm tired of Love: I'm still more tired of Rhyme.
But Money gives me pleasure all the time.
Hilaire Belloc 1870–1953: 'Fatigued' (1923); cf. **Pleasure 4**

2 Let us have wine and women, mirth and laughter,
Sermons and soda-water the day after.
Lord Byron 1788–1824: *Don Juan* (1819–24)

3 In love, as in gluttony, pleasure is a matter of the utmost precision.
Italo Calvino 1923–85: Charles Fourier *Theory of the Four Movements* (1971)

4 I hardly ever tire of love or rhyme—
That's why I'm poor and have a rotten time.
Wendy Cope 1945– : 'Variation on Belloc's "Fatigued"' (1992); cf. **Pleasure 1**

5 If we seek the pleasures of love, passion should be occasional, and common sense continual.
Robertson Davies 1913–95: *The Enthusiasms of Robertson Davies* (1990)

6 Time is short and we must seize
Those pleasures found above the knees.
habitual comment made to his son Richard's girlfriends
Richard Eyre 1916–92: Richard Eyre *Utopia and Other Places* (1993)

7 This being in love is great—you get a lot of compliments and begin to think you are a great guy.
F. Scott Fitzgerald 1896–1940: *The Crack-Up* (1945)

8 I didn't wind up in the grotto with a bunch of Playmates; I
   wound up in bed with my wife and children at 10.30 pm
   watching Murder One. What people don't understand
   about me is that there is no dark side to my life.
   on his seventieth birthday celebrations
   Hugh Hefner 1926– : in *Guardian* 25 April 1996

9 If I had no duties, and no reference to futurity, I would
   spend my life in driving briskly in a post-chaise with a
   pretty woman.
   Samuel Johnson 1709–84: James Boswell *Life of Johnson* (1791) 19
   February 1777

10 The pleasure of love is loving, and we get more happiness
   from the passion we feel than from the passion we inspire.
   Duc de la Rochefoucauld 1613–80: *Maximes* (1678)

11 Brother, do you know a nicer occupation,
   Matter of fact, neither do I,
   Than standing on the corner
   Watching all the girls go by?
   Frank Loesser 1910–69: 'Standing on the Corner' (1956 song)

12 Who loves not woman, wine, and song
   Remains a fool his whole life long.
   Martin Luther 1483–1546: attributed (later inscribed, in German, in the
   Luther room in the Wartburg)

13 No, there's nothing half so sweet in life
   As love's young dream.
   Thomas Moore 1779–1852: 'Love's Young Dream' (1807)

14 Blest is the man who loves and after early play
   Whereby his limbs are supple made and strong,
   Retiring to his house, with wine and song
   Toys with a fair boy on his breast the livelong day!
   Solon c.640– after 556 BC: 'Blest is the man'

(P)

Poets see also Books and Literature, Words

1 Men can write good love poems because they are always
   aware that the girl they happen to be in love with might be
   someone else (and often one suspects that they are thinking
   of several girls at the same time).
   W. H. Auden 1907–73: Phyllis McGinley *Times Three* (1960) foreword

2 There's many a would-be poet at this hour,
   Rhymes of a love that he hath never woo'd,
   And o'er his lamp-lit desk in solitude
   Deems that he sitteth in the Muses' bower.
   Robert Bridges 1844–1930: 'Growth of Love'

3 I was only a poor poet, made for singing at her casement,
   As the finches or the thrushes, while she thought of other
      things.
   Elizabeth Barrett Browning 1806–61: 'Lady Geraldine's Courtship' (1844)

4 She that with poetry is won,
   Is but a desk to write upon.
   Samuel Butler 1612–80: *Hudibras* pt. 2 (1664)

5 When amatory poets sing their loves
   In liquid lines mellifluously bland,
   And pair their rhymes as Venus yokes her doves,
   They little think what mischief is in hand.
   Lord Byron 1788–1824: *Don Juan* (1819–24)

6 Is it not *life*, is it not *the thing?*—Could any man have
   written it—who has not lived in the world?—and tooled in
   a post-chaise? in a hackney coach? in a gondola? Against a
   wall? in a court carriage? in a *vis-à-vis?*—on a table?—and
   under it?
   of Don Juan
   Lord Byron 1788–1824: letter to Douglas Kinnaird, 26 October 1819

7 A poet without love were a physical and metaphysical
   impossibility.
   Thomas Carlyle 1795–1881: in *Edinburgh Review* 1928

8   O love, how thou art tired out with rhyme!
    Thou art a tree whereon all poets climb;
    And from thy branches every one takes some
    Of thy sweet fruit, which Fancy feeds upon.
    But now thy tree is left so bare and poor,
    That they can scarcely gather one plum more.
    Margaret Cavendish c.1624–74: 'Love and Poetry' (1664)

9   I used to think all poets were Byronic.
    They're mostly wicked as a ginless tonic
    And wild as pension plans.
    Wendy Cope 1945– : 'Triolet' (1986)

10 You!
    Gavin Ewart 1916–95: 'The Lover Writes a One-word Poem'

11 Poets should never marry. The world should thank me for
    not marrying you.
    to W. B. Yeats
    Maud Gonne 1867–1953: Nancy Cardozo *Maud Gonne* (1978)

12 Wherever you've got to in the tunnel of love, remember
    that some poet has been there before you.
    Daisy Goodwin: *The Nation's Favourite Love Poems* (1997) introduction

13 Beware, madam, of the witty devil,
    The arch intriguer who walks disguised
    In a poet's cloak, his gay tongue oozing evil.
    Robert Graves 1895–1985: 'Beware, Madam!'

14 I suspect
    There would be more poems
    About sex
    If it rhymed with more than
    Pecks
    Necks
    Erects and ejects.
    Lynn Peters: Susan Roberts (ed.) *Making Love to Marilyn* (1998)

15 Every man is a poet when he is in love.
    Plato 429–347 BC: *Symposium*

16 I court others in verse: but I love thee in prose:
And they have my whimsies, but thou hast my heart.
Matthew Prior 1664–1721: 'A Better Answer' (1718)

17 Never durst poet touch a pen to write
Until his ink were tempered with Love's sighs.
William Shakespeare 1564–1616: *Love's Labour's Lost* (1595)

18 Chameleons feed on light and air:
Poets' food is love and fame.
Percy Bysshe Shelley 1792–1822: 'An Exhortation' (1820)

Politics

1 The sadness of the women's movement is that they don't
allow the necessity of love. See, I don't personally trust any
revolution where love is not allowed.
Maya Angelou 1928– : in *California Living* 14 May 1975

2 If Í were the Héad of the Chúrch or the Státe,
I'd pówder my nóse and just téll them to wáit.

For lóve's more impórtant and pówerful than
Éven a príest or a pólitícián.
W. H. Auden 1907–73: 'Calypso'

3 Women—one half the human race at least—care fifty times
more for a marriage than a ministry.
Walter Bagehot 1826–77: *The English Constitution* (1867)

4 No man is regular in his attendance at the House of
Commons until he is married.
Benjamin Disraeli 1804–81: Hesketh Pearson *Dizzy* (1951)

5 Palmerston is now seventy. If he could prove evidence of
his potency in his electoral address he'd sweep the country.
*to the suggestion that a Palmerston romance should be made
public*
Benjamin Disraeli 1804–81: Hesketh Pearson *Dizzy* (1951); attributed,
probably apocryphal

(P)

6   I have found it impossible to carry the heavy burden of
    responsibility and to discharge my duties as King as I would
    wish to do without the help and support of the woman I
    love.
    following his abdication
    Edward VIII (Duke of Windsor) 1894–1972: radio broadcast, 11 December
    1936

7   Like all successful politicians I married above myself.
    Dwight D. Eisenhower 1890–1969: attributed; Richard Nixon *Six Crises*
    (1962)

8   I don't think matrimony consistent with the liberty of the
    subject.
    George Farquhar 1678–1707: *The Twin Rivals* (1703)

9   A great party is not to be brought down because of a
    scandal by a woman of easy virtue and a proved liar.
    on the Profumo affair
    Lord Hailsham 1907– : BBC television interview; in *The Times* 14 June
    1963

10 My Lord, if it were not to satisfy the world, and my realm, I
    would not do that I must do this day for none earthly
    thing.
    on his marriage to Anne of Cleves
    Henry VIII 1491–1547: to Thomas Cromwell, 5 January 1540

11 I regret to say that we of the FBI are powerless to act in
    cases of oral-genital intimacy, unless it has in some way
    obstructed interstate commerce.
    J. Edgar Hoover 1895–1972: Irving Wallace et al. *Intimate Sex Lives of
    Famous People* (1981)

12 Power is the great aphrodisiac.
    Henry Kissinger 1923– : in *New York Times* 19 January 1971

13 I still love you, but in politics there is no heart, only head.
    to Josephine, on their divorce
    Napoleon I 1769–1821: C. Barnett *Bonaparte* (1978)

14 It is now known, however, that men enter local politics solely as a result of being unhappily married.
C. Northcote Parkinson 1909–93: *Parkinson's Law* (1958)

15 The state has no place in the nation's bedrooms.
Pierre Trudeau 1919– : interview, Ottawa, 22 December 1967

Poverty see Wealth and Poverty

The Power of Love

1 How in hell can you handle love without turning your life upside down? That's what love does, it changes everything.
Lauren Bacall 1924– : *By Myself* (1978)

2 Love seeks to escape from itself, to mingle itself with its victim, as a victor nation with the vanquished—and yet at the same time to retain the privileges of a conqueror.
Charles Baudelaire 1821–67: *Fusées* (1862)

3 How easy it is for a man to reduce women of a certain age to imbecility. All he has to do is give an impersonation of desire, or, better still, of secret knowledge, for a woman to feel herself a source of power.
Anita Brookner 1938– : *A Family Romance* (1993)

4 No cord nor cable can so forcibly draw, or hold so fast, as love can do with a twined thread.
Robert Burton 1577–1640: *The Anatomy of Melancholy* (1621–51)

5 Love wol nat been constreyned by maistrye.
When maistrie comth, the God of Love anon
Beteth his wynges, and farewel, he is gon!
Geoffrey Chaucer c.1343–1400: *The Canterbury Tales* 'The Franklin's Tale'

6 *L'amor che muove il sole e l'altre stelle.*
The love that moves the sun and the other stars.
Dante Alighieri 1265–1321: *Divina Commedia* 'Paradiso'

7 I felt it my duty to put you in *yr place* (on yr knees at my
feet) and *that* I flatter myself I have thoroughly done.
Lady Elcho 1866–1914: letter to Arthur Balfour, 30 October 1903

8 Whoever said love conquers all was a fool. Because almost
everything conquers love—or tries to.
Edna Ferber 1887–1968: *Giant* (1952)

9 Bid me to live, and I will live
Thy Protestant to be:
Or bid me love, and I will give
A loving heart to thee.
Robert Herrick 1591–1674: 'To Anthea, Who May Command Him Anything'
(1648)

10 Nature has given women so much power that the law has
very wisely given them little.
Samuel Johnson 1709–84: letter to John Taylor, 18 August 1763

11 Where love rules, there is no will to power, and where
power predominates, love is lacking. The one is the shadow
of the other.
Carl Gustav Jung 1875–1961: 'On the Psychology of the Unconscious'
(1917)

12 *Omnia vincit Amor: et nos cedamus Amori.*

Love conquers all things: let us too give in to Love.
Virgil 70–19 BC: *Eclogues*

13 Love conquers all things—except poverty and toothache.
Mae West 1892–1980: attributed

14 Our deepest fear is not that we are inadequate. Our deepest
fear is that we are powerful beyond measure. It is our light,
not our darkness, that most frightens us.
Marianne Williamson 1953– : *A Return to Love* (1992)

Pregnancy and Children

1 A fast word about oral contraception. I asked a girl to go to
bed with me and she said 'no'.
Woody Allen 1935– : *Woody Allen Volume Two*

2 So for the mother's sake the child was dear,
And dearer was the mother for the child.
Samuel Taylor Coleridge 1772–1834: 'Sonnet to a Friend Who Asked How I
Felt When the Nurse First Presented My Infant to Me' (1797)

3 If men had to have babies, they would only ever have one
each.
Diana, Princess of Wales 1961–97: in *Observer* 29 July 1984

4 Batt he gets children, not for love to rear 'em;
But out of hope his wife might die to bear 'em.
Robert Herrick 1591–1674: 'Upon Batt'

5 We have long passed the Victorian Era when asterisks were
followed after a certain interval by a baby.
W. Somerset Maugham 1874–1965: *The Constant Wife* (1926)

6 Contraceptives should be used on all conceivable occasions.
Spike Milligan 1918– : *The Last Goon Show of All* (1972)

7 KATH: Can he be present at the birth of his child? . . .
ED: It's all any reasonable child can expect if the dad is
present at the conception.
Joe Orton 1933–67: *Entertaining Mr Sloane* (1964)

8 Love set you going like a fat gold watch.
The midwife slapped your footsoles, and your bald cry
Took its place among the elements.
Sylvia Plath 1932–63: 'Morning Song' (1965)

9 If you have a great passion it seems that the logical thing is
to see the fruit of it, and the fruit are children.
Roman Polanski 1933– : in *Independent on Sunday* 12 May 1991

10 Do not breed. Nothing gives less pleasure than
childbearing. Pregnancies are damaging to health, spoil the
figure, wither the charms, and it's the cloud of uncertainty
forever hanging over these events that darkens a husband's
mood.
Marquis de Sade 1740–1814: *Juliette* (1797)

11 She was an extremely beautiful girl and as innocent as a
rose. When Watts kissed her, she took for granted she was
going to have a baby.
of Ellen Terry
George Bernard Shaw 1856–1950: Stephen Winston *Days with Bernard
Shaw* (1949)

12 He says that when men first meet women they want to be
getting the sort of signals that say, 'I can't wait to be naked
with you.' He says I look like I'm thinking, 'Do you fancy a
stroll past the local Mothercare?' He also said I hadn't got
'bedroom eyes', I'd got 'pram eyes'.
Arabella Weir: *Does My Bum Look Big in This?* (1997)

13 No test tube can breed love and affection. No frozen packet
of semen ever read a story to a sleepy child.
Shirley Williams 1930– : in *Daily Mirror* 2 March 1978

Promises

1 O where are you going? stay with me here!
Were the vows you swore me deceiving, deceiving?
No, I promised to love you, dear,
But I must be leaving.
W. H. Auden 1907–73: 'O what is that sound which so thrills the ear'
(1936)

2 Lovers' vows do not reach the ears of the gods.
Callimachus *c.*305–*c.*240 BC: *Epigrams*

3 But what a woman says to her lusting lover it is best to
   write in wind and swift-flowing water.
   Catullus *c.*84–*c.*54 BC: *Carmina*

4 Why should a foolish marriage vow
   Which long ago was made,
   Oblige us to each other now
   When passion is decayed?
   John Dryden 1631–1700: *Marriage à la Mode* (1672)

5 The moment I swear to love a woman, a certain woman,
       all my life
   that moment I begin to hate her.
   D. H. Lawrence 1885–1930: 'The Mess of Love'

6 By the time you say you're his,
   Shivering and sighing
   And he vows his passion is
   Infinite, undying—
   Lady, make a note of this:
   One of you is lying.
   Dorothy Parker 1893–1967: 'Unfortunate Coincidence' (1937)

7 O! swear not by the moon, the inconstant moon,
   That monthly changes in her circled orb,
   Lest that thy love prove likewise variable.
   William Shakespeare 1564–1616: *Romeo and Juliet* (1595)

8 I beg your pardon: I never promised you a rose garden.
   I could ring you a tune and promise you the moon,
   But if that's what it takes to hold you I'd just as soon let
       you go.
   Joe South: 'Rose Garden' (1970 song)

9 To swear new oaths from this place, were but to weaken
   the credit of those I have sworn in another: if heaven be to
   forgive you now for not believing of them then (as sure as it
   was a sin), heaven forgive me now for swearing of them
   then (for that was double sin).
   John Suckling 1609–42: letter to Anne Willoughby, 1633

Promises

Proposals see also Declarations

1 Oh Bernard muttered Ethel this is so sudden. No no cried
   Bernard and taking the bull by both horns he kissed her
   violently on her dainty face. My bride to be he murmered
   several times.
   Daisy Ashford 1881–1972: *The Young Visiters* (1919)

2 When the waltz throbbed out on the long promenade
   His eyes and his smile they went straight to my heart;
   'O marry me, Johnny—I'll love and obey':
   But he frowned like thunder and he went away.
   W. H. Auden 1907–73: 'Johnny'

3 It is always incomprehensible to a man that a woman
   should ever refuse an offer of marriage. A man always
   imagines a woman to be ready for anybody who asks her.
   Jane Austen 1775–1817: *Emma* (1816)

4 What did she say?—Just what she ought, of course. A lady
   always does.—She said enough to show there need not be
   despair—and to invite him to say more himself.
   Jane Austen 1775–1817: *Emma* (1816)

5 Till it does come, you know, we women never mean to
   have anybody. It is a thing of course among us, that every
   man is refused—until he offers.
   Jane Austen 1775–1817: *Persuasion* (1818)

6 You—you strange, you almost unearthly thing!—I love
   you as I love my own flesh. You—poor and obscure, and
   small and plain as you are—I entreat you to accept me as a
   husband.
   Mr Rochester to Jane Eyre
   Charlotte Brontë 1816–55: *Jane Eyre* (1847)

7 God and nature intended you for a missionary's wife. It is
   not personal, but mental endowments they have given
   you: you are formed for labour, not for love. A missionary's

wife you must—you shall be. You shall be mine: I claim
you—not for my pleasure, but for my Sovereign's service.
St John Rivers to Jane Eyre
Charlotte Brontë 1816–55: *Jane Eyre* (1847)

8 In the mythic schema of all relations between men and
women, man proposes, and woman is disposed of.
Angela Carter 1940–92: *The Sadeian Woman* (1979)

9 Do you think not being married to me might maybe be
something you could consider doing for the rest of your
life?
Richard Curtis 1956– : *Four Weddings and a Funeral* (1994 film)

10 Barkis is willin'.
Charles Dickens 1812–70: *David Copperfield* (1850)

11 Oh, Mrs Corney, what a prospect this opens! What a
opportunity for a jining of hearts and house-keepings!
Charles Dickens 1812–70: *Oliver Twist* (1838)

12 Come live with me, and be my love,
And we will some new pleasures prove
Of golden sands, and crystal brooks,
With silken lines, and silver hooks.
John Donne 1572–1631: 'The Bait'

13 'The choice is open to you. Either you go to America with
Mrs Van Hopper or you come home to Manderley with me.'
   'Do you mean you want a secretary or something?'
   'No, I'm asking you to marry me, you little fool.'
Daphne Du Maurier 1907–89: *Rebecca* (1938)

14 I'm afraid I was very much the traditionalist. I went down
on one knee and dictated a proposal which my secretary
faxed over straight away.
Stephen Fry 1957– and **Hugh Laurie**: *A Bit More Fry and Laurie* (1991)

15 But if it pleases you to play the part of a true, loyal mistress
and friend, and to give yourself body and heart to me, who
will be, and has been, your most loyal servant (if your

(P)

rigour does not forbid me), I promise you that not only will
you deserve the name, but also that I will take you for my
only mistress, casting all others, that are in competition
with you, out of my thoughts and affection, and serving
only you.
Henry VIII 1491–1547: letter to Anne Boleyn, 1527

16 He also reminded her that she was at a time of life when
she could hardly expect to pick and choose, and that her
spiritual condition was one of, at least, great uncertainty.
These combined statements are held, under the law of
Scotland at any rate, to be equivalent to an offer of
marriage.
Stephen Leacock 1869–1944: *Arcadian Adventures with the Idle Rich*
(1914)

17 Use any form of proposal you like. Try to avoid abstract
nouns.
Joe Orton 1933–67: *Loot* (1967)

18 The hardest task of a girl's life is to prove to a man that his
intentions are serious.
Helen Rowland 1875–1950: *Reflections of a Bachelor Girl* (1903)

19 She searched for the word that should carry her over the
last difficult breach.
It was he who found it for her . . .
'*Placetne, magistra?*'
'*Placet.*'
Lord Peter Wimsey and Harriet Vane
Dorothy L. Sayers 1893–1957: *Gaudy Night* (1935)

20 You were better speak first, and when you were gravelled
for lack of matter, you might take occasion to kiss.
William Shakespeare 1564–1616: *As You Like It* (1599)

21 Miss Madeleine Phillips was making it very manifest to
    Captain Douglas that she herself was a career; that a lover
    with any other career in view need not—as the
    advertisements say—apply.
    H. G. Wells 1866–1946: *Bealby* (1925)

22 You require but a simple 'Yes'? Such a small word—but
    such an important one. But should not a heart so full of
    unutterable love as mine utter this little word with all its
    might? I do so and my innermost soul whispers always to
    you.
    Clara Wieck 1819–96: letter to Robert Schumann, 15 August 1837

23 Once a week is quite enough to propose to anyone, and it
    should always be done in a manner that attracts some
    attention.
    Oscar Wilde 1854–1900: *An Ideal Husband* (1895)

24 Yes, but men often propose for practice. All my girl friends
    tell me so.
    Oscar Wilde 1854–1900: *The Importance of Being Earnest* (1895)

Quarrels and Forgiveness

1 Let's contend no more, Love,
   Strive nor weep:
   All be as before, Love,
   —Only sleep!
   Robert Browning 1812–89: 'A Woman's Last Word' (1855)

2 Once a woman has forgiven her man, she must not reheat
   his sins for breakfast.
   Marlene Dietrich 1901–92: *Marlene Dietrich's ABC* (1962)

3 Never go to bed mad. Stay up and fight.
Phyllis Diller 1917– : *Phyllis Diller's Housekeeping Hints* (1966)

4 The concept of two people living together for 25 years without having a cross word suggests a lack of spirit only to be admired in sheep.
A. P. Herbert 1890–1971: in *News Chronicle*, 1940

5 Forgive you?—Oh of course, dear,
A dozen times a week!
We women were created
Forgiveness but to speak.
Ella Higginson 1862–1940: 'Wearing Out Love'

6 We pardon to the extent that we love.
Duc de la Rochefoucauld 1613–80: *Maximes* (1678)

7 Some men dash for the shelter of a local hostelry at the first gathering clouds of a domestic argument. Not me. I slip out quietly and head for the local Homebase, where I scan the shelves until I think the coast is clear at home.
Terry Major-Ball 1932– : in *Independent on Sunday* 18 April 1998

8 The more I love, the more I quarrel.
Marguerite d'Angoulême 1492–1549: *Dizains* (1547)

9 Love-quarrels oft in pleasing concord end.
John Milton 1608–74: *Samson Agonistes* (1671)

10 Moments of kindness and reconciliation are worth having, even if the parting has to come sooner or later.
Alice Munro 1931– : *The Progress of Love* (1986)

11 To keep your marriage brimming
With love in the loving cup,
Whenever you're wrong, admit it,
Whenever you're right, shut up.
Ogden Nash 1902–71: 'A Word to Husbands' (1957)

12 Love is a kind of warfare.
Ovid 43 BC– AD c.17: *Ars Amatoria*

13 Sir, I have quarrelled with my wife; and a man who has quarrelled with his wife is absolved from all duty to his country.
Thomas Love Peacock 1785–1866: *Nightmare Abbey* (1818)

14 A married couple are well suited when both partners usually feel the need for a quarrel at the same time.
Jean Rostand 1894–1977: *Le Mariage* (1927)

15 Never feel remorse for what you have thought about your wife; she has thought much worse things about you.
Jean Rostand 1894–1977: *Le Mariage* (1927)

16 Love means not ever having to say you're sorry.
'not ever' was replaced by 'never' in the 1970 film
Erich Segal 1937– : *Love Story* (1970)

17 The test of a man or woman's breeding is how they behave in a quarrel.
George Bernard Shaw 1856–1950: *The Philanderer* (1893)

18 And blessings on the falling out
That all the more endears,
When we fall out with those we love
And kiss again with tears!
Alfred, Lord Tennyson 1809–92: *The Princess* (1847), song (added 1850)

19 Lovers' rows make love whole.
Terence *c.*190–159 BC: *Andria*

20 A husband should not insult his wife publicly, at parties. He should insult her in the privacy of the home.
James Thurber 1894–1961: *Thurber Country* (1953)

21 The fights are the best part of married life. The rest is merely so-so.
Thornton Wilder 1897–1975: *The Merchant of Yonkers* (1939)

Religion see God and Religion

Remarriage

1   Housbondes at chirche dore she hadde fyve,
    Withouten oother compaignye in youthe—
    But thereof nedeth nat to speke as nowthe.
    Geoffrey Chaucer c.1343–1400: *The Canterbury Tales* 'The General Prologue'

2   The first wives' club.
    Olivia Goldsmith: title of novel (1992)

3   The others were only my wives. But you, my dear, will be
    my widow.
    Sacha Guitry 1885–1957: attributed remark to his fifth wife, c.1950

4   I married many men,
    A ton of them,
    And yet I was untrue to none of them
    Because I bumped off ev'ry one of them
    To keep my love alive.
    Lorenz Hart 1895–1943: 'To Keep My Love Alive' (1943 song)

5   He loves his bonds, who when the first are broke,
    Submits his neck unto a second yoke.
    Robert Herrick 1591–1674: 'To Love' (1648)

6   The triumph of hope over experience.
    of a man who remarried immediately after the death of a wife
    with whom he had been unhappy
    Samuel Johnson 1709–84: James Boswell *Life of Samuel Johnson* (1791)

7 If I were young and handsome as I was, instead of old and
faded as I am, and you could lay the empire of the world at
my feet, you should never share the heart and hand that
once belonged to John, Duke of Marlborough.
refusing an offer of marriage from the Duke of Somerset
Sarah, Duchess of Marlborough 1660–1744: W. S. Churchill *Marlborough:
His Life and Times* vol. 4 (1938)

8 I have no wish for a second husband. I had enough of the
first. I like to have my own way—to lie down mistress, and
get up master.
Susanna Moodie 1803–85: *Roughing It in the Bush* (1852)

9 I'm Henery the Eighth, I am!
Henery the Eighth, I am, I am!
I got married to the widow next door,
She's been married seven times before.
Every one was a Henery,
She wouldn't have a Willie or a Sam.
I'm her eighth old man named Henery
I'm Henery the Eighth, I am!
Fred Murray: 'I'm Henery the Eighth, I Am!' (1911 song)

10 There are moments when the meanest of women may feel a
sisterly sympathy for her husband's first wife.
Helen Rowland 1875–1950: *Reflections of a Bachelor Girl* (1903)

11 Anyone who marries three girls from St Louis hasn't
learned much.
of Ernest Hemingway
Gertrude Stein 1874–1946: J. R. Mellow *Charmed Circle: Gertrude Stein and
Company* (1974)

12 I think every woman's entitled to a middle husband she
can forget.
Adela Rogers St Johns 1894–1988: in *Los Angeles Times* 13 October 1974

13 Thrift, thrift, Horatio! the funeral baked meats
Did coldly furnish forth the marriage tables.
William Shakespeare 1564–1616: *Hamlet* (1601)

Remarriage

14 That's my first wife up there and this is the *present* Mrs Harris.
James Thurber 1894–1961: cartoon caption in *New Yorker* 16 March 1933

15 When a woman marries again it is because she detested her first husband. When a man marries again it is because he adored his first wife. Women try their luck; men risk theirs.
Oscar Wilde 1854–1900: *The Picture of Dorian Gray* (1891)

Rings

1 With this Ring I thee wed, with my body I thee worship, and with all my worldly goods I thee endow.
The Book of Common Prayer 1662: *Solemnization of Matrimony* Wedding

2 I did hate so, to have to take off the ring. You will have to take the trouble of putting it on again, some day.
following their secret marriage
Elizabeth Barrett Browning 1806–61: letter to Robert Browning, 14 September 1846

3 Surely the whole point of an engagement is the ring! It's a get-out clause with accompanying jewellery.
Jean Buchanan 1947– : *The Wild House* (1998) BBC TV series

4 Too many rings around Rosie
Never got Rosie a ring.
Irving Caesar 1895– : 'Too Many Rings around Rosie' (1925 song)

5 Oh! how many torments lie in the small circle of a wedding-ring!
Colley Cibber 1671–1757: *The Double Gallant* (1707)

6 The ring so worn, as you behold,
So thin, so pale, is yet of gold.
George Crabbe 1754–1832: 'His Mother's Wedding Ring'

7 'Dear Pig, are you willing to sell for one shilling
Your ring?' Said the Piggy, 'I will.'
Edward Lear 1812–88: 'The Owl and the Pussy-Cat' (1871)

8 Now that you've gone
   All that's left is a band of gold.
   Bob Musel: 'Band of Gold' (1956 song)

9 He has married me with a ring, a ring of bright water
   Whose ripples spread from the heart of the sea,
   He has married me with a ring of light, the glitter
   Broadcast on the swift river.
   Kathleen Raine 1908– : 'The Marriage of Psyche' (1952)

10 We will have rings, and things, and fine array;
   And kiss me Kate, we will be married o' Sunday.
   William Shakespeare 1564–1616: *The Taming of the Shrew* (1592)

11 Look, how my ring encompasseth thy finger,
   Even so thy breast encloseth my poor heart;
   Wear both of them, for both of them are thine.
   William Shakespeare 1564–1616: *Venus and Adonis* (1593)

12 Opportunity knocks for every man, but you have to give a
   woman a ring.
   Mae West 1892–1980: Joseph Weintraub *Peel Me a Grape* (1975)

Romance

1 She had been forced into prudence in her youth, she
   learned romance as she grew older—the natural sequel of
   an unnatural beginning.
   Jane Austen 1775–1817: *Persuasion* (1818)

2 Marianne would have felt herself very inexcusable had she
   been able to sleep at all the first night after parting from
   Willoughby.
   Jane Austen 1775–1817: *Sense and Sensibility* (1811)

3 One is never too old for romance.
   Ingrid Bergman 1915–82: in *Sunday Mirror* 5 May 1974

4 A romantic man often feels more uplifted with two women than with one: his love seems to hit the ideal mark somewhere between two different faces.
Elizabeth Bowen 1899–1973: *The Death of the Heart* (1938)

5 Reader, I married him.
Charlotte Brontë 1816–55: *Jane Eyre* (1847)

6 The essence of romantic love is that wonderful beginning, after which sadness and impossibility may become the rule.
Anita Brookner 1938– : *A Friend From England* (1987)

7 This isn't at all your idea of a proposal, is it? It should be in a conservatory, you in a white frock with a red rose in your hand and a violin playing in the distance, and I should be making violent love to you behind a palm tree—poor darling, never mind.
Daphne Du Maurier 1907–89: *Rebecca* (1938)

8 Any walk through a park that runs between a double line of mangy trees and passes brazenly by the ladies' toilet is invariably known as 'Lover's Lane'.
F. Scott Fitzgerald 1896–1940: Edmund Wilson (ed.) *The Crack-Up* (1945) 'Note-Books E'

9 'Confound Romance!' . . . And all unseen
Romance brought up the nine-fifteen.
Rudyard Kipling 1865–1936: 'The King' (1896)

10 And what's romance? Usually, a nice little tale where you have everything As You Like It, where rain never wets your jacket and gnats never bite your nose and it's always daisy-time.
D. H. Lawrence 1885–1930: *Studies in Classic American Literature* (1924)

11 Love is not the dying moan of a distant violin—it's the triumphant twang of the bedspring.
S. J. Perelman 1904–79: attributed

12 ELAINE: *Romantic?* In your mother's clean apartment with two glasses from Bloomingdale's and your rubbers dripping on the newspaper?
BARNEY: It was my belief that romance is inspired by the participants and not the accoutrements.
Neil Simon 1927– : *Last of the Red Hot Lovers* (1970)

13 It's our *own* story *exactly*! He bold as a hawk, she soft as the dawn.
James Thurber 1894–1961: cartoon caption in *New Yorker* 25 February 1939

14 Men are so romantic, don't you think? They look for a perfect partner when what they should be looking for is perfect love.
Fay Weldon 1931– : in *Sunday Times* 6 September 1987

15 Twenty years of romance make a woman look like a ruin; but twenty years of marriage make her something like a public building.
Oscar Wilde 1854–1900: *A Woman of No Importance* (1893)

Sacrifice

1   And she for him had given
Her all on earth, and more than all in heaven!
Lord Byron 1788–1824: *The Corsair* (1814)

2 Any great love involves sacrifice. You feel that as a father, as a husband. You give up all your freedom. But the love is so much greater than the freedom.
Nicholas Cage 1964– : in *The Times* 17 June 1998

3 If you want to sacrifice the admiration of many men for the criticism of one, go ahead, get married.
to her daughter Katharine, 1928
Katharine Houghton Hepburn: Anne Edwards *A Remarkable Woman* (1985)

4 A woman will always sacrifice herself if you give her the opportunity. It is her favourite form of self-indulgence.
W. Somerset Maugham 1874–1965: *The Circle* (1921)

5 A woman can forgive a man for the harm he does her, but she can never forgive him for the sacrifices he makes on her account.
W. Somerset Maugham 1874–1965: *The Moon and Sixpence* (1919)

6 Each one of an affectionate couple may be willing, as we say, to die for the other, yet unwilling to utter the agreeable word at the right moment.
George Meredith 1828–1909: 'The Idea of Comedy'; lecture at the London Institution, 1 February 1877

Screen see Stage and Screen

The Seasons

1 What men call gallantry, and gods adultery,
Is much more common where the climate's sultry.
Lord Byron 1788–1824: *Don Juan* (1819–24)

2 The Summer hath his joys,
And Winter his delights.
Though Love and all his pleasures are but toys,
They shorten tedious nights.
Thomas Campion 1567–1620: 'Now Winter Nights Enlarge'

3 I'll see you again,
Whenever spring breaks through again.
Noël Coward 1899–1973: 'I'll See You Again' (1929 song)

4 Now the peak of summer's past, the sky is overcast.
And the love we swore would last for an age seems deceit.
C. Day-Lewis 1904–72: 'Hornpipe'

5 April is the cruellest month, breeding
Lilacs out of the dead land, mixing
Memory and desire, stirring
Dull roots with spring rain.
T. S. Eliot 1888–1965: *The Waste Land* (1922)

6 A man has every season, while a woman has only the right to spring.
Jane Fonda 1937– : in *Daily Mail* 13 September 1989

7 Every year, in the fulness o' summer, when the sukebind hangs heavy from the wains . . . 'tes the same. And when the spring comes her hour is upon her again. 'Tes the hand of Nature and we women cannot escape it.
Stella Gibbons 1902–89: *Cold Comfort Farm* (1932)

8 June is bustin' out all over
The sheep aren't sleepin' any more!
All the rams that chase the ewe sheep
Are determined there'll be new sheep
And the ewe sheep aren't even keepin' score!
Oscar Hammerstein II 1895–1960: 'June is Bustin' Out All Over' (1945 song) from *Carousel*

9 In the spring a young man's fancy lightly turns to thoughts of love;
And in summer,
and in autumn,
and in winter—
See above.
E. Y. Harburg 1898–1981: 'Tennyson Anyone?' (1965); cf. **Seasons 18**

10 Never hath absence been more grievous to me than this. To spend the month of April far from one's beloved, 'tis not to live at all.
Henri IV (of Navarre) 1553–1610: letter to Gabrielle d'Estrées

11 I sing of brooks, of blossoms, birds, and bowers:
Of April, May, of June, and July-flowers.
I sing of May-poles, Hock-carts, wassails, wakes,
Of bride-grooms, brides, and of their bridal-cakes.
Robert Herrick 1591–1674: *Hesperides* (1648)

12 Blossoms crowd the branches: too beautiful to endure.
Thinking of you, I break into bloom again.
Hsueh T'ao 768–831: 'Spring-Gazing Song'

13 Another bride, another June,
Another sunny honeymoon,
Another season, another reason,
For makin' whoopee!
Gus Kahn 1886–1941: 'Makin' Whoopee' (1928)

14 For like as herbs and trees bringeth forth fruit and flourish in May, in likewise every lusty heart that is in any manner a lover, springeth and flourisheth in lusty deeds.
Thomas Malory d. 1471: *Le Morte D'Arthur* (1485)

15 Sailings and weddings and births and showers!
My fate is sealed for the month of flowers.
When the first June wind blows soft and south,
I'll be looking a gift shop in the mouth.
Phyllis McGinley 1905– : 'Song for an Engraved Invitation'

16 But I miss you most of all my darling
When autumn leaves start to fall.
Johnny Mercer 1909–76: 'Autumn Leaves' (1947 song)

17 It was a lover and his lass,
With a hey, and a ho, and a hey nonino,
That o'er the green cornfield did pass,
In the spring time, the only pretty ring time,

When birds do sing, hey ding a ding, ding;
Sweet lovers love the spring.
William Shakespeare 1564–1616: *As You Like It* (1599)

18 In the spring a livelier iris changes on the burnished dove;
In the spring a young man's fancy lightly turns to thoughts
of love.
Alfred, Lord Tennyson 1809–92: 'Locksley Hall' (1842)

Secrets

1 To hide a passion is inconceivable: not because the human
subject is too weak, but because passion is in its essence
made to be seen: *I want you to know that I am hiding
something from you*, that is the active paradox I must
resolve.
Roland Barthes 1915–80: *A Lover's Discourse* (1977)

2 Love ceases to be a pleasure, when it ceases to be a secret.
Aphra Behn 1640–89: *The Lover's Watch* (1686)

3 So let us melt, and make no noise,
No tear-floods, nor sigh-tempests move,
'Twere profanation of our joys
To tell the laity our love.
John Donne 1572–1631: 'A Valediction: forbidding mourning'

4 I am the Love that dare not speak its name.
Lord Alfred Douglas 1870–1945: 'Two Loves' (1896)

5 If a man cannot keep a measly affair secret, what is he
doing in charge of the Intelligence Service?
*on the break-up of the marriage of Foreign Secretary Robin
Cook*
Frederick Forsyth 1938– : in *Guardian* 14 January 1998

6 A lover without indiscretion is no lover at all.
Thomas Hardy 1840–1928: *The Hand of Ethelberta* (1876)

7 A man nearly always loves for other reasons than he thinks. A lover is apt to be as full of secrets from himself as is the object of his love from him.
Ben Hecht 1894–1964: in *Think* February 1963

8 Love and a cough cannot be hid.
George Herbert 1593–1633: *Outlandish Proverbs* (1640)

9 If men knew how women pass the time when they are alone, they'd never marry.
O. Henry 1862–1910: *Four Million* (1906)

10 I always ask a husband, or a wife, as the case may be, is there anything you have done in the course of your married life of which you are now thoroughly ashamed? The witness usually finds that a tricky one to answer.
on questioning a witness in the divorce court
Clifford Mortimer: John Mortimer *Clinging to the Wreckage* (1982)

11 Prince or commoner, tenor or bass,
Painter or plumber or never-do-well,
Do me a favour and shut your face—
Poets alone should kiss and tell.
Dorothy Parker 1893–1967: 'Ballade of a Talked-Off Ear'

12 Traditionally, sex has been a very private, secretive activity. Herein perhaps lies its powerful force for uniting people in a strong bond. As we make sex less secretive, we may rob it of its power to hold men and women together.
Thomas Szasz 1920– : *The Second Sin* (1973)

13 I doubt whether any girl would be satisfied with her lover's mind if she knew the whole of it.
Anthony Trollope 1815–82: *The Small House at Allington* (1864)

14 An affair wants to spill, to share its glory with the world.
No act is so private it does not seek applause.
John Updike 1932– : *Couples* (1968)

15 And I'm so afraid that the treasures I long to unpack for
you, that have come to me in magic ships from enchanted
islands, are only, to you, the old familiar red calico and
beads of the clever trader, who has had dealings in every
latitude, and knows just what to carry in the hold to please
the simple native—I'm so afraid of this, that often and
often I stuff my shining treasures back into their box, lest I
should see you smiling at them!
Edith Wharton 1862–1937: letter to W. Morton Fullerton, March 1908

Seduction

1 He said it was artificial respiration, but now I find I am to
have his child.
Anthony Burgess 1917–93: *Inside Mr Enderby* (1963)

2 A little still she strove, and much repented,
And whispering 'I will ne'er consent'—consented.
Lord Byron 1788–1824: *Don Juan* (1819–24)

3 A gentleman doesn't pounce . . . he glides.
Quentin Crisp 1908– : *Manners from Heaven* (1984)

4 Seduction is often difficult to distinguish from rape. In
seduction, the rapist bothers to buy a bottle of wine.
Andrea Dworkin 1946– : in 1976; *Letters from a War Zone* (1988)

5 He in a few minutes ravished this fair creature, or at least
would have ravished her, if she had not, by a timely
compliance, prevented him.
Henry Fielding 1707–54: *Jonathan Wild* (1743)

6 Mad, bad, and dangerous to know.
of Byron
Lady Caroline Lamb 1785–1828: diary, March 1812

7 The trouble with Ian is that he gets off with women
because he can't get on with them.
of Ian Fleming
Rosamond Lehmann 1903–90: John Pearson *The Life of Ian Fleming*
(1966)

8 Pursuit and seduction are the essence of sexuality. It's part
of the sizzle.
Camille Paglia 1947– : in *Playboy* October 1991

9 The chief trouble, for man or girl, is that everything in a
bedsitter is so *visible*. Unless you work it all out with
greatest care, your visitor can see at a glance just exactly
what you expect or hope for or hope to avoid.
Katharine Whitehorn 1928– : *Cooking in a Bedsitter* (1963)

Selfishness

1 I married several times with my ends in view and I didn't
reckon on the ends of the wives.
Saul Bellow 1915– : in *Guardian* 10 September 1997

2 Selfishness is one of the qualities apt to inspire love.
Nathaniel Hawthorne 1804–64: *American Notebooks* (1837–40)

3 In marriage, a man becomes slack and selfish, and
undergoes a fatty degeneration of his moral being.
Robert Louis Stevenson 1850–94: *Virginibus Puerisque* (1881)

4 We had a lot in common. I loved him and he loved him.
Shelley Winters 1922– : attributed, 1952; Susan Strasberg *Bittersweet*
(1980)

Sex see also **Seduction, Sexuality**

1 That was the most fun I ever had without laughing.
Woody Allen 1935– : *Annie Hall* (1977 film, with Marshall Brickman)

2 Is sex dirty? Only if it's done right.
Woody Allen 1935– : *Everything You Always Wanted to Know about Sex* (1972 film)

3 In the old days a lot of people, men as well as women, didn't quite know what to expect from sex so they didn't worry when it didn't work too well.
Kingsley Amis 1922–95: *Jake's Thing* (1979)

4 One failure on
Top of another.
A. R. Ammons 1926– : 'Their Sex Life'

5 *Post coitum omne animal triste.*
After coition every animal is sad.
Anonymous: post-classical saying

6 My mother used to say, Delia, if S-E-X ever rears its ugly head, close your eyes before you see the rest of it.
Alan Ayckbourn 1939– : *Bedroom Farce* (1978)

7 I don't know what I am, darling. I've tried several varieties of sex. The conventional position makes me claustrophobic. And the others give me either stiff neck or lockjaw.
Tallulah Bankhead 1903–68: Lee Israel *Miss Tallulah Bankhead* (1972)

8 I don't want to give you the idea I'm trying to hide anything, or that anything unorthodox goes on between my wife and me. It doesn't. Nothing goes on at all . . . No foreplay. No afterplay. And fuck all in between.
Alan Bennett 1934– : *Enjoy* (1980)

9 Sex has never been an obsession with me. It's just like eating a bag of crisps. Quite nice, but nothing marvellous. Sex is not simply black and white. There's a lot of grey.
Boy George 1961– : in *Sun* 21 October 1982

10   I could be content that we might procreate like trees,
     without conjunction, or that there were any way to
     perpetuate the world without this trivial and vulgar way of
     coition; it is the foolishest act a wise man commits in all his
     life.
     Sir Thomas Browne 1605–82: *Religio Medici* (1643)

11   She gave me a smile I could feel in my hip pocket.
     Raymond Chandler 1888–1959: *Farewell, My Lovely* (1940)

12   The pleasure is momentary, the position ridiculous, and the
     expense damnable.
     Lord Chesterfield 1694–1773: attributed

13   may i feel said he
     (i'll squeal said she
     just once said he)
     it's fun said she

     (may i touch said he
     how much said she
     a lot said he)
     why not said she
     e. e. cummings 1894–1962: *Complete Poems* (1935)

14   Licence my roving hands, and let them go,
     Behind, before, above, between, below.
     O my America, my new found land,
     My kingdom, safeliest when with one man manned.
     John Donne 1572–1631: 'To His Mistress Going to Bed' (c.1595)

15   I'll have what she's having.
     woman to waiter, seeing Sally acting an orgasm
     Nora Ephron 1941– : *When Harry Met Sally* (1989 film)

16   How a man must hug, and dandle, and kittle, and play a
     hundred little tricks with his bedfellow when he is disposed
     to make that use of her that nature designed for her.
     Erasmus c.1469–1536: *In Praise of Folly* (1509)

17 Older women are best because they always think they may
be doing it for the last time.
Ian Fleming 1908–64: John Pearson *Life of Ian Fleming* (1966)

18 The contemplation of the erotic is a joyous frame in life's
rich comic strip.
Stephen Fry 1957– : in *Tatler* December 1986

19 Personally I know nothing about sex because I've always
been married.
Zsa Zsa Gabor 1919– : in *Observer* 16 August 1987 'Sayings of the Week'

20 Only the lion and the cock,
As Galen says, withstand love's shock,
So, dearest, do not think me rude
If I yield now to lassitude,
But sympathise with me, I know
You would not have me roar, or crow.
Oliver St John Gogarty 1878–1957: 'After Galen'

21 But did thee feel the earth move?
Ernest Hemingway 1899–1961: *For Whom the Bell Tolls* (1940)

22 I am happy now that Charles calls on my bedchamber less
frequently than of old. As it is, I now endure but two calls a
week and when I hear his steps outside my door I lie down
on my bed, close my eyes, open my legs, and think of
England.
Lady Hillingdon 1857–1940: said to derive from a 1912 entry in her
journal, but the journal has never been traced; J. Gathorne-Hardy *The Rise
and Fall of the British Nanny* (1972)

23 Sex and taxes are in many ways the same. Tax does to cash
what males do to genes. It dispenses assets among the
population as a whole. Sex, not death, is the great leveller.
Steve Jones 1944– : speech to the Royal Society; in *Independent* 25
January 1997

24 The zipless fuck is the purest thing there is. And it is rarer
than the unicorn.
Erica Jong 1942– : *Fear of Flying* (1973)

Sex

25 He kissed me under the Moorish wall and I thought well as
well him as another and then I asked him with my eyes to
ask again yes and then he asked me would I yes to say yes
my mountain flower and first I put my arms around him
yes and drew him down to me so he could feel my breasts
all perfume yes and his heart was going like mad and yes I
said yes I will Yes.
James Joyce 1882–1941: *Ulysses* (1922)

26 The only unnatural sex act is that which you cannot
perform.
Alfred Kinsey 1894–1956: in *Time* 21 January 1966

27 Sexual intercourse began
In nineteen sixty-three
(Which was rather late for me)—
Between the end of the *Chatterley* ban
And the Beatles' first LP.
Philip Larkin 1922–85: 'Annus Mirabilis' (1974)

28   While we think of it, and talk of it
Let us leave it alone, physically, keep apart.
For while we have sex in the mind, we truly have none in
   the body.
D. H. Lawrence 1885–1930: 'Leave Sex Alone' (1929)

29 You mustn't force sex to do the work of love or love to do
the work of sex.
Mary McCarthy 1912–89: *The Group* (1954)

30 Sex annihilates identity, and the space given to sex in
contemporary novels is an avowal of the absence of
character.
Mary McCarthy 1912–89: George Plimpton (ed.) *The Writer's Chapbook*
(1989)

31 There is nothing safe about sex. There never will be.
Norman Mailer 1923– : in *International Herald Tribune* 24 January 1992

32 Bed. No woman is worth more than a fiver unless you're in love with her. Then she's worth all she costs you.
W. Somerset Maugham 1874–1965: *A Writer's Notebook* (1949) written in 1903

33 Sex is one of the nine reasons for reincarnation . . . The other eight are unimportant.
Henry Miller 1891–1980: *Sexus* (1945)

34 I know it [sex] does make people happy, but to me it is just like having a cup of tea.
Cynthia Payne: in *Observer* 8 February 1987 'Sayings of the Week'

35 Delight of lust is gross and brief
And weariness treads on desire.
Petronius d. AD 65: A. Baehrens (ed.) *Latini Minores* (1882, tr. Helen Waddell)

36 If sex is a war, I am a conscientious objector: I will not play.
Marge Piercy 1936– : *Braided Lives* (1982)

37 Modest? My word, no . . . He was an all-the-lights-on man.
Henry Reed 1914–86: *A Very Great Man Indeed* (1953 radio play)

38 Love is two minutes fifty-two seconds of squishing noises.
Johnny Rotten 1957– : in *Daily Mirror*, 1983

39 That pathetic short-cut suggested by Nature the supreme joker as a remedy for our loneliness, that ephemeral communion which we persuade ourselves to be of the spirit when it is in fact only of the body—durable not even in memory!
Vita Sackville-West 1892–1962: *No Signposts in the Sea* (1961)

40 This is the monstruosity in love, lady, that the will is infinite, and the execution confined; that the desire is boundless, and the act a slave to limit.
William Shakespeare 1564–1616: *Troilus and Cressida* (1602)

Sex

41 The expense of spirit in a waste of shame
Is lust in action.
William Shakespeare 1564–1616: sonnet 129 (1609)

42 Someone asked Sophocles, 'How is your sex-life now? Are
you still able to have a woman?' He replied, 'Hush, man;
most gladly indeed am I rid of it all, as though I had
escaped from a mad and savage master.'
Sophocles c.496–406 BC: Plato *Republic*

43 'Pray, my dear,' quoth my mother, 'have you not forgot to
wind up the clock?'—'Good G—!' cried my father, making
an exclamation, but taking care to moderate his voice at
the same time,—'Did ever woman, since the creation of the
world, interrupt a man with such a silly question?'
Laurence Sterne 1713–68: *Tristram Shandy* (1759–67)

44 Chasing the naughty couples down the grassgreen
gooseberried double bed of the wood.
Dylan Thomas 1914–53: *Under Milk Wood* (1954)

45 Sex is like money; only too much is enough.
John Updike 1932– : *Couples* (1968)

46 All this fuss about sleeping together. For physical pleasure
I'd sooner go to my dentist any day.
Evelyn Waugh 1903–66: *Vile Bodies* (1930)

47 Sex is an emotion in motion.
Mae West 1892–1980: Diane Arbus *Show* (1965)

48 Sex has never been an act of freedom for me. Robert and I
climb into the bath together, but we tend to talk about
quantum physics.
Toyah Wilcox: in *Independent on Sunday* 29 December 1996 'Comment'

49 Sex is the tabasco sauce which an adolescent national
palate sprinkles on every course in the menu.
Mary Day Winn 1888–1965: *Adam's Rib* (1931)

Sexuality

1 On bisexuality: It immediately doubles your chances for a
date on Saturday night.
Woody Allen 1935– : in *New York Times* 18 December 1975

2 A gender bender I
A creature of illusion,
Of genital confusion,
A gorgeous butterfly.
Alistair Beaton and Ned Sherrin 1931– : *The Metropolitan Mikado* (1985)

3 The world dictates that heteros make love while gays have
sex.
Boy George 1961– : in *New Musical Express Book of Quotes* (1995)

4 If homosexuality were the normal way, God would have
made Adam and Bruce.
Anita Bryant 1940– : in *New York Times* 5 June 1977

5 Now the whole dizzying and delirious range of sexual
possibilities has been boiled down to that one big, boring,
bulimic word. RELATIONSHIP.
Julie Burchill 1960– : *Sex and Sensibility* (1992)

6 In homosexual sex you know exactly what the other
person is feeling, so you are identifying with the other
person completely. In heterosexual sex you have no idea
what the other person is feeling.
William S. Burroughs 1914–97: Victor Bockris *With William Burroughs: A
Report from the Bunker* (1981)

7 I think what we call love is a fraud perpetrated by the
female sex, and that the point of sexual relations between
men is nothing that we could call love, but rather what we
might call *recognition*.
William S. Burroughs 1914–97: in *Soho News* 18 February 1981

8 In heterosexual love there's no solution. Man and woman
are irreconcilable, and it's the doomed attempt to do the
impossible, repeated in each new affair, that lends
heterosexual love its grandeur.
Marguerite Duras 1914- : *Practicalities* (1990)

9 In homosexual love the passion is homosexuality itself.
What a homosexual loves, as if it were his lover, his
country, his art, his land, is homosexuality.
Marguerite Duras 1914- : *Practicalities* (1990)

10 You're neither unnatural, nor abominable, nor mad;
you're as much a part of what people call nature as anyone
else; only you're unexplained as yet—you've not got your
niche in creation.
Radclyffe Hall 1883-1943: *The Well of Loneliness* (1928)

11 Our history master . . . was also known to possess a pair of
suede shoes, a sure sign in the Melbourne of this period of
sexual ambivalence.
Barry Humphries 1934- : *More Please* (1992)

12 Heterosexuality isn't normal — it's just common.
Derek Jarman 1942-94: in *Observer* 6 March 1994

13 I know nothing about Platonic love except that it is not to
be found in the works of Plato.
Edgar Jepson 1863-1938: James Agate *Ego 5* (1942) 24 August 1940

14 There is probably no sensitive heterosexual alive who is not
preoccupied with his latent homosexuality.
Norman Mailer 1923- : *Advertisement for Myself* (1959)

15 At Oxford after Dunkirk the fashion was to be homosexual.
It seems that it was only after the war, with the return of
the military, that heterosexuality came to be completely
tolerated.
John Mortimer 1923- : *Clinging to the Wreckage* (1982)

16 Gay men may seek sex without emotion; lesbians often end up in emotion without sex.
Camille Paglia 1947– : in *Esquire* October 1991

17 Competence in heterosexuality, or at least the appearance or pretence of such competence, is as much a public affair as a private one. Thus, going steady is a high school diploma in heterosexuality; engagement a BA; marriage an MA; and children a PhD.
Thomas Szasz 1920– : *The Second Sin* (1973)

Shape see Size and Shape

Sickness and Health

1 Love's a thin diet, nor will keep out cold.
Aphra Behn 1640–89: *The Lucky Chance* (1686)

2 Love? What is it? Most natural painkiller. What there is . . . LOVE.
final entry in journal, 1 August 1997, the day before he died
William S. Burroughs 1914–97: in *New Yorker* 18 August 1997

3 If this be not love, it is madness, and then it is pardonable.
William Congreve 1670–1729: *The Old Bachelor* (1693)

4 The true index of a man's character is the health of his wife.
Cyril Connolly 1903–74: *The Unquiet Grave* (1944)

5 In other words just from waiting around
For that plain little band of gold
A person . . . can develop a cold.
You can spray her wherever you figure the streptococci lurk.
You can give her a shot for whatever she's got but it just won't work.
If she's tired of getting the fish-eye from the hotel clerk,

A person . . . can develop a cold.
Frank Loesser 1910–69: 'Adelaide's Lament' (1950 song) from *Guys and Dolls*

6 Love's a disease. But curable.
Rose Macaulay 1881–1958: *Crewe Train* (1926)

7 There are worse occupations in this world than feeling a woman's pulse.
Laurence Sterne 1713–68: *A Sentimental Journey* (1768)

8 Why so pale and wan, fond lover?
Prithee, why so pale?
Will, when looking well can't move her,
Looking ill prevail?
John Suckling 1609–42: *Aglaura* (1637)

9 It is sad that my emotional dependence on the man I love should have killed so much of my energy and ability; there was certainly once a great deal of energy in me.
Sonya Tolstoy 1844–1919: diary, 31 December 1890

10 When people discussed tonics, pick-me-ups after a severe illness, she kept to herself the prescription of a quick dip in bed with someone you liked but were not in love with. A shock of sexual astonishment which could make you feel astonishingly well and high spirited.
Mary Wesley 1912– : *Not That Sort of Girl* (1987)

The Single Life see also Bachelors, Without Love

1 Single women have a dreadful propensity for being poor— which is one very strong argument in favour of matrimony.
Jane Austen 1775–1817: letter to Fanny Knight, 13 March 1817

2 He was reputed one of the wise men that made answer to the question when a man should marry? 'A young man not yet, an elder man not at all.'
Francis Bacon 1561–1626: *Essays* (1625) 'Of Marriage and the Single Life'

3 Even quarrels with one's husband are preferable to the ennui of a solitary existence.
Elizabeth Patterson Bonaparte 1785–1879: Eugene L. Didier *The Life and Letters of Madame Bonaparte* (1879)

4 I am that twentieth-century failure, a happy undersexed celibate.
Denise Coffey: Ned Sherrin *Cutting Edge* (1984)

5 At Christmas little children sing and merry bells jingle,
The cold winter air makes our hands and faces tingle
And happy families go to church and cheerily they mingle
And the whole business is unbelievably dreadful, if you're
    single.
Wendy Cope 1945– : 'A Christmas Poem' (1992)

6 I would be married, but I'd have no wife,
I would be married to a single life.
Richard Crashaw c.1612–49: 'On Marriage' (1646)

7 All these years we've been single and proud of it—never noticed that two of us were to all intents and purposes married all this time.
Richard Curtis 1956– : *Four Weddings and a Funeral* (1994 film)

8 And how can I make up my mind to become a wife before I shall have enjoyed for some years my virgin state and arrived at years of discretion?
Elizabeth I 1533–1603: letter to Thomas Seymour, 27 February 1547

9 If I am to disclose to you what I should prefer if I follow the inclination of my nature, it is this: beggar-woman and single, far rather than queen and married!
Elizabeth I 1533–1603: attributed reply to an imperial envoy, 1563; J. E. Neale *Queen Elizabeth I* (1979)

Single

10 Being an old maid is like death by drowning, a really
delightful sensation after you cease to struggle.
Edna Ferber 1887–1968: R. E. Drennan *Wit's End* (1973)

11 I will not . . . sulk about having no boyfriend, but develop
inner poise and authority and sense of self as woman of
substance, complete *without* boyfriend, as best way to
obtain boyfriend.
Helen Fielding 1958– : *Bridget Jones's Diary* (1996)

12 When you live alone, you can be sure that the person who
squeezed the toothpaste tube in the middle wasn't
committing a hostile act.
Ellen Goodman 1941– : *Close to Home* (1979)

13 Marriage has many pains, but celibacy has no pleasures.
Samuel Johnson 1709–84: *Rasselas* (1759)

14 He travels fastest who travels alone, and that goes double
for she. Real feminism is spinsterhood.
Florence King 1936– : *Reflections in a Jaundiced Eye* (1989)

15 'Always be civil to the girls, you never know who they may
marry' is an aphorism which has saved many an English
spinster from being treated like an Indian widow.
Nancy Mitford 1904–73: *Love in a Cold Climate* (1949)

16 Bachelorhood, like being alive, is more depressing than
anything but the known alternative.
P. J. O'Rourke 1947– : *The Bachelor Home Companion* (1987)

17 Marriage may often be a stormy lake, but celibacy is almost
always a muddy horsepond.
Thomas Love Peacock 1785–1866: *Melincourt* (1817)

18 Your virginity, your old virginity, is like one of our French
withered pears; it looks ill, it eats drily.
William Shakespeare 1564–1616: *All's Well that Ends Well* (1603–4)

19 But earthlier happy is the rose distilled,
Than that which withering on the virgin thorn
Grows, lives, and dies, in single blessedness.
William Shakespeare 1564–1616: *A Midsummer Night's Dream* (1595–6)

20 A woman without a man is like a fish without a bicycle.
Gloria Steinem 1934– : attributed

21 Be nobody's darling;
Be an outcast.
Alice Walker 1944– : 'Be Nobody's Darling' (1970)

22 It makes me wince when I hear Mum refer to me as 'her
independent daughter'. (Query: why does the word
'independent' sound more like 'lesbian' or 'on the shelf' or
'no idea how to hold down a relationship' or 'a complete
disappointment to me in every way' when uttered by a
mother?)
Arabella Weir: *Does My Bum Look Big in This?* (1997)

Size and Shape see also The Body

1 I repent of my diets, the delicious dishes rejected out of
vanity, as much as I lament the opportunities for making
love that I let go by because of pressing tasks or puritanical
virtue.
Isabel Allende 1942– : in *The Times* 25 April 1998

2 Have you ever noticed, Harry, that many jewels make
women either incredibly fat or incredibly thin?
J. M. Barrie 1860–1937: *The Twelve-Pound Look and Other Plays* (1921)

3 After forty a woman has to choose between losing her
figure or her face. My advice is to keep your face, and stay
sitting down.
Barbara Cartland 1901– : Libby Purves 'Luncheon à la Cartland'; in *The
Times* 6 October 1993; similar remarks have been attributed since *c.*1980

4 I shall grow skinnier as you grow paunched,
a Laurel to your Hardy.
Elaine Feinstein 1930– : 'Valentine for a Middle-Aged Spouse' (1990)

5 As long as a woman's flesh is clean and healthy what does
it matter what shape she is?
Ian Fleming 1908–64: from his private notebooks; Frank Pepper (ed.) *20th Century Quotations* (1984)

6 it's a sex object if you're pretty
and no love
or love and no sex if you're fat
Nikki Giovanni 1943– : 'Woman Poem' (1970)

7 Yes behold me literally in love with this great horse-faced
blue-stocking . . . Altogether, she has a larger
circumference than any woman I have ever seen.
of George Eliot
Henry James 1843–1916: letter to his father Henry James, 10 May 1869

8 Eating doesn't make you fat. Marriage does. Compare the
waistlines of married and single friends for proof.
P. J. O'Rourke 1947– : *The Bachelor Home Companion* (1987)

9 When self-indulgence has reduced a man to the shape of
Lord Hailsham, sexual continence requires no more than a
sense of the ridiculous.
Reginald Paget 1908–90: speech in the House of Commons during the
Profumo affair, 17 June 1963

10 Going to marry her! Going to marry her! Impossible! You
mean, a part of her; he could not marry her all himself. It
would be a case, not of bigamy, but of trigamy; the
neighbourhood or the magistrates should interfere. There is
enough of her to furnish wives for a whole parish.
Sydney Smith 1771–1845: attributed

11 Does my bum look big in this?
Arabella Weir: title of book (1997)

12 A woman has all too much substance in a man's eyes at
the best of times. That is why men like women to be slim.
Her lack of flesh negates her. The less of her there is, the
less notice he need take of her. The more like a male she
appears to be, the safer he feels.
Fay Weldon 1931– : *The Fat Woman's Joke* (1967)

13 You can never be too rich or too thin.
Duchess of Windsor 1896–1986: attributed

14 I know I weigh seventeen stone and my missus looks like a
ninepenny rabbit, and yet we're as happy as can be.
P. G. Wodehouse 1881–1975: *Summer Lightning* (1929)

15 To ask women to become unnaturally thin is to ask them
to relinquish their sexuality.
Naomi Wolf 1962– : *The Beauty Myth* (1990)

The Skies see also Night

1 Busy old fool, unruly sun,
Why dost thou thus,
Through windows, and through curtains call on us?
John Donne 1572–1631: 'The Sun Rising'

2 The moon is nothing
But a circumambulating aphrodisiac
Divinely subsidized to provoke the world
Into a rising birth-rate.
Christopher Fry 1907– : *The Lady's not for Burning* (1949)

3 . . . The evening star,
Love's harbinger.
John Milton 1608–74: *Paradise Lost* (1667)

4 When the moon is in the seventh house,
And Jupiter aligns with Mars,
Then peace will guide the planets,
And love will steer the stars;

This is the dawning of the age of Aquarius.
James Rado 1939– and **Gerome Ragni** 1942– : 'Aquarius' (1967 song)
from *Hair*

5 Give me my Romeo: and, when he shall die,
Take him and cut him out in little stars,
And he will make the face of heaven so fine
That all the world will be in love with night,
And pay no worship to the garish sun.
William Shakespeare 1564–1616: *Romeo and Juliet* (1595)

6 My girl, thou gazest much
upon the golden skies:
Would I were heaven! I would behold
thee with all mine eyes.
George Turberville *c.*1540–*c.*98: 'The Lover to his Lady, that Gazed Much
up to the Skies'

Sleep

1 Lay your sleeping head, my love,
Human on my faithless arm.
W. H. Auden 1907–73: 'Lullaby' (1940)

2 Ay waukin, Oh,
Waukin still and weary:
Sleep I can get nane,
For thinking on my dearie.
Robert Burns 1759–96: 'Ay Waukin O' (1790)

3 O the pleasure of counting the melancholy clock by a
snoring husband!
George Farquhar 1678–1707: *The Beaux' Stratagem* (1707)

4 Love, hopeless love, my ardent soul encumbers:
Love, nightmare-like, lies heavy on my chest,
And weaves itself into my midnight slumbers!
W. S. Gilbert 1836–1911: *Iolanthe* (1882)

5 Take him, I won't put a price on him
   Take him, he's yours
   Take him, pyjamas look nice on him
   But how he snores!
   Lorenz Hart 1895–1943: 'Take Him' (1940)

6   Husband, I sleep with you every night
   And like it; but each morning when I wake
   I've dreamed of my first love, the subtle serpent.
   Randall Jarrell 1914–65: 'In Nature There is Neither Right nor Left nor Wrong'

7 But be, as you have been, my happiness;
   Let me sleep beside you each night, like a spoon;
   When, starting from my dreams, I groan to you,
   May your 'I love you' send me back to sleep.
   Randall Jarrell 1914–65: 'Woman' (1966)

8 In thy youth thou wast as true a lover
   As ever sighed upon a midnight pillow.
   William Shakespeare 1564–1616: *As You Like It* (1599)

9 My brother Toby, quoth she, is going to be married to Mrs Wadman.
      Then he will never, quoth my father, lie *diagonally* in his bed again as long as he lives.
   Laurence Sterne 1713–68: *Tristram Shandy* (1759–67)

10 Sleeping as quiet as death, side by wrinkled side, toothless, salt and brown, like two old kippers in a box.
   Dylan Thomas 1914–53: *Under Milk Wood* (1954)

Solitude and Loneliness

1 In human intimacy there is a secret boundary; neither the experience of being in love nor passion can cross it, though lips be joined together in awful silence, and the heart break asunder with love.
   Anna Akhmatova 1889–1966: 'In Human Intimacy' (1915)

Solitude

2 Somewhere there waiteth in this world of ours
For one lone soul another lonely soul,
Each choosing each through all the weary hours,
and meeting strangely at one sudden goal.
Edwin Arnold 1832–1904: 'Somewhere There Waiteth'

3 Please fence me in baby the world's too big out here and I
don't like it without you.
Humphrey Bogart 1899–1957: telegram to Lauren Bacall; Lauren Bacall *By Myself* (1978)

4 Now I go to films alone
watch a silent telephone
send myself a valentine
whisper softly 'I am mine'
Louise Hudson 1958– : Wendy Cope (ed.) *Is That the New Moon* (1989)

5 Many a housewife staring at the back of her husband's
newspaper, or listening to his breathing in bed is lonelier
than any spinster in a rented room.
Germaine Greer 1939– : *The Female Eunuch* (1970)

6 Loneliness is never more cruel than when it is felt in close
propinquity with someone who has ceased to
communicate.
Germaine Greer 1939– : *The Female Eunuch* (1970)

7 Being alone and liking it is, for a woman, an act of
treachery, an infidelity far more threatening than adultery.
Molly Haskell 1940– : *Love and Other Infectious Diseases* (1990)

8 The onset and the waning of love make themselves felt in
the uneasiness experienced at being alone together.
Jean de la Bruyère 1645–96: *Les Caractères ou les moeurs de ce siècle* (1688) 'Du Coeur'

9 All the lonely people, where do they all come from?
John Lennon 1940–80 and **Paul McCartney** 1942– : 'Eleanor Rigby' (1966 song)

10   This, to ponder:
     A heart that's solitary
     Is a heart no longer.
     Antonio Machado 1878–1939: attributed

11   My heart is a lonely hunter that hunts on a lonely hill.
     Fiona McLeod (William Sharp) 1855–1905: 'The Lonely Hunter' (1896)

12   There is nothing like the bootless solitude of those who are
     caged together.
     Iris Murdoch 1919– : *The Black Prince* (1973)

13   The breeze is chasing the zephyr,
     The moon is chasing the sea,
     The bull is chasing the heifer,
     But nobody's chasing me.
     Cole Porter 1891–1964: 'Nobody's Chasing Me' (1950 song)

14   What we take, in the presence of the beloved object, is
     merely a negative, which we develop later, when we are
     back at home, and have once again found at our disposal
     that inner darkroom the entrance to which is barred to us
     so long as we are with other people.
     Marcel Proust 1871–1922: *Within a Budding Grove* (1918)

15   I hold this to be the highest task for a bond between two
     people: that each protects the solitude of the other.
     Rainer Maria Rilke 1875–1926: letter to Paula Modersohn-Becker, 12
     February 1902

16   We had the same gait, the same habits and lived in the
     same rhythm; our bodies suited each other, and all was
     well. I had no right to regret his failure to make the
     tremendous effort required of love, the effort to know and
     shatter the solitude of another.
     Françoise Sagan 1935– : *A Certain Smile* (1956)

17   Do not allow yourself to be imprisoned by any affection.
     Keep your solitude. The day, if it ever comes, when you are
     given true affection there will be no opposition between

interior solitude and friendship, quite the reverse. It is even
by this infallible sign that you will recognize it.
Simone Weil 1909–43: *Gravity and Grace* (1947)

18 He had discovered that the time he had in the train going
to work was the only time a married man ever got to
himself.
Katharine Whitehorn 1928– : *Roundabout* (1962)

19 The wind blows out of the gates of the day,
The wind blows over the lonely of heart,
And the lonely of heart is withered away.
W. B. Yeats 1865–1939: *The Land of Heart's Desire* (1894)

Sorrow see also **Heartbreak, Loss**

1 Oh! too convincing—dangerously dear—
In woman's eye the unanswerable tear!
Lord Byron 1788–1824: *The Corsair* (1814)

2 There is no despair so absolute as that which comes with
the first moments of our first great sorrow, when we have
not yet known what it is to have suffered and be healed, to
have despaired and have recovered hope.
George Eliot 1819–80: *Adam Bede* (1859)

3 Now laughing friends deride tears I cannot hide,
So I smile and say 'When a lovely flame dies,
Smoke gets in your eyes.'
Otto Harbach 1873–1963: 'Smoke Gets in your Eyes' (1933 song)

4 No one ever told me that grief felt so like fear.
C. S. Lewis 1898–1963: *A Grief Observed* (1961)

5 The joy of love is too short, and the sorrow thereof, and
what cometh thereof, dureth over long.
Thomas Malory d. 1471: *Le Morte D'Arthur* (1485)

6 Give sorrow words: the grief that does not speak
Whispers the o'er-fraught heart, and bids it break.
William Shakespeare 1564–1616: *Macbeth* (1606)

7 A widow bird sat mourning for her love
Upon a wintry bough;
The frozen wind crept on above,
The freezing stream below.
Percy Bysshe Shelley 1792–1822: *Charles the First* (1822)

Stage and Screen

1 Egghead weds hourglass.
on the marriage of Arthur Miller and Marilyn Monroe
Anonymous: headline in *Variety* 1956; attributed

2 All I need to make a comedy is a park, a policeman and a pretty girl.
Charlie Chaplin 1889–1977: *My Autobiography* (1964)

3 Sexuality is such a part of life, but sexuality in the movies—I have a hard time finding it.
Catherine Deneuve 1943– : in *Première* April 1993

4 I love Mickey Mouse more than any woman I've ever known.
Walt Disney 1901–66: John Walker (ed.) *Halliwell's Filmgoer's Companion* (1995)

5 It struck me that the movies had spent more than half a century saying 'They lived happily ever after' and the following quarter-century warning that they'll be lucky to make it through the weekend. Possibly now we are entering a third era in which the movies will be sounding a note of cautious optimism: You know it just might work.
on her screenplay for When Harry Met Sally
Nora Ephron 1941– : in *Los Angeles Times* 27 July 1989

6 Is it Colman's smile
   That makes life worth while
   Or Crawford's significant form?
   Is it Lombard's lips
   Or Mae West's hips
   That carry you through the storm?
   Gavin Ewart 1916–95: 'Verse from an Opera' (1939)

7 If, sir, I possessed, as you suggest, the power of conveying
   unlimited sexual attraction through the potency of my
   voice, I would not be reduced to accepting a miserable
   pittance from the BBC for interviewing a faded female in a
   damp basement.
   reply to Mae West's manager who asked 'Can't you sound a bit
   more sexy when you interview her?'
   Gilbert Harding 1907–60: S. Grenfell *Gilbert Harding by his Friends* (1961)

8 I'll come no more behind your scenes, David; for the silk
   stockings and white bosoms of your actresses excite my
   amorous propensities.
   to David Garrick, in 1750
   Samuel Johnson 1709–84: James Boswell *Life of Samuel Johnson* (1791)

9 The words 'Kiss Kiss Bang Bang' which I saw on an Italian
   movie poster, are perhaps the briefest statement imaginable
   of the basic appeal of movies.
   Pauline Kael 1919– : *Kiss Kiss Bang Bang* (1968)

10 I've been around so long, I knew Doris Day before she was
   a virgin.
   Groucho Marx 1895–1977: Max Wilk *The Wit and Wisdom of Hollywood*
   (1972)

11 Brush up your Shakespeare,
   Start quoting him now.
   Brush up your Shakespeare
   And the women you will wow.
   Cole Porter 1891–1964: 'Brush Up your Shakespeare' (1948 song)

12 Thro' all the drama—whether damned or not—
    Love gilds the scene, and women guide the plot.
    Richard Brinsley Sheridan 1751–1816: *The Rivals* (1775)

13 I can do you blood and love without the rhetoric, and I can
    do you blood and rhetoric without the love, and I can do
    you all three concurrent or consecutive, but I can't do you
    love and rhetoric without the blood. Blood is compulsory—
    they're all blood, you see.
    Tom Stoppard 1937– : *Rosencrantz and Guildenstern are Dead* (1967)

14 To Raoul Walsh a tender love scene is burning down a
    whorehouse.
    Jack Warner 1892–1978: P. F. Boller and R. L. Davis *Hollywood Anecdotes*
    (1988)

15 Being a sex symbol is rather like being a convict.
    Raquel Welch 1940– : in *Observer* 25 February 1979

16 It's not what I do, but the way I do it. It's not what I say,
    but the way I say it.
    Mae West 1892–1980: G. Eells and S. Musgrove *Mae West* (1989)

Suffering see Pain and Suffering

Talking see also Words

1 Though a very few hours spent in the hard labour of
   incessant talking will dispatch more subjects than can
   really be in common between any two rational creatures,
   yet with lovers it is different. Between *them* no subject is

finished, no communication is even made, till it has been
made at least twenty times over.
Jane Austen 1775–1817: *Sense and Sensibility* (1811)

2 You must come to our house next time. Absolute peace.
Neither of us ever says a word to each other. That's the
secret of a successful union.
Alan Ayckbourn 1939– : *Absent Friends* (1975)

3 The speaking in a perpetual hyperbole is comely in nothing
but in love.
Francis Bacon 1561–1626: *Essays* (1625) 'Of Love'

4 The devil's in her tongue, and so 'tis in most women of her
age; for when it has quitted the tail, it repairs to the upper
tier.
Aphra Behn 1640–89: *The Town Fop* (1677)

5 The particular charm of marriage is the duologue, the
permanent conversation between two people who talk over
everything and everyone till death breaks the record. It is
this back-chat which, in the long run, makes a reciprocal
equality more intoxicating than any form of servitude or
domination.
Cyril Connolly 1903–74: *The Unquiet Grave* (1944)

6 This evening when I spake with thee, beloved,
as in thy face and in thy mien I saw
that I could not persuade thee with my words,
the longing came for thee to see my heart.
Juana Inés de la Cruz 1651–95: 'This evening when I spake with thee,
beloved'

7 For God's sake hold your tongue, and let me love.
John Donne 1572–1631: 'The Canonization'

8 Their relationship consisted
In discussing if it existed.
Thom Gunn 1929– : 'Jamesian' (1992)

9 I wasn't allowed to speak while my husband was alive, and since he's gone no one has been able to shut me up.
Hedda Hopper 1890–1966: attributed

10 I think men talk to women so they can sleep with them and women sleep with men so they can talk to them.
Jay McInerney 1955– : *Brightness Falls* (1992)

11 Whenever a husband and wife begin to discuss their marriage they are giving evidence at a coroner's inquest.
H. L. Mencken 1880–1956: *Chrestomathy* (1949)

12 Talking is excellent exercise for the mouth's all-important oral sex muscles.
P. J. O'Rourke 1947– : *Modern Manners* (1984)

13 Our passions are most like to floods and streams;
The shallow murmur, but the deep are dumb.
Walter Ralegh c.1552–1618: 'Sir Walter Ralegh to the Queen' (1655)

14 For these fellows of infinite tongue, that can rhyme themselves into ladies' favours, they do always reason themselves out again.
William Shakespeare 1564–1616: *Henry V* (1599)

15 How silver-sweet sound lovers' tongues by night,
Like softest music to attending ears!
William Shakespeare 1564–1616: *Romeo and Juliet* (1595)

16 Speech happens not to be his language.
*on being asked what she found to talk about with her new lover,
a hussar*
Mme de Staël 1766–1817: attributed

17 It is well within the order of things
That man should listen when his mate sings;
But the true male never yet walked
Who liked to listen when his mate talked.
Anna Wickham 1884–1947: 'The Affinity' (1915)

Talking

Time see also **Lasting Love, Transience**

1 Love, all alike, no season knows, nor clime,
  Nor hours, days, months, which are the rags of time.
  John Donne 1572–1631: 'The Sun Rising'

2 Time, which strengthens friendship, weakens love.
  Jean de la Bruyère 1645–96: *Les Caractères ou les moeurs de ce siècle*
  (1688)

3 Time has transfigured them into
  Untruth. The stone fidelity
  They hardly meant has come to be
  Their final blazon, and to prove
  Our almost-instinct almost true:
  What will survive of us is love.
  Philip Larkin 1922–85: 'An Arundel Tomb' (1964)

4 For love that time was not as love is nowadays.
  Thomas Malory d. 1471: *Le Morte D'Arthur* (1485)

5 Had we but world enough, and time,
  This coyness, lady, were no crime.
  Andrew Marvell 1621–78: 'To His Coy Mistress' (1681)

6 Time does not bring relief; you all have lied
  Who told me time would ease me of my pain!
  I miss him in the weeping of the rain;
  I want him at the shrinking of the tide.
  Edna St Vincent Millay 1892–1950: 'Time does not bring relief'

7 Time turns the old days to derision,
  Our loves into corpses or wives;
  And marriage and death and division
  Make barren our lives.
  Algernon Charles Swinburne 1837–1909: 'Dolores' (1866)

8 Any time that is not spent on love is wasted.
  Torquato Tasso 1544–95: attributed

9 Time is
   Too slow for those who wait,
   Too swift for those who fear,
   Too long for those who grieve,
   Too short for those who rejoice;
   But for those who love,
   Time is eternity.
   Henry Van Dyke 1852–1933: 'Time is too slow for those who wait' (1905),
   read at the funeral of Diana, Princess of Wales; Nigel Rees in 'Quote . . .
   Unquote' October 1997 notes that the original form of the last line is 'Time
   is not'

Toasts

1 Go fetch to me a pint o' wine,
   An' fill it in a silver tassie;
   That I may drink, before I go,
   A service to my bonnie lassie.
   Robert Burns 1759–96: 'My Bonnie Mary'

2 Here's looking at you, kid.
   Julius J. Epstein 1909– : *Casablanca* (1942 film)

3 Drink to me only with thine eyes,
   And I will pledge with mine;
   Or leave a kiss but in the cup,
   And I'll not look for wine.
   Ben Jonson c.1573–1637: 'To Celia' (1616)

4 Fat, fair and forty were all the toasts of the young men.
   John O'Keeffe 1747–1833: *The Irish Mimic* (1795)

5 Here's to the maiden of bashful fifteen
   Here's to the widow of fifty
   Here's to the flaunting, extravagant quean;
   And here's to the housewife that's thrifty.
   Let the toast pass—
   Drink to the lass—

I'll warrant she'll prove an excuse for the glass!
Richard Brinsley Sheridan 1751–1816: *The School for Scandal* (1777)

Transience see also Lasting Love

1 Let us live, my Lesbia, and let us love, and let us reckon all
the murmurs of more censorious old men as worth one
farthing. Suns can set and come again: for us, when once
our brief light has set, one everlasting night is to be slept.
Catullus *c.*84–*c.*54 BC: *Carmina*

2 Gather ye rosebuds while ye may,
Old Time is still a-flying:
And this same flower that smiles to-day,
To-morrow will be dying.
Robert Herrick 1591–1674: 'To the Virgins, to Make Much of Time' (1648)

3 Love. Of course, love. Flames for a year, ashes for thirty.
Guiseppe di Lampedusa 1896–1957: *The Leopard* (1957)

4 Fidelity and love are two different things, like a flower and
a gem.
and love, like a flower, will fade, will change into
something else,
or it would not be flowery.
D. H. Lawrence 1885–1930: 'Fidelity'

5 Even newlyweds don't spend much time together, now that
few marriages outlast the appliance warranties.
P. J. O'Rourke 1947– : *The Bachelor Home Companion* (1987)

6 What is love? 'tis not hereafter;
Present mirth hath present laughter;
What's to come is still unsure.
William Shakespeare 1564–1616: *Twelfth Night* (1601)

Travel see also Places and Peoples

1 Adieu to disappointment and spleen. What are men to
rocks and mountains?
Jane Austen 1775–1817: *Pride and Prejudice* (1813)

2 There is much to be said for exotic marriages. If your
husband is a bore, it takes years longer to discover.
Saul Bellow 1915– : *Mr Sammler's Planet* (1969)

3 My message to the businessmen of this country when they
go abroad on business is that there is one thing above all
they can take with them to stop them catching Aids—and
that is the wife.
Edwina Currie 1946– : speech at Runcorn, 12 February 1987

4 And I would love you all the day,
Every night would kiss and play,
If with me you'd fondly stray
Over the hills and far away.
John Gay 1685–1732: *The Beggar's Opera* (1728)

5 Standing among savage scenery, the hotel offers
stupendous revelations. There is a French widow in every
bedroom, affording delightful prospects.
supposedly quoting a letter from a Tyrolean landlord
Gerard Hoffnung 1925–59: speech at the Oxford Union, 4 December 1958

6 I'd love to get you
On a slow boat to China,
All to myself, alone.
Frank Loesser 1910–69: 'On a Slow Boat to China' (1948 song)

7 The fabric of my faithful love
No power shall dim or ravel
While I stay here—but oh, my dear,
If I should ever travel!
Edna St Vincent Millay 1892–1950: 'To the Not Impossible Him'

8 Born under different skies we have neither the same
   thoughts nor the same language—have we, perhaps,
   hearts that resemble one another?
   George Sand 1804–76: letter to Pietro Pagello, 10 July 1834

9 O mistress mine! where are you roaming?
   O! stay and hear; your true love's coming,
   That can sing both high and low.
   Trip no further, pretty sweeting;
   Journeys end in lovers meeting,
   Every wise man's son doth know.
   William Shakespeare 1564–1616: *Twelfth Night* (1601)

10 A journey is like marriage. The one certain way to be
   wrong is to think you control it.
   John Steinbeck 1902–68: *Travels with Charley* (1961)

Trust and Betrayal see also Deception, Fidelity

1 There is no infidelity when there has been no love.
   Honoré de Balzac 1799–1850: letter to Mme Hanska, August 1833

2 Behind almost every woman you ever heard of stands a
   man who let her down.
   Naomi Bliven 1925– : Regina Barreca (ed.) *The Penguin Book of Women's
   Humour* (1996)

3 And my fause luver stole my rose,
   But ah! he left the thorn wi' me.
   Robert Burns 1759–96: 'The Banks o' Doon' (1792)

4 If anyone sends me a card with a robin on it I'll never
   speak to them again. It is strange that such an aggressive
   creature has come to symbolise the season of goodwill.
   after her husband Robin left her
   Margaret Cook: in *Independent on Sunday* 18 January 1998

5 Anyone who hasn't experienced the ecstasy of betrayal
   knows nothing about ecstasy at all.
   Jean Genet 1910–86: *Prisoner of Love* (1986)

6 When lovely woman stoops to folly
And finds too late that men betray,
What charm can soothe her melancholy,
What art can wash her guilt away?
Oliver Goldsmith 1728–74: *The Vicar of Wakefield* (1766)

7 '*Pone seram, cohibe.*' *Sed quis custodiet ipsos
Custodes? Cauta est et ab illis incipit uxor.*

'Bolt her in, keep her indoors.' But who is to guard the
guards themselves? Your wife is prudent and begins with
them.
Juvenal AD c.60–c.130: *Satires*

8 In every question and every remark tossed back and forth
between lovers who have not played out the last fugue,
there is one question and it is this: 'Is there someone new?'
Edna O'Brien 1936– : *Lantern Slides* (1990)

9 It is the property of love to make us at once more distrustful
and more credulous, to make us suspect the loved one,
more readily than we should suspect anyone else, and be
convinced more easily by her denials.
Marcel Proust 1871–1922: *Cities of the Plain* (1922)

10 The shackles of an old love straitened him,
His honour rooted in dishonour stood,
And faith unfaithful kept him falsely true.
Alfred, Lord Tennyson 1809–92: *Idylls of the King* 'Lancelot and Elaine'
(1859)

11 And trust me not at all or all in all.
Alfred, Lord Tennyson 1809–92: *Idylls of the King* 'Merlin and Vivien'
(1859)

12 Women and fortune are truest still to those that trust 'em.
William Wycherley c.1640–1716: *The Country Wife* (1675)

Unrequited Love

1 When late I attempted your pity to move,
What made you so deaf to my prayers?
Perhaps it was right to dissemble your love,
But—why did you kick me downstairs?
Isaac Bickerstaffe 1733–*c.*1808: 'An Expostulation' (1789)

2 What is this recompense you'd have from me?
Melville asked no compassion of the sea.
Roll to and fro, forgotten in my wrack,
Love as you please—I owe you nothing back.
Norman Cameron 1905–53: 'From a Woman to a Greedy Lover'

3 Heaven has no rage, like love to hatred turned,
Nor Hell a fury, like a woman scorned.
William Congreve 1670–1729: *The Mourning Bride* (1697)

4 It is very hard to be in love with someone who no longer
loves you, but it is far worse to be loved by someone with
whom you are no longer in love.
Georges Courteline 1858–1929: *La Philosophie de Georges Courteline*
(1948)

5 If you could see my legs when I take my boots off, you'd
form some idea of what unrequited affection is.
Charles Dickens 1812–70: *Dombey and Son* (1848)

6 If only the strength of the love that people feel when it is
reciprocated could be as intense and obsessive as the love
we feel when it is not; then marriages would be truly made
in heaven.
Ben Elton 1959– : *Stark* (1989)

7   When someone leaves you . . . the worst is the thought that
they tried you out and, in the end, the whole sum of parts
which adds up to you got stamped REJECT by the one you
love. How can you not be left with the personal confidence
of a passed-over British Rail sandwich?
Helen Fielding 1958– : *Bridget Jones's Diary* (1996)

8   With love to lead the way,
I've found more clouds of grey
Than any Russian play
Could guarantee . . .
  . . . When ev'ry happy plot
Ends with the marriage knot—
And there's no knot for me.
Ira Gershwin 1896–1983: 'But Not For Me' (1930 song)

9   Of all pains, the greatest pain
Is to love, and love in vain.
George Granville, Lord Lansdowne 1666–1735: 'Happiest Mortals Once We
Were'

10   Love without hope, as when the young bird-catcher
Swept off his tall hat to the Squire's own daughter,
So let the imprisoned larks escape and fly
Singing about her head, as she rode by.
Robert Graves 1895–1985: 'Love Without Hope'

11   Pray, let me beg of you, my much loved Greville, only one
line from your dear, dear hands. You don't know how
thankful I shall be for it. For if you knew the misery [I] feel,
oh! your heart would not be entirely shut up against me,
for I love you with the truest affection.
Emma Hamilton *c.*1765–1815: letter to Charles Greville, 22 July 1786

12   Perhaps a great love is never returned.
Dag Hammarskjöld 1905–61: *Markings* (1964)

Unrequited

(U)

13 There aren't many irritations to match the condescension
which a woman metes out to a man who she believes has
loved her vainly for the past umpteen years.
Edward Hoagland 1932– : *Heart's Desire* (1988)

14 Less than the dust, beneath thy Chariot wheel,
Less than the rust, that never stained thy Sword . . .
Less than the need thou hast in life of me.
Even less am I.
Laurence Hope (Adela Florence Nicolson) 1865–1904: *The Garden of
Kama* (1901) 'Less than the Dust'

15 The rainy Pleiads wester
And seek beyond the sea
The head that I shall dream of
That will not dream of me.
A. E. Housman 1859–1936: *More Poems* (1936) no. 11

16 I saw pale kings and princes too,
Pale warriors, death-pale were they all;
Who cried—'La Belle Dame sans Merci
Hath thee in thrall!'
John Keats 1795–1821: 'La belle dame sans merci' (1820)

*advising someone rejected in love to be cheerful, forgiving, and
unavailable:*
17 Such behaviour will have two rewards. First, it will take
the sufferer's mind off suffering and begin the recovery.
Second, it will make the former lover worry that this
supposed act of cruelty was actually a relief to the person it
should have hurt. That hurts.
Judith Martin 1938– : 'Advice from Miss Manners', column in *Washington
Post* 1979–82

18 The love that lasts longest is the love that is never returned.
W. Somerset Maugham 1874–1965: *A Writer's Notebook* (1949) written in
1894

19 I wanted your soft verges
But you gave me the hard shoulder.
Adrian Mitchell 1932– : 'Song for a Beautiful Girl Petrol-Pump Attendant
on the Motorway'

20 Not tonight, Josephine.
Napoleon I 1769–1821: attributed, but probably apocryphal; the phrase
does not appear in contemporary sources, but was current by the early
twentieth century

21 Disdain me still, that I may ever love,
For who his Love enjoys, can love no more;
The war once past, with peace men cowards prove,
And ships returned do rot upon the shore.
William Herbert, Lord Pembroke c.1501–70: 'Disdain me still, that I may
ever love'

22 VIOLA: My father had a daughter loved a man,
As it might be, perhaps, were I a woman,
I should your lordship.
DUKE: And what's her history?
VIOLA: A blank, my lord. She never told her love,
But let concealment, like a worm i' the bud,
Feed on her damask cheek: she pined in thought;
And with a green and yellow melancholy,
She sat like patience on a monument,
Smiling at grief.
William Shakespeare 1564–1616: *Twelfth Night* (1601)

23 Come away, come away, death,
And in sad cypress let me be laid;
Fly away, fly away, breath:
I am slain by a fair cruel maid.
William Shakespeare 1564–1616: *Twelfth Night* (1601)

24 She only said, 'My life is dreary,
He cometh not,' she said;
She said, 'I am aweary, aweary,
I would that I were dead!'
Alfred, Lord Tennyson 1809–92: 'Mariana' (1830)

Unrequited

25 Yes, I am a fatal man, Madame Fribsbi. To inspire hopeless
    passion is my destiny.
    William Makepeace Thackeray 1811–63: *Pendennis* (1848–50)

26 It is not that I love you less
    Than when before your feet I lay:
    But, to prevent the sad increase
    Of hopeless love, I keep away.
    In vain, alas! for every thing
    Which I have known belong to you,
    Your form does to my fancy bring
    And makes my old wounds bleed anew.
    Edmund Waller 1606–87: 'Self-Banished'

Valentines

1 Is it all too much, this Valentine fuss, or is it wonderful and
   symbolic? Does it mean that 364 days a year your loved
   one does not think about you, but that's OK if there's one
   day that the loved one does make a fuss?
   Maeve Binchy 1940– : in *Irish Times* 14 February 1998

2 Right worshipful and well-beloved Valentine, I commend
   myself to you with all my heart, wishing to hear that all is
   well with you: I beseech Almighty God to keep you well
   according to his pleasure and your heart's desire.
   Margery Brews: letter to John Paston, 1477

3 The particular picture . . . was a highly coloured
   representation of a couple of human hearts skewered
   together with an arrow, cooking before a cheerful fire,
   while a male and female cannibal in modern attire, the
   gentleman being clad in a blue coat and white trousers,

and the lady in a deep red pelisse with a parasol of the same, were approaching the meal with hungry eyes, up a serpentine gravel path leading thereunto. A decidedly indelicate young gentleman, in a pair of wings and nothing else, was depicted as superintending the cooking; a representation of the spire of the church in Langham Place, London, appeared in the distance; and the whole formed a 'valentine'.
Charles Dickens 1812–70: *Pickwick Papers* (1837)

4 Except of me Mary my dear as your walentine and think over what I've said.
Charles Dickens 1812–70: *Pickwick Papers* (1837)

5 Hail, Bishop Valentine, whose day this is,
All the air is thy Diocese.
John Donne 1572–1631: 'An Epithalamion . . . on the Lady Elizabeth and Count Palatine being Married on St Valentine's Day' (1613)

6 Oh God. Valentine's Day tomorrow. Why? Why? Why is entire world geared to make people not involved in romance feel stupid when everyone knows romance does not work anyway.
Helen Fielding 1958– : *Bridget Jones's Diary* (1996)

7 The things about you I appreciate
May seem indelicate:
I'd like to find you in the shower
and chase the soap for half an hour.
John Fuller 1937– : 'Valentine'

8 Anonymous, unseen—
You're dealing with the all-time king or queen
Of undercover loves.
The author of this valentine wore gloves.
Sophie Hannah 1971– : 'Poem for a Valentine Card' (1995)

9 Stay, little Valentine, stay,
Each day is Valentine's day.
Lorenz Hart 1895–1943: 'My Funny Valentine' (1937 song)

10 I wouldn't thank you for a Valentine
I won't wake up early wondering if the postman's been.
Should 10 red-padded satin hearts arrive with a sticky
    sickly saccharine
Sentiments in very vulgar verses I wouldn't wonder if you
    meant them.
Liz Lochhead 1947– : 'I Wouldn't Thank You for a Valentine' (1985)

11 If you hired a plane and blazed our love in a banner across
    the skies;
If you bought me something flimsy in a flatteringly wrong
    size;
If you sent me a postcard with three Xs and told me how
    you felt
I wouldn't thank you, I'd melt.
Liz Lochhead 1947– : 'I Wouldn't Thank You for a Valentine' (1985)

12 I sing Saint Valentine, his day,
I spread abroad his rumour—
A gentleman, it's safe to say,
Who owned a sense of humour.
Most practical of jokers, he,
Who bade sweethearts make merry
With flowers and birds and amorous words,
In the month of February.
The antic, frantic,
Unromantic
Middle of February.
Phyllis McGinley 1905– : 'Poor Timing'

13 I'll bet he doesn't realize that the 14th is Valentine's Day.
The whole restaurant will be filled with couples in love not
panicking about their fat knees throughout their meals.
Arabella Weir: *Does My Bum Look Big in This?* (1997)

Violence

1 Some women . . . enjoy tremendously being told they look a
   mess—and they actually thrill to the threat of physical
   violence. I've never met one that does, mind you, but they
   probably do exist. In books. By men.
   Alan Ayckbourn 1939– : *Round and Round the Garden* (1975)

2 Women are made for loving not hitting.
   on female boxing
   Henry Cooper 1934– : in *Independent on Sunday* 'For the Record' 5
   October 1997

3 Aristocrats spend their childhood being beaten by fierce
   nannies and their later years murdering wildlife, so it's
   hardly surprising their sex lives are a bit cock-eyed.
   Jilly Cooper 1937– : *Men and Super-Men* (1972)

4 Certain women should be struck regularly, like gongs.
   Noël Coward 1899–1973: *Private Lives* (1930)

5 There are only about 20 murders a year in London and not
   all are serious—some are just husbands killing their wives.
   a view from a Commander at Scotland Yard
   G. H. Hatherill: news reports, 1 July 1954

6 Every woman adores a Fascist,
   The boot in the face, the brute
   Brute heart of a brute like you.
   Sylvia Plath 1932–63: 'Daddy' (1963)

7 Bricklayers kick their wives to death, and dukes betray
   theirs; but it is among the small clerks and shopkeepers
   nowadays that it comes most often to the cutting of
   throats.
   H. G. Wells 1866–1946: *Short Stories* 'The Purple Pileus'

Virtue and Chastity

1 Give me chastity and continency—but not yet!
St Augustine of Hippo AD 354–430: *Confessions* (AD 397–8)

2 I'm as pure as the driven slush.
Tallulah Bankhead 1903–68: in *Saturday Evening Post* 12 April 1947

3 What is it that constitutes virtue, Mrs Graham? Is it the circumstance of being able and willing to resist temptation; or that of having no temptation to resist?
Anne Brontë 1820–49: *The Tenant of Wildfell Hall* (1848)

4 I begin to find out that nothing but virtue will do in this damned world. I am tolerably sick of vice which I have tried in its agreeable varieties, and mean on my return to cut all my dissolute acquaintance and leave off wine and 'carnal company', and betake myself to politics and decorum.
Lord Byron 1788–1824: letter, 5 May 1810

5 I'll wager you that in 10 years it will be fashionable again to be a virgin.
Barbara Cartland 1901– : in *Observer* 20 June 1976

6 Logic and a sense of justice tell me that there is more love in electricity and steam than there is in chastity and abstention from eating meat.
on Tolstoy as celibate and vegetarian
Anton Chekhov 1860–1904: Donald Rayfield *Anton Chekhov* (1997)

7 I have never seen anyone who loved virtue as much as sex.
Confucius 551–479BC: *The Analects*

8 Would I were free from this restraint,
Or else had hopes to win her;
Would she could make of me a saint,
Or I of her a sinner.
William Congreve 1670–1729: 'Pious Selinda Goes to Prayers' (song)

9 There's nothing wrong with being innocent or high-
minded
But I'm glad you're not.
Wendy Cope 1945– : 'From June to December' (1986)

10 What most men desire is a virgin who is a whore.
Edward Dahlberg 1900–77: *Reasons of the Heart* (1965)

11 I'm just a fool when lights are low,
I cain't be prissy and quaint.
I ain't the type thet c'n faint,
How c'n I be whut I ain't,
I cain't say no!
Oscar Hammerstein II 1895–1960: 'I Cain't Say No' (1943 song)

12 A woman's chastity consists, like an onion, of a series of
coats.
Nathaniel Hawthorne 1804–64: diary, 16 March 1854

13 A woman would no doubt need a great deal of imagination
to love a man for his virtue.
John Oliver Holmes 1867–1906: *Sinner's Comedy*

14 Remember, you're fighting for this woman's honour . . .
which is probably more than she ever did.
Bert Kalmar 1884–1947 et al.: *Duck Soup* (1933 film); spoken by Groucho
Marx

15 There are few virtuous women who are not bored with
their trade.
Duc de la Rochefoucauld 1613–80: *Maximes* (1678)

16 Feminine virtue is nothing but a convenient masculine
invention.
Ninon de Lenclos 1616–1705: attributed remark, *c.*1660; *Letters* (1870)

17 The woman who goes to bed with a man should put off her
modesty with her skirt and put it on again with her
petticoats.
Montaigne 1533–92: *Essays* (1580)

Virtue

18 Home is heaven and orgies are vile,
But you *need* an orgy, once in a while.
Ogden Nash 1902–71: 'Home, 99⁴⁴⁄₁₀₀% Sweet Home' (1935)

19 These people abstain, it is true: but the bitch Sensuality
glares enviously out of all they do.
Friedrich Nietzsche 1844–1900: *Thus Spake Zarathrustra* (1883)

20 Whose love is given over-well
Shall look on Helen's face in hell
Whilst they whose love is thin and wise
Shall see John Knox in Paradise.
Dorothy Parker 1893–1967: 'Partial Comfort' (1937)

21 Most good women are hidden treasures who are only safe
because nobody looks for them.
Dorothy Parker 1893–1967: attributed; in *New York Times* 8 June 1967

22 No, no; for my virginity,
When I lose that, says Rose, I'll die:
Behind the elms last night, cried Dick,
Rose, were you not extremely sick?
Matthew Prior 1664–1721: 'A True Maid' (1718)

23   Change in a trice
The lilies and languors of virtue
For the raptures and roses of vice.
Algernon Charles Swinburne 1837–1909: 'Dolores' (1866)

24 When I'm good, I'm very, very good, but when I'm bad,
I'm better.
Mae West 1892–1980: *I'm No Angel* (1933 film)

25 'Goodness, what beautiful diamonds!'
'Goodness had nothing to do with it.'
Mae West 1892–1980: *Night After Night* (1932 film)

26 When women go wrong, men go right after them.
Mae West 1892–1980: *She Done Him Wrong* (1933 film)

27 I used to be Snow White . . . but I drifted.
Mae West 1892–1980: Joseph Weintraub *Peel Me a Grape* (1975)

28 I can resist everything except temptation.
Oscar Wilde 1854–1900: *Lady Windermere's Fan* (1892)

Waiting

1 What is insane about love is that one wishes to precipitate and to *lose* the days of waiting. Thus one desires to approach the end. So by one of its characteristics love coincides with death.
Albert Camus 1913–60: diary, April 1950

2 Where the blue of the night
Meets the gold of the day,
Someone waits for me.
Bing Crosby 1903–77: 'Where the Blue of the Night meets the Gold of the Day' (1931 song, with Roy Turk and Fred Ahlert)

3 Why be in haste? You've nothing to waste,
The best things come without rhyme or reason.
Sit in the sun, the sun, the sun,
And you might be in love by the end of the season.
Dorothy Reynolds and Julian Slade 1930– : 'I Sit in the Sun' (1954 song)

4 How men hate waiting while their wives shop for clothes and trinkets; how women hate waiting, often for much of their lives, while their husbands shop for fame and glory.
Thomas Szasz 1920– : *The Second Sin* (1973)

5 There has fallen a splendid tear
From the passion-flower at the gate.
She is coming, my dove, my dear;

She is coming, my life, my fate;
The red rose cries, 'She is near, she is near;'
And the white rose weeps, 'She is late;'
The larkspur listens, 'I hear, I hear;'
And the lily whispers, 'I wait.'
Alfred, Lord Tennyson 1809–92: *Maud* (1855)

Wealth and Poverty see also Money

1 She was poor but she was honest
 Victim of a rich man's game.
 First he loved her, then he left her,
 And she lost her maiden name.
 Anonymous: 'She was Poor but she was Honest' (sung by British soldiers in the First World War)

2 There are certainly not so many men of large fortune in the world, as there are pretty women to deserve them.
 Jane Austen 1775–1817: *Mansfield Park* (1814)

3 Your portion is unhappily so small that it will in all likelihood undo the effects of your loveliness and amiable qualifications.
 Mr Collins to Elizabeth Bennet
 Jane Austen 1775–1817: *Pride and Prejudice* (1813)

4 O, gie me the lass that has acres o' charms,
 O, gie me the lass wi' the weel-stockit farms.
 Robert Burns 1759–96: 'Hey for a Lass wi' a Tocher' (1799)

5 Maidens, like moths, are ever caught by glare,
 And Mammon wins his way where Seraphs might despair.
 Lord Byron 1788–1824: *Childe Harold's Pilgrimage* (1812–18)

6 When the glowing of passion's over, and pinching winter comes, will amorous sighs supply the want of fire, or kind looks and kisses keep off hunger?
 Susanna Centlivre c.1669–1723: *Artifice*

7 Love and a cottage! Eh, Fanny! Ah, give me indifference
and a coach and six!
George Colman, the Elder 1732–94: *The Clandestine Marriage* (1766)

8 No woman can be a beauty without a fortune.
George Farquhar 1678–1707: *The Beaux' Stratagem* (1707)

9 The minute you walked in the joint,
I could see you were a man of distinction,
A real big spender . . .
Hey! big spender, spend a little time with me.
Dorothy Fields 1905–74: 'Big Spender' (1966 song)

10 I want an old-fashioned house
With an old-fashioned fence
And an old-fashioned millionaire.
Marve Fisher: 'An Old-Fashioned Girl' (1954 song)

11 So I fell in love with a rich attorney's
Elderly ugly daughter.
W. S. Gilbert 1836–1911: *Trial by Jury* (1875)

12 Love in a hut, with water and a crust,
Is—Love, forgive us!—cinders, ashes, dust;
Love in a palace is perhaps at last
More grievous torment than a hermit's fast.
John Keats 1795–1821: 'Lamia' (1820)

13 A woman unsatisfied must have luxuries. But a woman
who loves a man would sleep on a board.
D. H. Lawrence 1885–1930: attributed; in *Ladies' Home Journal* February
1949

14 Battles and sex are the only free diversions in slum life.
Alexander McArthur and H. Kingsley Long: *No Mean City* (1935)

15 HE: Who wants to be a millionaire?
SHE: I don't.
HE: Have flashy flunkeys ev'rywhere?
SHE: I don't . . .
HE: Who wants a marble swimming pool too?

Wealth

SHE: I don't.
HE: And I don't,
BOTH: 'Cause all I want is you.
Cole Porter 1891–1964: 'Who Wants to be a Millionaire?' (1956 song)

16 I was too rich in possessions whilst I possessed him.
of her husband, Lord William Russell, first Duke of Bedford
Rachel Russell 1636–1723: letter to Dr Fitzwilliam

17 PAUL: You want me to be rich and famous, don't you?
CORRIE: During the day. At night I want you to be here and sexy.
Neil Simon 1927– : *Barefoot in the Park* (1964)

18 Remember, it is as easy to marry a rich woman as a poor woman.
William Makepeace Thackeray 1811–63: *Pendennis* (1848–50)

19 Love is like any other luxury. You have no right to it unless you can afford it.
Anthony Trollope 1815–82: *The Way We Live Now* (1875)

20 I would worship the ground you walk on, Audrey, if you only lived in a better neighbourhood.
when courting his future wife
Billy Wilder 1906– : M. Zolotow *Billy Wilder in Hollywood* (1977)

Wedding Dresses

1 I have no dress except the one I wear every day. If you are going to be kind enough to give me one, please let it be practical and dark so that I can put it on afterwards to go to the laboratory.
when offered a dress for her wedding
Marie Curie 1867–1934: letter to a friend; attributed

2 She looks like a big meringue.
Richard Curtis 1956– : *Four Weddings and a Funeral* (1994 film)

3 I . . . chose my wife, as she did her wedding gown, not for a
fine glossy surface, but such qualities as would wear well.
Oliver Goldsmith 1728-74: *The Vicar of Wakefield* (1766)

4 In your pink wool knitted dress
Before anything had smudged anything
You stood at the altar.
Ted Hughes 1930-98: *Birthday Letters* (1998) 'A Pink Wool Knitted Dress'

5 So gloomy to have your bride, however bigamous, insisting
on grey alpaca or merino or whatever it was.
of Jane Eyre's choice of wedding dress
Dorothy L. Sayers 1893-1957: *Busman's Honeymoon* (1937); cf. **Books
and Literature 4**

6 It is true that the moment I'm interested in someone I start
doodling dresses with trains in tulle and taffeta and I don't
even know what tulle is.
Arabella Weir: *Does My Bum Look Big in This?* (1997)

Weddings see also The Best Man, Bridegrooms, Brides, Bridesmaids, Rings, Wedding Dresses

1 If it were not for the presents, an elopement would be
preferable.
George Ade 1886-1944: *Forty Modern Fables* (1901)

2 I think weddings is sadder than funerals, because they
remind you of your own wedding. You can't be reminded
of your own funeral because it hasn't happened. But
weddings always make me cry.
Brendan Behan 1923-64: *Richard's Cork Leg*

3 All weddings are similar but every marriage is different.
Death comes to everyone but one mourns alone.
John Berger: *The White Bird* (1985)

4 No man is in love when he marries. He may have loved
before; I have even heard he has sometimes loved after: but
at the time never. There is something in the formalities of
the matrimonial preparations that drive away all the little
cupidons.
Fanny Burney 1752–1840: *Camilla* (1796)

5 O! how short a time does it take to put an end to a
woman's liberty!
of a wedding
Fanny Burney 1752–1840: diary, 20 July 1768

6 All tragedies are finished by a death,
All comedies are ended by a marriage;
The future states of both are left to faith.
Lord Byron 1788–1824: *Don Juan* (1819–24)

7 It's pretty easy. Just say 'I do' whenever anyone asks you a
question.
Richard Curtis 1956– : *Four Weddings and a Funeral* (1994 film)

8 It won't be a stylish marriage,
I can't afford a carriage,
But you'll look sweet upon the seat
Of a bicycle made for two.
Harry Dacre: 'Daisy Bell' (1892 song)

9 Halloa! Here's a church! . . . Let's go in! . . . Here's Miss
Skiffins! Let's have a wedding!
Charles Dickens 1812–70: *Great Expectations* (1861)

10 I love to cry at weddings, anybody's weddings anytime!
. . . anybody's weddings just so long as it's not mine!
Dorothy Fields 1905–74: 'I Love to Cry at Weddings' (1966)

11 We have a committed relationship but we haven't married.
We want to set this straight because we've started getting
wedding presents.
on rumours that he had married his partner, Elton John
David Furnish: in *The Times* 13 June 1998

12 I'm not getting married today. I'm in bed.
after his rumoured wedding to Patsy Kensit failed to take place
Liam Gallagher 1972– : in *Independent* 15 February 1997

13 I can't stand these modern hymns. They're so socialist.
at a society wedding
Hugh Grant 1960– : in *Daily Telegraph* 12 May 1998

14 Eleanor Rigby picks up the rice in the church where a
wedding has been,
Lives in a dream.
John Lennon 1940–80 and **Paul McCartney** 1942– : 'Eleanor Rigby' (1966 song)

15 O wha's the bride that cairries the bunch
O' thistles blinterin' white?
Her cuckold bridegroom little dreids
What he sall ken this nicht.
Hugh MacDiarmid 1892–1978: *A Drunk Man Looks at the Thistle* (1926)

16 I tremble for what we are doing. Are you sure you will love
me for ever? Shall we never repent? I fear, and I hope.
before her elopement
Lady Mary Wortley Montagu 1689–1762: letter to Edward Wortley
Montagu, 15 August 1712

17 Saw a wedding in the church . . . and strange to say what
delight we married people have to see these poor fools
decoyed into our condition.
Samuel Pepys 1633–1703: diary, 25 December 1665

18 I said 'Yes'. Isn't that enough?
asked for a comment on her wedding
Françoise Sagan 1935– : in *New York Mirror* 16 March 1958

19 It was one of those weddings where the bride's and groom's
families stand out like opposing football teams, wearing
their colours. All the decent hats were, thank God, on our
side.
Barbara Trapido 1941– : *Brother of the More Famous Jack* (1982)

20 What a holler there would be if people had to pay the minister as much to marry them as they have to pay a lawyer to get them a divorce.
Claire Trevor: in *New York Journal-American* 12 October 1960

21 FEAR I MAY NOT BE ABLE TO REACH YOU IN TIME FOR THE CEREMONY. DON'T WAIT.
telegram of apology for missing Oscar Wilde's wedding
James McNeill Whistler 1834–1903: E. J. and R. Pennell *The Life of James McNeill Whistler* (1908)

22 A man looks pretty small at a wedding, George. All those good women standing shoulder to shoulder, making sure that the knot's tied in a mighty public way.
Thornton Wilder 1897–1975: *Our Town* (1938)

23 Her veil blows across my face
as we cling together in the porch.
Propped on the mantelpiece,
The photograph distils our ecstasy.
Hugo Williams 1942– : 'Love-Life'

Widows and Widowers

1 Give unto them beauty for ashes, the oil of joy for mourning.
Bible: Isaiah

2 Take example by your father, my boy, and be wery careful o' vidders all your life.
Charles Dickens 1812–70: *Pickwick Papers* (1837)

3 When widows exclaim loudly against second marriage, I would always lay a wager that the man, if not the wedding-day, is absolutely fixed on.
Henry Fielding 1707–54: *Amelia* (1751)

4 The comfortable estate of widowhood, is the only hope that keeps up a wife's spirits.
John Gay 1685–1732: *The Beggar's Opera* (1728)

5   Easy-crying widows take new husbands soonest; there's
    nothing like wet weather for transplanting.
    Oliver Wendell Holmes 1809–94: attributed

6   My last Good-night! Thou wilt not wake
    Till I thy fate shall overtake:
    Till age, or grief, or sickness must
    Marry my body to that dust
    It so much loves; and fill the room
    My heart keeps empty in thy tomb.
    written for his wife Anne, d. 1624
    Henry King 1592–1669: 'An Exequy' (1657)

7   For a season there must be pain—
    For a little, little space
    I shall lose the sight of her face,
    Take back the old life again
    While She is at rest in her place.
    Rudyard Kipling 1865–1936: 'The Widower'

8   I can't remember if I cried
    When I read about his widowed bride.
    Something touched me deep inside
    The day the music died.
    Don McLean 1945– : 'American Pie' (1972 song)

9   Thirty years is a very long time to live alone and life doesn't
    get any nicer.
    at the age of 92
    Frances Partridge 1900– : G. Kinnock and F. Miller (eds.) *By Faith and
    Daring* (1993)

10 Widow. The word consumes itself.
    Sylvia Plath 1932–63: 'Widow' (1971)

11 Widows are divided into two classes—the bereaved and
    relieved.
    Victor Robinson 1886–1947: in *Truth Seeker* 6 January 1906

12 My most neglected wife, till you are a much respected widow, I find you will scarce be a contented woman, and to say no more than the plain truth, I do endeavour so fairly to do you that last good service.
Lord Rochester 1647–80: letter to his wife, 20 November 1677

13 A widow is a fascinating being with the flavour of maturity, the spice of experience, the piquancy of novelty, the tang of practised coquetry, and the halo of one man's approval.
Helen Rowland 1875–1950: *A Guide to Men* (1922)

14 He first deceased; she for a little tried
To live without him: liked it not, and died.
Henry Wotton 1568–1639: 'Upon the Death of Sir Albertus Moreton's Wife' (1651)

Without Love see also The Single Life

1 Nobody dies from lack of sex. It's lack of love we die from.
Margaret Atwood 1939– : *The Handmaid's Tale* (1986)

2 Why was I made for Love and Love denied to me?
Samuel Taylor Coleridge 1772–1834: 'The Blossoming of the Solitary Date-Tree'

3 I wonder by my troth, what thou, and I
Did, till we loved, were we not weaned till then?
But sucked on country pleasures, childishly?
Or snorted we in the seven sleepers den?
John Donne 1572–1631: 'The Good-Morrow'

4 The broken dates,
The endless waits,
The lovely loving and the hateful hates,
The conversation and the flying plates—
I wish I were in love again.
Lorenz Hart 1895–1943: 'I Wish I Were in Love Again' (1937)

5 I can live without it all—
   love with its blood pump,
   sex with its messy hungers,
   men with their peacock strutting,
   their silly sexual baggage,
   their wet tongues in my ear.
   Erica Jong 1942– : 'Becoming a Nun'

6 Those that go searching for love
   only make manifest their own lovelessness,

   and the loveless never find love,
   only the loving find love,
   and they never have to seek for it.
   D. H. Lawrence 1885–1930: 'Search for Love'

7 My father was a man as unacquainted with love as a Scots
   pine tree and what's wrong with that? It makes a change,
   these days, when love slops out all over the place from any
   old bucket.
   Jill Tweedie 1936–93: *Eating Children* (1993)

8 When you really want love you will find it waiting for you.
   Oscar Wilde 1854–1900: *De Profundis* (1905)

9 A man can be happy with any woman as long as he does
   not love her.
   Oscar Wilde 1854–1900: *The Picture of Dorian Gray* (1891)

Wives

1 My wife was an immature woman . . . I would be home in
   the bathroom, taking a bath, and my wife would walk in
   whenever she felt like it and sink my boats.
   Woody Allen 1935– : 'I Had a Rough Marriage' (monologue, 1964)

2 Wives are young men's mistresses, companions for middle
   age, and old men's nurses.
   Francis Bacon 1561–1626: *Essays* (1625) 'Of Marriage and the Single Life'

3 A man's mother is his misfortune, but his wife is his fault.
on being urged to marry by his mother
Walter Bagehot 1826–77: in Norman St John Stevas *Works of Walter Bagehot* (1986) vol. 15 'Walter Bagehot's Conversation'

4 A married woman is a slave whom one must put on a throne.
Honoré de Balzac 1799–1850: *Physiology of Marriage* (1829)

5 The woman whose life is of the head will strive to inspire her husband with indifference; the woman whose life is of the heart, with hatred; the passionate woman, with disgust.
Honoré de Balzac 1799–1850: *Physiology of Marriage* (1829)

6 When a man has married a wife, he finds out whether
Her knees and elbows are only glued together.
William Blake 1757–1827: 'When a man has married a wife'

7 Meek wifehood is no part of my profession;
I am your friend, but never your possession.
Vera Brittain 1893–1970: 'Married Love'

8 Think you, if Laura had been Petrarch's wife,
He would have written sonnets all his life?
Lord Byron 1788–1824: *Don Juan* (1819–24)

9 Variability is one of the virtues of a woman. It avoids the crude requirement of polygamy. So long as you have one good wife you are sure to have a spiritual harem.
G. K. Chesterton 1874–1936: *Alarms and Discursions* (1910)

10 It's my old girl that advises. She has the head. But I never own to it before her. Discipline must be maintained.
Charles Dickens 1812–70: *Bleak House* (1853)

11 It's only my child-wife.
of Dora
Charles Dickens 1812–70: *David Copperfield* (1850)

12 If you want to know about a man you can find out an awful lot by looking at who he married.
Kirk Douglas 1916– : in *Daily Mail* 9 September 1988

13 Nature meant me
A wife, a silly harmless dove,
Fond without art; and kind without deceit.
John Dryden 1631–1700: *All for Love* (1678)

14 A woman dictates before marriage in order that she may have an appetite for submission afterwards.
George Eliot 1819–80: *Middlemarch* (1871–2)

15 He knows little, who will tell his wife all he knows.
Thomas Fuller 1608–61: *The Holy State and the Profane State*

16 The trouble with my wife is that she is a whore in the kitchen and a cook in bed.
Geoffrey Gorer 1905–85: 'Exploring the English Character'; cf. **Wives 17**

17 My mother said it was simple to keep a man, you must be a maid in the living room, a cook in the kitchen and a whore in the bedroom. I said I'd hire the other two and take care of the bedroom bit.
Jerry Hall: in *Observer* 6 October 1985; cf. **Wives 16**

18 It is probably no mere chance that in legal textbooks the problems relating to married women are usually considered immediately after the pages devoted to idiots and lunatics.
A. P. Herbert 1890–1971: *Misleading Cases* (1935)

19 We were married.
                    'A wife is a wife,'
Some husband said. If only it were true!
My wife is a girl playing house
With the girl next door.
Randall Jarrell 1914–65: 'Hope' (1966)

20 I've been married six months. She looks like a million
dollars, but she only knows a hundred and twenty words
and she's only got two ideas in her head.
Eric Linklater 1899–1974: *Juan in America* (1931)

21 Happy is the man with a wife to tell him what to do and a
secretary to do it.
Lord Mancroft 1917–87: in *Observer* 18 December 1966

22 No slave is a slave to the same lengths, and in so full a
sense of the word, as a wife is.
John Stuart Mill 1806–73: *The Subjection of Women* (1869)

23 My wife, who, poor wretch, is troubled with her lonely life.
Samuel Pepys 1633–1703: diary 19 December 1662

24 The clog of all pleasure, the luggage of life,
Is the best can be said for a very good wife.
Lord Rochester 1647–80: 'On a Wife'

25 You must either be house-Wives or house-Moths;
remember that. In the deep sense, you must either weave
men's fortunes, and embroider them; or feed upon, and
bring them to decay.
John Ruskin 1819–1900: *The Ethics of the Dust* (1866)

26 She is so naked and singular.
She is the sum of yourself and your dream.
Climb her like a monument, step after step.
She is solid.
Anne Sexton 1928–74: 'For my Lover, returning to his Wife'

27 You are my true and honourable wife,
As dear to me as are the ruddy drops
That visit my sad heart.
William Shakespeare 1564–1616: *Julius Caesar* (1599)

28 Such duty as the subject owes the prince,
Even such a woman oweth to her husband.
William Shakespeare 1564–1616: *The Taming of the Shrew* (1592)

29 He will hold thee, when his passion shall have spent its
       novel force,
    Something better than his dog, a little dearer than his
       horse.
    Alfred, Lord Tennyson 1809–92: 'Locksley Hall' (1842)

30 I am a source of satisfaction to him, a nurse, a piece of
    furniture, a *woman*—nothing more.
    Sonya Tolstoy 1844–1919: diary, 13 November 1893

31 What man thinks of changing himself so as to suit his wife?
    And yet men expect that women shall put on altogether
    new characters when they are married, and girls think that
    they can do so.
    Anthony Trollope 1815–82: *Phineas Redux* (1874)

32 After my marriage, she edited everything I wrote. And
    what is more—she not only edited my works—she edited
    me!
    of his wife, Livy
    Mark Twain 1835–1910: Van Wyck Brooks *The Ordeal of Mark Twain* (1920)

33 She was the kind of wife, who looks out of her front door in
    the morning and, if it's raining, apologizes.
    Fay Weldon 1931– : *Heart of the Country* (1987)

Women see also Men and Women, The Single Life, Wives

1 Long and lazy, little and loud; fat and fulsome, pretty and
   proud.
   Anonymous: proverb

2 All the privilege I claim for my own sex . . . is that of loving
   longest, when existence or when hope is gone.
   Jane Austen 1775–1817: *Persuasion* (1818)

3 You will find that the woman who is really kind to dogs is always one who has failed to inspire sympathy in men.
Max Beerbohm 1872–1956: *Zuleika Dobson* (1911)

4 Women who love the same man have a kind of bitter freemasonry.
Max Beerbohm 1872–1956: *Zuleika Dobson* (1911)

5 It is the only major omission that the parents have made in our upbringing . . . I don't know what they are interested in, what they think about, and when I do meet them I feel most embarrassed.
on females
Tony Benn 1925– : letter to his brother, 12 March 1942

6 Green grow the rashes, O,
Green grow the rashes, O;
The sweetest hours that e'er I spend,
Are spent among the lasses, O.
Robert Burns 1759–96: 'Green Grow the Rashes' (1787)

7 If *Miss* means respectably unmarried, and *Mrs* respectably married, then *Ms* means nudge, nudge, wink, wink.
Angela Carter 1940–92: 'The Language of Sisterhood' in Christopher Ricks (ed.) *The State of the Language* (1980)

8 Women are much more like each other than men: they have, in truth, but two passions, vanity and love; these are their universal characteristics.
Lord Chesterfield 1694–1773: *Letters to his Son* (1774) 19 December 1749

9 She knows her man, and when you rant and swear, Can draw you to her *with a single hair*.
John Dryden 1631–1700: translation of Persius *Satires*

10 There are only three things to be done with a woman. You can love her, suffer for her, or turn her into literature.
Lawrence Durrell 1912–90: *Justine* (1957)

11 She takes just like a woman, yes, she does
She makes love just like a woman, yes, she does
And she aches just like a woman
But she breaks like a little girl.
Bob Dylan 1941– : 'Just Like a Woman' (1966 song)

12 I should like to know what is the proper function of
women, if it is not to make reasons for husbands to stay at
home, and still stronger reasons for bachelors to go out.
George Eliot 1819–80: *The Mill on the Floss* (1860)

13 The great question that has never been answered and
which I have not yet been able to answer, despite my thirty
years of research into the feminine soul, is 'What does a
woman want?'
Sigmund Freud 1856–1939: letter to Marie Bonaparte, in Ernest Jones
Sigmund Freud: Life and Work (1955)

14 As you are woman, so be lovely:
As you are lovely, so be various.
Robert Graves 1895–1985: 'Pygmalion to Galatea' (1927)

15 Not huffy, or stuffy, not tiny or tall,
But fluffy, just fluffy, with no brains at all.
A. P. Herbert 1890–1971: 'I Like them Fluffy' (1927)

16 I do think better of womankind than to suppose they care
whether Mister John Keats five feet high likes them or not.
John Keats 1795–1821: letter to Benjamin Bailey, 18 July 1818

17 When you get to a man in the case,
They're like as a row of pins—
For the Colonel's Lady an' Judy O'Grady
Are sisters under their skins!
Rudyard Kipling 1865–1936: 'The Ladies' (1896)

18 Thank heaven for little girls!
For little girls get bigger every day.
Alan Jay Lerner 1918–86: 'Thank Heaven for Little Girls' (1958 song)

19 Personally, I don't see why a man can't have a dog AND a
girl. But if you can only afford one, get a dog.
Groucho Marx 1895–1977: *Memoirs of a Mangy Lover* (1963)

20 Because women can do nothing except love, they've given
it a ridiculous importance.
W. Somerset Maugham 1874–1965: *The Moon and Sixpence* (1919)

21 Love is the delusion that one woman differs from another.
H. L. Mencken 1880–1956: *Chrestomathy* (1903)

22 Love is based on a view of women that is impossible to
those who have had any experience with them.
H. L. Mencken 1880–1956: attributed, 1956

23 Women would rather be right than be reasonable.
Ogden Nash 1902–71: 'Frailty, Thy Name is a Misnomer' (1942)

24 God created woman. And boredom did indeed cease from
that moment—but many other things ceased as well!
Woman was God's *second* mistake.
Friedrich Nietzsche 1844–1900: *The Antichrist* (1888)

25 Amo, amas, I love a lass,
As a cedar tall and slender;
Sweet cowslip's grace
Is her nom'native case,
And she's of the feminine gender.
John O'Keeffe 1747–1833: *The Agreeable Surprise* (1781)

26 Women are around all the time but World Cups come only
every four years.
Peter Osgood: in *The Times* 9 May 1998

27 There are two kinds of women—goddesses and doormats.
Pablo Picasso 1881–1973: attributed, 1973

28 A woman's love for us increases
The less we love her, sooth to say—
She stoops, she falls, her struggling ceases;

Caught fast, she cannot get away.
Alexander Pushkin 1799–1837: *Eugene Onegin* (1833)

29 Love a woman! y'are an ass,
'Tis a most insipid passion,
To choose out for your happiness
The silliest part of God's creation.
Lord Rochester 1647–80: 'Song'

30 The plain truth is that there are as many types of lover
among women of all classes as among men, and that
nothing but honesty and freedom will make instinctive
satisfaction possible for all.
Dora Russell 1894–1986: *Hypatia* (1925)

31 Only the male intellect, clouded by sexual impulse, could
call the undersized, narrow-shouldered, broad-hipped, and
short-legged sex the fair sex.
Arthur Schopenhauer 1788–1860: 'On Women' (1851)

32 Age cannot wither her, nor custom stale
Her infinite variety; other women cloy
The appetites they feed, but she makes hungry
Where most she satisfies.
William Shakespeare 1564–1616: *Antony and Cleopatra* (1606–7)

33 She is a woman, therefore may be wooed;
She is a woman, therefore may be won.
William Shakespeare 1564–1616: *Titus Andronicus* (1590)

34 Like all young men, you greatly exaggerate the difference
between one young woman and another.
George Bernard Shaw 1856–1950: *Major Barbara* (1907)

35   The woman is so hard
Upon the woman.
Alfred, Lord Tennyson 1809–92: *The Princess* (1847)

36 A woman with fair opportunities and without a positive
hump, may marry whom she likes.
William Makepeace Thackeray 1811–63: *Vanity Fair* (1847–8)

37 From whom indeed do we derive sensuality, effeminacy, frivolity in everything and a multitude of other vice, if it is not from women? Who is to blame for the fact that we lose our inner feelings of boldness, resolution, judiciousness, etc., if not from women? . . . They are worse than us.
Leo Tolstoy 1828–1910: diary, 14 June 1847

38 With many women I doubt whether there be any more effectual way of touching their hearts than ill-using them and then confessing it. If you wish to get the sweetest fragrance from the herb at your feet, tread on it and bruise it.
Anthony Trollope 1815–82: *Miss Mackenzie* (1865)

39 When once a woman has given you her heart, you can never get rid of the rest of her body.
John Vanbrugh 1664–1726: *The Relapse* (1696)

40 a woman is not
a potted plant
her leaves trimmed
to the contours
of her sex.
Alice Walker 1944– : 'A woman is not a potted plant'

Words see also Books and Literature, Endearments, Talking

1 The best sentence in the English language is not 'I love you' but 'It's benign'.
Woody Allen 1935– : *Deconstructing Harry* (1998 film)

2 The Eskimos had fifty-two names for snow because it was important to them: there ought to be as many for love.
Margaret Atwood 1939– : attributed

3 To try to write love is to confront the *muck* of language: that region of hysteria where language is both *too much* and *too little*, excessive . . . and impoverished.
Roland Barthes 1915–80: *A Lover's Discourse* (1977)

4 Love. In that word, beautiful in all languages, but most so in yours—*Amor mio*—is comprised my existence here and hereafter.
Lord Byron 1788–1824: letter to Teresa Guiccioli, 1819

5 Language has not the power to speak what love indites:
The soul lies buried in the ink that writes.
John Clare 1793–1864: 'Language has not the power'

6 If a lady says No, she means Perhaps; if she says Perhaps, she means Yes; if she says Yes, she is no Lady.
Lord Dawson of Penn 1864–1945: Francis Watson *Dawson of Penn* (1950)

7 Only connect! . . . Only connect the prose and the passion, and both will be exalted, and human love will be seen at its height.
E. M. Forster 1879–1970: *Howards End* (1910)

8 Maybe just whistle. You know how to whistle, don't you, Steve? You just put your lips together and blow.
Jules Furthman 1888–1960 and **William Faulkner** 1897–1962: *To Have and Have Not* (1944 film); spoken by Lauren Bacall

9 In my youth there were words you couldn't say in front of a girl; now you can't say 'girl'.
Tom Lehrer 1928– : interview in *The Oldie* 1996

10 Ah fair Zenocrate, divine Zenocrate,
Fair is too foul an epithet for thee.
Christopher Marlowe 1564–93: *Tamburlaine the Great* (1590)

11 If you want to find out some things about yourself—and in vivid detail, too—just try calling your wife 'fat'.
P. J. O'Rourke 1947– : *Age and Guile* (1995)

12 That woman speaks eighteen languages, and can't say No
in any of them.
Dorothy Parker 1893–1967: Alexander Woollcott *While Rome Burns* (1934)

13 O! know, sweet love, I always write of you,
And you and love are still my argument;
So all my best is dressing old words new,
Spending again what is already spent.
William Shakespeare 1564–1616: sonnet 76

14 Man is a creature who lives not upon bread alone, but
principally by catchwords; and the little rift between the
sexes is astonishingly widened by simply teaching one set of
catchwords to the girls and another to the boys.
Robert Louis Stevenson 1850–94: *Virginibus Puerisque* (1881)

15 Why is it that the most unoriginal thing we can say to one
another is still the thing we long to hear? 'I love you' is
always a quotation. You did not say it first and neither did
I, yet when you say it and when I say it we speak like
savages who have found three words and worship them.
Jeanette Winterson 1959– : *Written on the Body* (1992)

16 There are men who fear repartee in a wife more keenly
than a sword.
P. G. Wodehouse 1881–1975: *Jill the Reckless* (1922)

Work

1 I could have stayed home and baked cookies and had teas.
But what I decided was to fulfil my profession, which I
entered before my husband was in public life.
Hillary Rodham Clinton 1947– : comment on questions raised by rival
Democratic contender Edmund G. Brown Jr.; in *Albany Times-Union* 17
March 1992

2 It has been my experience that one cannot, in any shape or form, depend on human relations for lasting reward. It is only work that truly satisfies.
Bette Davis 1908–89: *The Lonely Life* (1962)

3 Sex suppressed will go berserk,
But it keeps us all alive.
It's a wonderful change from wives and work
And it ends at half past five.
Gavin Ewart 1916–95: 'Office Friendships' (1966)

4 Today the problem that has no name is how to juggle work, love, home and children.
Betty Friedan 1921– : *The Second Stage* (1987)

5 When I got married again I said, 'Oh my God, this is going to be the end of the work', but actually it has had the opposite effect . . . I'm glad to say that being happy hasn't proved fatal to my career.
David Hare 1947– : in *Independent* 21 March 1998

6 Powerful men often succeed through the help of their wives. Powerful women only succeed in spite of their husbands.
Lynda Lee-Potter: in *Daily Mail* 16 May 1984

7 I gave up screwing around a long time ago. I came to the conclusion that sex is a sublimation of the work instinct.
David Lodge 1935– : *Small World* (1984)

8 Take away leisure and Cupid's bow is broken.
Ovid 43 BC– AD *c.*17: *Remedia Amoris*

9 When you see what some girls marry, you realize how they must hate to work for a living.
Helen Rowland 1875–1950: *Reflections of a Bachelor Girl* (1909)

10 I have yet to hear a man ask for advice on how to combine marriage and a career.
Gloria Steinem 1934– : attributed

Work

11 An office party is not, as is sometimes supposed, the
Managing Director's chance to kiss the tea-girl. It is the tea-
girl's chance to kiss the Managing Director.
Katharine Whitehorn 1928– : *Roundabout* (1962) 'The Office Party'

Youth see also **Age**

1 When you're young, you think of marriage as a train you
simply have to catch. You run and run until you've caught
it, and then you sit back and look out of the window and
realize you're bored.
Elizabeth Bowen 1899–1973: attributed

2 It's that second time you hear your love song sung,
Makes you think perhaps, that
Love like youth is wasted on the young.
Sammy Cahn 1913–93: 'The Second Time Around' (1960 song)

3 It was the kind of desperate, headlong, adolescent calf love
that he should have experienced years ago and got over.
Agatha Christie 1890–1976: *Remembered Death* (1945)

4 When a man of forty falls in love with a girl of twenty, it
isn't her youth he is seeking but his own.
Lenore Coffee c.1897–1984: John Robert Colombo *Popcorn in Paradise*
(1979)

5 Then be not coy, but use your time;
And while ye may, go marry:
For having lost but once your prime,
You may for ever tarry.
Robert Herrick 1591–1674: 'To the Virgins, to Make Much of Time' (1648)

6 Mom and Pop were just a couple of kids when they got
married. He was eighteen, she was sixteen, and I was
three.
Billie Holiday 1915–59: *Lady Sings the Blues* (1956, with William Duffy)

7 When I was one-and-twenty
I heard a wise man say,
'Give crowns and pounds and guineas
But not your heart away;
Give pearls away and rubies,
But keep your fancy free.'
But I was one-and-twenty,
No use to talk to me.
A. E. Housman 1859–1936: *A Shropshire Lad* (1896)

8 Most mothers think that to keep young people away from
love making it is enough never to speak of it in their
presence.
Madame de La Fayette 1634–93: *The Princess of Clèves* (1678)

9 In delay there lies no plenty;
Then come kiss me, sweet and twenty,
Youth's a stuff will not endure.
William Shakespeare 1564–1616: *Twelfth Night* (1601)

10 You've got to understand, in a way a thirty-three-year-old
guy is a lot younger than a twenty-four-year-old girl. That
is, he may not be ready for marriage yet.
Neil Simon 1927– : *Come Blow Your Horn* (1961)-

Index of Authors

Campbell, Naomi
(1970–)
Gossip 1

Campbell, Roy (1901–57)
Fidelity 5

Campion, Thomas
(1567–1620)
Seasons 2

Camus, Albert (1913–60)
Happiness 2
Waiting 1

Carew, Thomas
(c.1595–1640)
Beauty 9
Passion 5

Carey, John (1934–)
Books 7

Carlyle, Jane (1801–66)
Affairs 7
Beloved 8
Letters 5

Carlyle, Thomas
(1795–1881)
Poets 7

Carpenter, Charlotte
(b. 1777)
Letters 6

Carter, Angela (1940–92)
Clothes 5
Proposals 8
Women 7

Carter, Jimmy (1924–)
Affairs 8

Cartland, Barbara
(1901–)
Food 6
Places 6
Size 3
Virtue 5

Cary, Joyce (1888–1957)
Affairs 9

Casals, Pablo (1876–1973)
Age 10

Casanova, Jacques
(1725–98)
Jealousy 4

Catullus (c.84–c.54 BC)
Breaking 5
Kissing 7
Promises 3
Transience 1

Caudwell, Sarah (1939–)
Beauty 10
Body 4
Deception 3
Desire 4

Cavafy, Constantine
(1863–1933)
Memories 1

Cavendish, Margaret
(c.1624–74)
Humour 4
Poets 8

Centlivre, Susanna
(c.1669–1723)
Money 6
Wealth 6

Cervantes (1547–1616)
Absence 4

**Chamfort, Nicolas-
Sébastien** (1741–94)
Imagination 2
Intelligence 6
Love 18

Chandler, Raymond
(1888–1959)
Alcohol 1
Body 5
Courtship 10
Hair 1
Sex 11

Chanel, Coco (1883–1971)
Clothes 6
Pain 6
Passion 6

Chang Ch'ao (fl. c.1650)
Passion 7

Chaplin, Charlie
(1889–1977)
Stage 2

Chapman, Tracy (1964–)
Declarations 1

Charles, Hugh (1907–)
see **Parker, Ross** and
Charles, Hugh

Charles, Prince of Wales
(1948–)
Falling 6

**Chateaubriand, François-
René** (1768–1848)
Body 6

Chaucer, Geoffrey
(c.1343–1400)
Alcohol 2
Beauty 11
Declarations 2
Power 5
Remarriage 1

Chekhov, Anton
(1860–1904)
Beauty 12
Friendship 7
Happiness 3
Lovers 2
Men and Women 6
Virtue 6

Cher (1946–)
Age 11
Cosmetics 2

Chesterfield, Lord
(1694–1773)
Advice 2
Arranged 3
Sex 12
Women 8

Chesterton, G. K.
(1874–1936)
Intelligence 7
Wives 9

Chetwode, Lord
(1869–1950)
In-Laws 6

Chevalier, Maurice
(1888–1972)
Mistakes 2

Christie, Agatha
(1890–1976)
Men 4
Old 2
Youth 3

Christine de Pisan
(1364–c.1430)
Deception 4

Chuo Wen-chun
(c.179–117 BC)
Husbands 11

Churchill, Winston
(1874–1965)
Food 7

Cibber, Colley
(1671–1757)
Absence 5
Rings 5

Clairmont, Claire
(1798–1879)
Beloved 9

Clare, John (1793–1864)
Falling 7
Words 5

Clark, Jane
Affairs 10

Clary, Julian (1959–)
Men 5

Clemenceau, Georges
(1841–1929)
Old 3

Cleopatra (69–30 BC)
Food 8

Clinton, Hillary Rodham
(1947–)
Fidelity 6
Marriage 13
Work 1

Clough, Arthur Hugh
(1819–61)
Affairs 11
Bridegrooms 3

Coffee, Lenore
(c.1897–1984)
Youth 4

Coffey, Denise
Single 4

Cohen, Leonard (1934–)
Body 7

Coleridge, Hartley
(1796–1849)
Beauty 13

Coleridge, Samuel Taylor
(1772–1834)
Brides 4
Compatibility 3
Desire 5
Love 19
Old 4
Pregnancy 2
Without 2

Colette (1873–1954)
Absence 6
Body 8
Brides 5
Clothes 7
Heart 3
Heartbreak 1

Collins, Joan (1933–)
Husbands 12

Collins, Mortimer
(1827–76)
Age 12

Collins, Wilkie (1824–89)
Money 7

Colman, George, the Elder
(1732–94)
Wealth 7

**Colman, George, the
Younger** (1762–1836)
Opposition 2

Colton, Charles Caleb
(1780–1832)
Marriage 14

Compton-Burnett, Ivy
(1884–1969)
Men and Women 7

Confucius (551–479BC)
Virtue 7

Congreve, William
(1670–1729)
Beauty 14
Behaviour 4, 5
Courtship 11
Desire 6
Endearments 2
Gossip 2
Imagination 3
Individuality 1
Letters 7
Loss 6
Marriage 15
Mistakes 3
Sickness 3
Unrequited 3
Virtue 8

Connolly, Billy (1942–)
Marriage 16

Connolly, Cyril (1903–74)
Books 8
Divorce 8
First 3
Men and Women 8
Sickness 4
Talking 5

Conran, Terence (1931–)
Divorce 9

Constant, Benjamin
(1767–1834)
Memories 2

Cook, Margaret
Trust 4

Cooper, Henry (1934–)
Violence 2

Cooper, Jilly (1937–)
Attraction 3
Home 1
In-Laws 7
Violence 3

Cope, Wendy (1945–)
Breaking 6
Declarations 3
Falling 8
Loss 7
Men 6, 7
Mistakes 4
Pain 7
Pleasure 4
Poets 9
Single 5
Virtue 9

Corelli, Marie
(1855–1924)
Husbands 13

Coren, Alan (1938–)
Divorce 10
Life Together 6

Cornford, Frances
(1886–1960)
Parting 2

Corso, Gregory (1930–)
Bridegrooms 4
In-Laws 8

Cosby, Bill (1937–)
Marriage 17

Coupland, Douglas
(1961–)
Individuality 2
Life Together 7

Courteline, Georges
(1858–1929)
Unrequited 4

Coward, Noël (1899–1973)
Armed Forces 3
Attraction 4
Behaviour 6
Honeymoon 3, 4
Men 8
Music 5
Passion 8
Seasons 3
Violence 4

Cowley, Abraham
(1618–67)
Deception 5

McCartney, Paul (1942–)
see **Lennon, John** and
McCartney, Paul
MacColl, Ewen (1915–89)
Meeting 8
McCullers, Carson
(1917–67)
Beloved 18
McCullough, Colleen
(1937–)
Age 20
MacDiarmid, Hugh
(1892–1978)
Weddings 15
McGinley, Phyllis
(1905–)
Bachelors 4
Bridesmaids 2
Gifts 6
Home 3
Honeymoon 6
Life Together 17
Old 14
Seasons 15
Valentines 12
McGough, Roger (1937–)
Honeymoon 7
Machado, Antonio
(1878–1939)
Solitude 10
McInerney, Jay (1955–)
Marriage 30
Talking 10
Mackenzie, Compton
(1883–1972)
Marriage 31
McLean, Don (1945–)
Widows 8
McLeod, Fiona (William
Sharp) (1855–1905)
Solitude 11
MacNeice, Louis
(1907–63)
Life Together 18
Madonna (1959–)
Hair 2
Mailer, Norman (1923–)
Divorce 16
Sex 31
Sexuality 14

Maintenon, Madame de
(1635–1719)
Behaviour 10
Major-Ball, Terry (1932–)
Quarrels 7
Malkovich, John (1953–)
Clothes 17
Mallet, Robert (1915–)
Intelligence 17
Malory, Thomas (d. 1471)
Friendship 13
Seasons 14
Sorrow 5
Time 4
Mancroft, Lord (1917–87)
Wives 21
Mandela, Nelson (1918–)
Indifference 4
Mann, Thomas
(1875–1955)
Kissing 19
Mansfield, Jayne
(1932–67)
Men 13
Mansfield, Katherine
(1888–1923)
Deception 10
Letters 15
Marguerite d'Angoulême
(1492–1549)
Fidelity 15
Jealousy 11
Quarrels 8
Marie de France
(fl. 1160–70)
Love 39
Marivaux, Pierre
(1688–1763)
Attraction 11
Marlborough, Sarah,
Duchess of (1660–1744)
Armed Forces 7
Remarriage 7
Marlowe, Christopher
(1564–93)
Beauty 24
Falling 11
Kissing 20
Words 10
Marquez, Gabriel Garcia
(1928–)
Marriage 32

Marston, John
(c.1575–1634)
Affairs 22
Martial (AD c.40–c.104)
Beloved 19
Martin, Hugh and Blane,
Ralph
Falling 12
Martin, Judith (1938–)
Unrequited 17
Martineau, Harriet
(1802–76)
Arranged 9
Places 13
Marvell, Andrew
(1621–78)
Death 10
Time 5
Marvell, Holt (1901–69)
Memories 6
Marx, Chico (1891–1961)
Kissing 21
Marx, Groucho
(1895–1977)
Mistakes 7
Stage 10
Women 19
Marx, Karl (1818–83) and
Engels, Friedrich
(1820–95)
Affairs 23
Mason, Jackie (1931–)
Music 15
Matlovich, Leonard
(d. 1988)
Armed Forces 8
Matson, Vera see **Presley,
Elvis** and **Matson, Vera**
Maugham, W. Somerset
(1874–1965)
Affairs 24
Humour 7
Letters 16
Men 14
Pregnancy 5
Sacrifice 4, 5
Sex 32
Unrequited 18
Women 20
Maxwell, James Clerk
(1831–79)
Declarations 10

Mayakovsky, Vladimir
(1893–1930)
  Love 40
Menander (342–*c*.292 BC)
  Hair 3
Mencken, H. L.
(1880–1956)
  Affairs 25
  Alcohol 7
  Attraction 12
  Bachelors 5
  Folly 4
  Love 41
  Men and Women 19
  Talking 11
  Women 21, 22
Mercer, Johnny (1909–76)
  Parting 9
  Seasons 16
Meredith, George
(1828–1909)
  Courtship 16
  Food 14
  Sacrifice 6
Meynell, Alice
(1847–1922)
  Memories 7
Mikes, George (1912–)
  Places 14
Mill, John Stuart
(1806–73)
  Wives 22
Millay, Edna St Vincent
(1892–1950)
  Absence 16
  Breaking 21
  Heart 9
  Loss 12
  Love 42
  Memories 8
  Time 6
  Travel 7
Miller, Arthur (1915–)
  Compatibility 6
Miller, Henry (1891–1980)
  Fickleness 5
  Passion 15
  Places 15
  Sex 33
Miller, Mitch
  Music 16

Milligan, Spike (1918–)
  Pregnancy 6
Milton, John (1608–74)
  Beauty 25
  God 5
  Parting 10
  Quarrels 9
  Skies 3
Mistinguette (1875–1956)
  Kissing 22
Mitchell, Adrian (1932–)
  Memories 9
  Unrequited 19
Mitchell, Margaret
(1900–49)
  Indifference 5
Mitford, Nancy (1904–73)
  Courtship 17
  Single 15
Monkhouse, William
Cosmo (1840–1901)
  Marriage 33
Monroe, Marilyn
(1926–62)
  Clothes 18
Montagu, Lady Mary
Wortley (1689–1762)
  Fear 6
  Life Together 19
  Weddings 16
Montaigne (1533–92)
  Falling 13
  Marriage 34
  Virtue 17
Montherlant, Henry de
(1896–1972)
  Attraction 13
  Intelligence 18
Montrose, James Graham,
Marquess of (1612–50)
  Declarations 11
  Fidelity 16
Montrose, Percy
  Fickleness 6
  Loss 13
Moodie, Susanna
(1803–85)
  Remarriage 8
Moore, Thomas
(1779–1852)
  Body 23
  Books 12

Moore, Thomas (cont.)
  Fidelity 17
  Pleasure 13
Morley, Christopher
(1890–1957)
  Dancing 7
Mortimer, Clifford
  Cars 3
  Secrets 10
Mortimer, John (1923–)
  Beauty 26
  Sexuality 15
Moss, Stirling (1929–)
  Cars 4
Muggeridge, Malcolm
(1903–90)
  God 6
Muir, Edwin (1887–1959)
  Declarations 12
Muir, Frank (1920–98)
  Brides 8
Muldoon, Paul (1951–)
  Death 11
Munro, Alice (1931–)
  Life Together 20
  Lovers 8
  Quarrels 10
Murasaki Shikibu
(*c*.978–*c*.1031)
  Memories 10
Murdoch, Iris (1919–)
  Books 13
  Charm 5
  Love 43
  Marriage 35
  Mistakes 8
  Solitude 12
Murray, Fred
  Remarriage 9
Murray, Jim
  Body 24
Murray, Les A. (1938–)
  Best Man 4
Musel, Bob
  Rings 8

▶**N**

Nabokov, Vladimir
(1899–1977)
  Attraction 14

W